Basic Tools of RESEARCH

An Annotated Guide for Students of English

THIRD EDITION

REVISED AND ENLARGED

PHILIP H. VITALE

Professor of English, De Paul University

BARRON'S EDUCATIONAL SERIES, INC.

WOODBURY, NEW YORK

Library of Congress Cataloging in Publication Data

Vitale, Philip H
  Basic tools of research.

  1. English literature—Bibliography. 2. American
literature—Bibliography. 3. Reference books—
Bibliography. I. Title.
Z2011.V48 1974   016.82'08   74-8827
ISBN 0-8120-0627-5

All inquiries should be addressed to:
Barron's Educational Series, Inc.
113 Crossways Park Drive
Woodbury, New York 11797

Library of Congress Catalog Card No. 74-8827

Paper Edition
International Standard Book No. 0-8120-0627-5

PRINTED IN THE UNITED STATES OF AMERICA

TABLE OF CONTENTS

PREFACE

BASIC TOOLS OF RESEARCH is a selective list intended to serve the needs of undergraduate and graduate English majors as a handy work of reference or as a text for courses in bibliography and research. It differs from similar bibliographic manuals principally in: (1) its principal of selection, including a rather full listing of tools — concordances, author bibliographies, and guides to book selection and book reviews — not normally found in the others; (2) its arrangement, designed to answer the requirements, not of the scholar or professional investigator, so much as the student who lacks general conversance with the essential works of reference in English and American literature; and (3) its emphasis upon annotation and upon works which are virtually as useful to the graduate as they are to the undergraduate student.

The number of works in this manual is smaller than that embraced in comparable manuals; it is, however, it seems to me, adequately representative. For I am convinced, after some twenty-two years of college teaching, that the typical undergraduate major — the same holds generally true of the graduate English major — has merely a nominal or titular knowledge of no more than one hundred of the approximately six hundred basic tools of research contained in this work, and a practical or working knowledge of perhaps less than fifty.

Much is made currently of the glaring inadequacies of our students in linguistic expression, of the crucial need to deepen and to expand the thresholds of knowledge, and of the difficult task faced by colleges and universities as they seek to correct these inadequacies. Comparatively little is said of the correlative weakness of students in bibliography. But to know where and how to gain access to certain facts and ideas is a form of knowledge in itself, as well as a knowledge which is indispensable to the acquisition of the facts and ideas themselves. Lacking a proper awareness of the essential tools of research, the searcher of fact or truth either fails completely to gain his end, or he gains it at an expenditure of time and energy quite incommensurate to the end.

BASIC TOOLS OF RESEARCH is the result of a belief that a greater service may be rendered the student by exposing him to a relatively short list of some six hundred items, which he can be expected to know well, and which will meet most if not all of his needs, than to expose him to a long list of, say, two thousand items or more, which he finds overwhelming and confusing, and which probably contains hundreds of works which he will never have occasion to consult.

A glance at the Table of Contents will reveal the principle of arrangement: from the most general to the most specific; from the earliest to the most current. When an item (usually a learned journal or a bibliography of dissertations) is listed a second time, the student is referred to the first listing for the annotation. Brief excerpts from reviews in most instances follow the formal annotation of the work.

The Second Edition of BASIC TOOLS OF RESEARCH represented substantial revision and expansion of the First Edition. Of the 285 items in the earlier edition, 71 items were revised or inserted, and three new sections were added: "Major Author Bibliographies"; "Major Work Concordances"; and "Guides to Book Reviews and Book Selection." These three sections constitute, I believe, the fullest annotated lists available in any comparable manual. In all, the First Edition of BASIC TOOLS OF RESEARCH embraced some 285 items; the Second Edition embraced some 500 items.

The Third Edition represents a revision, expansion or updating of some forty entries, and the addition of some 150 new reference sources. The First Edition of BASIC TOOLS OF RESEARCH contained 285 sources; the Third Edition of BASIC TOOLS OF RESEARCH contains approximately 650 sources.

GUIDES

DOWNS, ROBERT B.
How to do Library Research. Urbana, Illinois: University of Illinois Press, 1967. 179 p.

Describes research facilities and the services of libraries, and the means to best utilize them. Useful prefatory essay on American libraries.

GALIN, SAUL.
Reference Books: How to Select and Use Them. New York: Random House, Inc., 1969. 312 p.

A description of about 200 basic reference books, divided into three parts: I. General Reference Works; II. Specialized Reference Works for the Humanities and Social Sciences; III. Specialized Reference Works for the Physical Sciences. Selection is excellent; summaries are quite informative.

GATES, JEAN KEY.
Guide to the Use of Books and Libraries. 2nd ed. New York: McGraw-Hill Book Co., 1969. 273 p.

A conventional presentation of "books and libraries, with emphasis upon . . . their organization and arrangement, and their usefulness for specific purposes. Particular attention is paid to academic libraries and to ways of using them . . . effectively." (Pref.) Among the significant omissions are the printed catalogues of the Library of Congress and the National Union Catalog.

MINTO, JOHN.
Reference Books: A Classified and Annotated Guide to the Principal Works of Reference. London: Library Association, 1929–1931. 2 vols., 356 p. and 140 p.

The "British Mudge"; standard for English students.

MUDGE, ISADORE.
A Guide to Reference Books. 6th ed. Chicago: American Library Association, 1936.

Appreciably fuller than the fifth edition and containing a valuable addition of business reference works. In many instances, however, the supplementary references remain dated.

MURPHEY, Robert W.
How and Where to Look it Up. New York: McGraw-Hill Book
Company, Inc., 1958. 721 p.

Intended "to fill the needs of . . . occasional or frequent users
of reference sources to whom the intricacies of library science
are largely a mystery."

ROBERTS, Arthur D.
Introduction to Reference Books. London: Library Association,
1956. 237 p.

Intended as a text for students taking the course in librarianship at the University College, London. Describes various kinds
of reference books, cites some titles as examples, but does not
attempt to list works in special subject fields. Useful, but from
the British point of view.

SHORES, Louis.
Basic Reference Books: A General Introduction to the Evaluation, Study, and Use of Reference Materials. Chicago: American Library Association, 1939. 472 p.

Basic Reference Sources: An Introduction to Materials and
Methods. With a Chapter on Science Reference Sources by
Helen Focke. Chicago: American Library Association, 1954.
378 p.

Based upon BASIC REFERENCE BOOKS (2nd ed. 1939 o.p.). Describes 147 types of source essentials; gives 554 basic reference
titles. Titles of works published after Dec. 1951 are not included.

WALFORD, Albert John and L. M. Payne.
Guide to Reference Material. London: Library Association, 1959.
543 p.

A list of 3000 principal titles, classified and annotated, and emphasizing current material and material published in Britain.

————— Supplement. London: Library Association, 1963. 370 p.
1500 additional items, exclusive of some 500 others in notes,
published mainly between 1957 and 1961.

——. 3d. ed., vol. 1. **Science and Technology,** 615 p. New York:
R.R. Bowker Company, 1973.

Aims to provide "signpost to reference books and bibliographies published mainly in recent years, international in scope, but with emphasis on items published in Britain." Critically describes or evaluates some 5000 reference works. Two subsequent volumes will cover the social sciences, humanities, arts, and bibliography.

WINCHELL, CONSTANCE M.
Guide to Reference Books. Chicago: American Library Association, 8th ed., 1967.

Incorporates much of the same material and many of the same titles as the seventh edition, but is generally reorganized and enlarged. The number of titles has been increased from some 5500 to about 7500. The year 1964 is the closing date for listing new works and new editions "except in a few instances where new titles were received early in 1965." Unlike the previous editions which, in general, followed the Dewey Decimal Classification order, the eighth edition "has been arranged to be more in keeping with the subject organization of many libraries and with the content courses in library schools, i.e., Part A, General Reference Works; Part B, The Humanities; Part C, Social Sciences; Part D, History and Area Studies; Part E, Pure and Applied Sciences." The third biennial supplement to the eighth edition by Eugene P. Sheehy (1969–70) contains nearly 1200 titles representing new words, new editions, and continuations of works in progress.

WYNAR, BOHDAN S., ed.
American Reference Books Annual. 2d. ed. Littleton, Colorado: Libraries Unlimited, 1971. 603 p.

The initial publication of a proposed annual record of new titles, reprints, and selected annuals which are published primarily in the United States but which include some British works. Volume one covers general reference, social sciences, history, economics, and business; volume two covers fine arts, humanities, science and engineering. Eighteen hundred and thirty-seven titles in all, with an improved index. In a general sense, AMERICAN REFERENCE BOOKS ANNUAL does much to keep the standard reference guides current. Useful for the quality of its descriptive and critical comments, its review citations, and its bibliographic notations.

DICTIONARIES

Unabridged

Century Dictionary and Cyclopedia: With a New Atlas of the World. New York: Century Company, 1911. 12 vols.

A very comprehensive, encyclopedic type of dictionary; too old for general and current use, but still valuable for its careful treatment of scientific and technical terms, especially those that have significantly altered in meaning, and for its excellent illustrations and plates. Volumes one to ten constitute the dictionary proper; volume eleven comprises a cyclopedia of names,—biographical, geographical, fictitious, mythological; volume twelve is an atlas.

A Dictionary of American English on Historical Principles. Chicago: University of Chicago Press, 1938–1944. 4 vols.

Aims to evidence those elements by which American English is distinguished from the English spoken elsewhere, and thus includes "not only words or phrases which are clearly or apparently of American origin, or have greater currency here than elsewhere, but also every word denoting something which has a real connection with the development of the country and the history of its people."—Cf. "Preface," p. v. A definitive study of American English and thus indispensable, but of limited value to the student of twentieth-century American English, since it does not generally include matter extending beyond the end of the nineteenth century.

Funk and Wagnalls New Standard Dictionary of the English Language. New York: Funk and Wagnalls, 1963. 2814 p.

A well-edited dictionary including within the same alphabet more than 450,000 words, as well as some 65,000 proper names, and about 30,000 geographical names. The "Appendix" contains a list of foreign words and phrases, disputed pronunciations, rules for simplified spelling, and population statistics.

4

New Century Dictionary of the English Language. New York: Appleton-Century, 1948. 2 vols., 2798 p.

Not an abridgement of the CENTURY DICTIONARY AND CYCLO-PEDIA as such. Although the vocabulary is selected from the CENTURY, the definitions are revised and the illustrative quotations are different. Includes more than 100,000 entries and more than 12,000 illustrative quotations.

Oxford English Dictionary. Editor-in-chief, James A.H. Murray. Oxford: Clarendon Press, 1933. 13 vols. Originally published as NEW ENGLISH DICTIONARY ON HISTORICAL PRINCIPALS.

Its main purpose is to trace the history of every word included from the date of its introduction into the language, and illustrating changes of meaning, spelling, pronunciation, and usage by quotations from the writings of more than 5000 authors of all periods. "The complete work has a total vocabulary of 414,-825 words and includes 1,827,306 quotations."

"To students of language the O.E.D. is a sort of recurring marvel which never ceases its glamour," but only those who use it intensively can "know how it improves volume by volume in scope, thoroughness, and elaboration of detail."—(Ernest Weekley in the ATLANTIC MONTHLY)

Oxford English Dictionary: A Supplement to the Oxford English Dictionary. vol. 1, A-G. Edited by R. W. Burchfield. New York: Oxford University Press, 1972.

The first of a projected three volume supplement to the thirteen volume OXFORD ENGLISH DICTIONARY. "When completed, the Supplement will contain about 50,000 main words (some new, some newly employed) that have become part of the language since 1884. "Its range exceeds that of the main work in that it provides older as well as newer citations of many words in the OED, incorporating the word uses of many of the modern writers, such as Joyce, Lawrence, Kipling and Yeats. The Supplement is clearly "a major event in the history of English lexicography and will be of enormous value . . . in establishing the vocabulary of the language as it exists today." (TLS)

The Compact Edition of the Oxford English Dictionary: Complete Text Reproduced Micrographically. 2 vols. Vol. 1: A–O.

Vol. 2: P–Z; Supplement and Bibliography. Oxford: Clarendon Press, 1971. 4116 p.

Allowing for the obvious disadvantages, the thirteen volumes of the original are well reproduced in the two-volume set. The principal advantage of the compact edition is the cost ($75.00 as against $300.00 for the thirteen-volume set).

The Random House Dictionary of the English Language. Editor-in-chief Jess Stein. New York: Random House, 1966. 2059 p.

Claims to contain "no fewer than 260,000 carefully selected entries" (Webster's third edition has some 450,000 entries). Includes definitions of slang and idiomatic expressions, technical terms, synonyms, etymologies, alphabet genealogies, and more than 2000 informative pictures and maps. Gives the most common meaning of a word first. Special features: political atlas, four concise foreign language dictionaries (French, Spanish, German, and Italian), "arranged in each case for two-way reference; that is, from the foreign language into English and vice-versa"; a chronology of world history; a directory of all United States colleges and universities and the major foreign universities; a chart of Indo-European languages; German, Hebrew, Arabic, Greek, and Russian alphabets.

Webster's New International Dictionary of the English Language. 2d ed., Unabridged. Editor-in-chief, Wilham Allan Neilson. Springfield, Massachusetts: G. & C. Merriam Co., 1961. 3149 p.

The oldest and most famous American dictionary, conservative, yet unbiased, ably edited, noted especially for the clearness of its definitions and for the explicitness of its rules and sanctions. A characteristic feature, introduced in the 1909 edition and continued in the second edition (1934), is the divided page, containing in the upper part the main words of the language and, in the lower part, in finer print, various minor words: different kinds of cross references, reformed spellings, some obsolete words or extremely rare words, foreign-language quotations, proverbs, special phrases, and such Biblical proper names as are entered only to show pronunciation. Definitions are given in historical sequence. Some 600,000 vocabulary entries.

Webster's Third New International Dictionary of the English Language, Unabridged. Editor-in-chief, Philip Babcock Gove. Springfield, Massachusetts: G. & C. Merriam Co. 1971. 2662 p.

Unlike its predecessors, the latest edition has been edited from the viewpoint of descriptive linguistics. Current usages and pronunciations are recorded, but the preferred form is not clearly indicated. Many of the pronunciation symbols of the earlier edition are retained, a few substitutions are made, and some have been dropped completely. According to the editors, 100,000 new words and definitions, using illustrative quotations from contemporary sources, have been added; but most of the new words and definitions, it must be noted, are in the area of scientific and technological reference. Instead of full treatment of a group of related terms, each term is defined at its own alphabetical place, and definition by synonym is carefully avoided. Among the special features, to follow the Preface, are: "(1) the recognition and separate entry (with part-of-speech label) of verb-plus-adverb compounds (as RUN DOWN) that function like one word verbs in every way except for having a separable suffix . . . (3) the recognition (by using the label OFTEN ATTRIB) of nouns that often function as adjectives but otherwise do not behave like the class of adjectives . . . (6) the recognition (by not using at all the status label COLLOQUIAL) that it is impossible to know whether a word out of context is colloquial or not, and (7) the incorporation of abbreviations alphabetically in the main vocabulary."

"The editors of the Third Edition have made a conscientious and usually successful attempt to determine the meanings and statuses of words by examination of their use in contexts and not by applying irrelevant historical, logical, or etymological criteria" — (HARPER'S, February, 1962).

"Instead, we have seen a century and a third of illustrious history largely jettisoned; we have seen a novel dictionary formula improvised, in great part out of snap judgments and the sort of theoretical improvement that in practice impairs; and we have seen the gates propped wide open in enthusiastic hospitality to miscellaneous confusions and corruptions. In fine, the anxiously awaited work that was to have crowned cisatlantic linguistic scholarship with a particular glory turns out to be a scandal and a disaster. Worse yet, it plumes itself on its faults and parades assiduously cultivated sins as virtues without precedent . . . We get dictionaries expressly that they may settle such problems for us. This dictionary seems to make a virtue of leaving them in flux, with the explanation that many matters are subjective and that the individual must decide for himself—a curious abrogation of authority in a work extolled as 'more useful and authoritative than any previous dictionary' "—(Wilson Follett, "Sabotage in Springfield," THE ATLANTIC, January, 1962).

"Most libraries will need both the 2d and 3d editions"— (LIBRARY JOURNAL, April 15, 1962).

Abridged Dictionaries

American College Dictionary, ed. by Clarence L. Barnhart, with the assistance of 355 authorities and specialists. New York: Random House, 1962. 1432 p.

Designed especially for use in schools, offices, and homes, and contains, in one alphabet about 120,000 entries, including proper names of persons and places, foreign words and phrases, abbreviations, etc. The current meanings are given first, the order for each entry being determined by the principle of frequency.

American Heritage Dictionary of the English Language, ed. by William Morris. Boston: American Heritage and Houghton, 1969. 1550 p.

A single alphabetical listing of about 155,000 entries, including new words from the world of science and technology, illustrative quotations from literature, and capsule biographies of leading figures. The preliminary section, following the publisher's note, contains articles on the origin, usage, dialects, grammar, spelling and pronunciation of the English language; and a discussion of the use of computers in language analysis and lexicography. A very handsome and impressively illustrated work.

The Concise Oxford Dictionary of Current English. Adapted from the original by H. W. and F. G. Fowler; 4th ed. rev. by E. McIntosh. New York: Oxford University Press, 1951. 1524 p.

Concerned principally with British words which are in current use or found frequently in quotations or proverbs; technical terms which are generally current, not purely erudite; and colloquialisms, slang, and vulgar expressions. Based upon the OXFORD ENGLISH DICTIONARY, but not an abridgement of it as such. Often cited as the C.O.D.

A Dictionary of Americanisms on Historical Principles. Ed. by Mitford McLeod Mathews. Chicago: University of Chicago Press, 1951. 2 vols., 1946 p.

Narrower in scope than A DICTIONARY OF AMERICAN ENGLISH ON HISTORICAL PRINCIPLES, embracing fewer words, but including those of more modern appearance and giving further emphasis to slang and dialect. Illustrated with some 400 line drawings.

"It is virtually a source book, continental in its range and diversity, of American experience in its most completely American aspects" — (NEW YORK HERALD TRIBUNE, 1951).

Americanisms: A Dictionary of Selected Americanisms on Historical Principles. Ed. by Mitford M. Mathews. Chicago: University of Chicago Press, 1966. 304 p.

An abridgement of Mitford M. Mathews' work A DICTIONARY OF AMERICANISMS ON HISTORICAL PRINCIPLES (see entry on page eight). The selection consists of approximately a thousand entries from the earlier work.

FOWLER, HENRY WATSON AND F. G. FOWLER.
Concise Oxford Dictionary of Current English. Oxford: Clarendon Press. 1964. 1558 p.

A complete revision and resetting of the fourth edition. The etymologies, given at the ends of the entries, have been thoroughly revised. In the Appendixes are found: General abbreviations; Pronunciation of non-English words; Tables of weights and measures. Sometimes cited as C.O.D.

Funk and Wagnalls New College Standard Dictionary of the English Language. Emphatype Edition. Ed. by Charles Earle Funk. New York: Funk and Wagnalls, 1947. 1404 p.

Based on the NEW STANDARD DICTIONARY OF THE ENGLISH LANGUAGE. The largest of the abridged "standard" dictionaries, it features a new system of pronunciation, following which

stressed syllables are underscored. Emphasis is on current usage.
Etymologies follow the definitions.

Funk and Wagnalls Standard College Dictionary. New York:
Funk and Wagnalls, 1963. 1605 p.

A complete revision of the earlier edition, containing more than
150,000 terms in one alphabet. Slang and colloquialisms are differentiated; order of definitions usually follows frequency of use,
rather than chronology; etymologies are given at the end of the
entry. Included in the Appendixes are: Colleges and Universities
in the United States and Canada; Common signs and symbols;
Vocabulary building; Punctuation; Guide to reference works;
Preparing a manuscript for publication and proof-readers' marks.

HALL, JOHN RICHARD CLARK.
A Concise Anglo-Saxon Dictionary. 4th ed. with a supplement by
Herbert D. Meritt. Cambridge: Cambridge University Press,
1960. 432 p.

References are to the headings in the NEW ENGLISH DICTIONARY,
under which quotations from the Anglo-Saxon texts are given;
hence the work serves as an index to a large body of valuable information on Old English words included in the NEW ENGLISH
DICTIONARY, "but often overlooked because it is found under the
head of words now obsolete."

KLEIN, ERNEST.
**A Comprehensive Etymological Dictionary of the English Lan-
guage:** dealing with the origin of words and their sense development, thus illustrating the history of civilization and culture.
Amsterdam: Slsevier, 1967, 2 vols.

The first volume, published in 1966, covers the letters A to K;
the second volume covers L to Z. The aim, according to the
author, is to show "the history of the humanities and sciences
. . . by giving the history of the technical terms . . . in a manner
that would enable the reader to reconstruct through them the
history of the various branches of the humanities and sciences."
Valuable for the large number of scientific and technical terms
and for the treatment of proper names.

KURATH, HANS AND SHERMAN M. KUHN.
Middle English Dictionary. Ann Arbor, Michigan: University of

Michigan Press, 1964–1970 (in progress)

The basis for the dictionary is a large collection of Middle English quotations which includes those assembled for the OXFORD ENGLISH DICTIONARY and those gathered for this work. The MIDDLE ENGLISH DICTIONARY is to be completed in some 65 parts over a period of ten years and will consist of about 8000 pages. The first three volumes were published during the years 1952–1964: vol. 1, A-B; vol. 2, C-D; vol. 3, pt. 1, E-F and pt. 2, G-Grith. The 1966–67 publication covers: pts. H. 4-H. 5, I. 1-I. 2. The 1969–70 volume covers: pts. J. 1, K. 1, L. 1-2.

The aim of the work is to cover the language from 1100 to 1475, providing the histories of words with many illustrative quotations arranged chronologically. Many cross references.

ONIONS, CHARLES TALBUT.
The Oxford Dictionary of English Etymology. New York: Oxford University Press, 1966. 1025 p.

Presents, in conventional form, an appreciable collection of the etymologies in the OXFORD ENGLISH DICTIONARY. Updates some words, but largely omits those originating in the twentieth century. "Notation of usage by century is a helpful feature."

Oxford Illustrated Dictionary. Edited by J. Coulson (and others). Illustrations edited by Helen Mary Petter. Oxford: Clarendon Press, 1962. 974 p.

Based on the CONCISE OXFORD DICTIONARY. All terms are in one alphabet, including proper nouns, abbreviations, foreign phrases, etc. Little or no etymology.

The Random House Dictionary of the English Language. College edition edited by Laurence Urdang. New York: Random House, Inc., 1968. 1568 p.

Based on the "unabridged" edition of the RANDOM HOUSE DICTIONARY, provides, in one alphabet, information on meaning, spelling, pronunciation, usage, and etymology. Includes foreign words and phrases, biographical terms, abbreviations, and other ypes of information. Introductions cover the history of the English language, phonetics, dialects. An impressive desk dictionary.

The Shorter Oxford English Dictionary on Historical Principles. 3d. ed. Oxford: The Clarendon Press, 1973. 2672 p.

An abridgement of THE OXFORD ENGLISH DICTIONARY, achieved principally by the omission of quotations and the extensive use of abbreviations. Includes "all words in regular literary and colloquial use" and a selected list of technical, archaic, and scientific words.

Although not a complete substitute for the O.E.D., it is "nevertheless an invaluable introduction to and aid in the use of the larger work" — (SATURDAY REVIEW OF LITERATURE).

This 1973 printing is still called the third edition; however, it has been reset in easier-to-read type, and the revised etymologies have been made a part of the text proper.

STRATMANN, FRANCIS HENRY.
Middle-English Dictionary: containing words used by English writers from the 12th to the 15th century. Ed. by Henry Bradley. Oxford: Clarendon Press, 1891. 708 p.

A standard work, providing etymologies and references to sources. Still useful and will remain so until the Kurath work is completed.

Webster's New World Dictionary of the American Language, College Edition. Ed. by Joseph H. Friend and David B. Guralnik. New York: The World Publishing Company, 1970. 1692 p.

A fully revised and updated edition, retaining format and arrangement of the 1953 edition. Usage labels continue to be used. New in the appendix is a "Guide to punctuation, mechanics, and manuscript form."

Differs from the two-volumed "encyclopedic edition," which has 2068 pages, in that the latter has more appendixes. The words, arranged in a single alphabet, include vocabulary; biographical, geographical, Biblical, and classical names; foreign words and phrases; abbreviations; and a relatively extensive list of synonyms and antonyms. The emphasis is on current American usage.

Webster's New Collegiate Dictionary. 8th ed. Springfield, Mass.: Merriam, 1973. 1563 p.

Includes over 152,000 revised and updated entries, with over 22,000 new entries; and, although reflecting the new concepts and policies of WEBSTER'S THIRD, retains many supplementary features found in the well-known sixth edition. Etymologies are adequate and given at the beginning of the entry; definitions are given chronologically, the modern meaning coming last; synonyms, but not antonyms, are included. "The expansion of the vocabulary consists primarily of . . . new words and meanings which have come into use since the previous edition of the dictionary was published in 1963."

Webster's New World Dictionary of the American Language, 2d. College Edition. Ed. by David B. Guralnik, ed. in chief. New York: The World Publishing Company, 1970. 1692 p.

Fully revised and updated. Retains format and arrangement of earlier edition, but, in place of forms of address in the appendix, now includes a "Guide to punctuation, mechanics, and manuscript form."

Differs from the two-volumed "encyclopedic edition," which has 2068 pages, in that the latter has more appendixes. The 142,000 words, arranged in a single alphabet, include vocabulary; biographical, geographical, Biblical, and classical names; foreign words and phrases; abbreviations; and a relatively extensive list of synonyms and antonyms. The emphasis is on current American usage.

WORDBOOKS

Acronyms and Initialisms Dictionary. 3d. ed. Ellen T. Crowley and Robert C. Thomas, eds. Detroit: Gale Research Company, 1970. 484 p.

More than 80,000 terms: alphabetic designations, contractions, acronyms, initialisms, and similar condensed appellations. Supplements entitled "New Acronyms and Initialisms" are planned for subsequent years.

ADAMS, RAMON F.
Western Words: A Dictionary of the Range, Cow Camp and Trail. Norman: University of Oklahoma Press, 1968. 355 p.
Coverage has been extended beyond the "cowman's language" of the 1944 edition; also includes the vocabulary of the "sheepman, the freighter and packer, the trapper, the buffalo hunter, the stagecoach driver, the western-river boatman, the logger, the sawmill worker, the miner, the western gambler—and the Indian."—Introd.

A delightful collection of words and phrases dealing "with the cattle business" and containing "extended discussions of the origins of such terms as 'maverick,' 'dogie,' etc."—(NEW YORKER)

A work "that will edify scholars and philologists and delight lay readers"—(BOOK WEEK, December 24, 1944).

ALLEN, EDWARD F.
A Dictionary of Abbreviations and Symbols. London: Cassell and Company, 1949. 224 p.
A collection of over 6,000 abbreviations and symbols usually encountered in literature, art, education, politics, religion, industry, war, and especially, business; but weak in the field of mathematics, specialized science, and foreign abbreviations. Includes more symbols than most of the better known dictionaries of abbreviations and symbols.

BERREY, L. V. AND M. VAN DEN BARK.
The American Thesaurus of Slang: A Complete Reference Book of Colloquial Speech. 2d ed. New York: Thomas Y. Crowell & Company, 1953. 1280 p.

Over 10,000 expressions arranged in parts, general slang and colloquialisms, and subdivided into categories determined by dominant ideas, occupations, etc.; contains an alphabetical word index for easy reference.

Presents "a vivid introduction to the past and present vitality of the American language. The synonyms and antonyms cover the broad subject of life from natural phenomena through social organization to individual acts and attributes"—(U.S. QUARTERLY BOOK LIST, June, 1947).

"It is obviously the result of vast and prolonged labor and it is a vast and imposing piece of work"—(NEW YORK TIMES, March 1, 1942).

BLISS, ALAN.
A Dictionary of Foreign Words and Phrases. New York: E. P. Dutton & Company, 1966. 389 p.

Contains over 5000 words and phrases which, used in English, are borrowed from many other languages. Fully defines each entry, clearly notes the language of origin, the century of its assimilation into English, and frequently provides an example of its current use. Quite current, the entries include words and phrases which have only recently become a part of our vocabulary.

CROWLEY, ELLEN T. AND ROBERT C. THOMAS.
Reverse Acronyms and Initialisms Dictionary: A Companion Volume to ACRONYMS AND INITIALISMS DICTIONARY, with Terms Arranged Alphabetically by Meaning of Acronym. Detroit: Gale Research Company, 1972. 485 p.

Based upon, and complements, the third edition of ACRONYMS AND INITIALISMS DICTIONARY (AID). By reversing the arrangement and providing an alphabetical listing by the full expanded term for which the abbreviation has been designated, REVERSE ACRONYMS AND INITIALISMS DICTIONARY (RAID) permits the user with a name, term or phrase in mind to determine the short-form alphabetic equivalent.

DE SOLA, RALPH.
Abbreviations Dictionary. International edition. New York: Meredith, 1967. 298 p.

Subtitle: Abbreviations, acronyms, anonyms, contractions, initials and nicknames, short forms and slang shortcuts, signs and symbols . . . automatic data-processing abbreviations for zip-coded mail; chemical element symbols . . . diacritical and punc-tuation marks . . . proofreader's marks . . . zodiacal signs.

FUNK, CHARLES E.
A Hog on Ice and Other Curious Expressions. New York: Har-per & Brothers, 1955. 214 p.

Readable and amusing explanations of the origin of, and for the most part, well known expressions, old and new.

The pleasing thing about Mr. Funk "is his willingness to turn his selections around slowly and have a look at them from all sides. . . . The reader will be amused almost always, sur-prised a good part of the time, and informed throughout" — (SAN FRANCISCO CHRONICLE, March 5, 1948).

Future lexicographers will acknowledge their indebtedness to the author for "the research he has done on old phrases and because he has set down in good time the origin of such mod-ern phrases as "Behind the Eight Ball" and "Bronx Cheer" — (SATURDAY REVIEW OF LITERATURE, May 22, 1948).

GOLDIN, HYMAN E., FRANK O'LEARY, M. LIPSIUS.
Dictionary of American Underworld Lingo. New York: Twayne Publishers, Inc., 1950. 327 p.

Perhaps the most authentic work on the language of the under-world, written as it is, from the point of view of those who have had personal contact with the criminal.

Deliberately avoids any attempt to define linguistic origin. Its aim is rather "to provide a source book for students, writers, and law-enforcement agencies. It may even help the general reader to understand modern fiction" — (NEW YORK TIMES, Nov. 26, 1950).

HARROD, LEONARD MONTAGUE.
The Librarians' Glossary of Terms Used in Librarianship and the Book Crafts and Reference Book. London: British Book Centre, 1971. 784 p.

The first edition was published in 1938, the second, in 1959. The 1971 edition is an expansion of the earlier ones having al-most twice as many pages as its immediate predecessor.

The terms are clearly and concisely defined; the cross refer-ences are judicious. An indispensable aid.

HARTMANN, R.R.K. AND E.C. STORK.
Dictionary of Language and Linguistics. Halsted Press Book, 1972. 302 p.

Defines many new terms in linguistics and related disciplines and relates them to the more familiar traditional grammatical forms. About 2600 entries, with the more important ones linked to the 26 page bibliography. Of definite usefulness to students of linguistics and to anyone interested in the study of language.

HAYAKAWA, SAMUEL ICHIYE / ET AL /.
Funk and Wagnalls Modern Guide to Synonyms and Related Words. New York: Funk and Wagnalls, 1968. 726 p.

Terms are defined, compared, and contrasted in essays that are readable and informative.

JOHNSON, BURGES.
New Rhyming Dictionary and Poets' Handbook. Rev. ed. New York: Harper & Brothers, 1957. 464 p.

Part I of the first edition, published in 1931, constitutes a discussion of the basic forms of English and French verse. Part II of the first edition constitutes a rhyming dictionary, in three parts: (1) one-syllable rhymes; (2) two-syllable rhymes; (3) three-syllable rhymes. The 1957 edition contains some revision in the introductory sections, "Forms of English versification," and slight alterations and additions in the rhyming sections. There is a brief appendix.

KENYON, JOHN S. AND THOMAS ALBERT.
A Pronouncing Dictionary of American English. Springfield, Massachusetts: Merriam, 1949.

Aims to record the phonetic pronunciation of words in common use by the people who set the standards in each community. In addition to ordinary words, it also lists proper names, and also names in literature and history that are likely to be encountered by college students. If the word has only one pronunciation throughout America, only one phonetic spelling is given; if the word has more than one pronunciation, the regional differences are indicated.

"It will probably long hold its place as an indispensable handbook on American-English pronunciation, both for natives and foreigners"—(MODERN LANGUAGE NOTES, Dec. 1944).

"This book is of great interest and value. It allows for broad regional differences . . . lets you say a lot of things that the purist considers incorrect but that everybody has been saying for decades"—(NEW YORKER, 1944).

"A definite addition to the field"—(SUBSCRIPTION BOOKS BULLETIN, October, 1944).

LEWIS, NORMAN, ed.
The New Roget's Thesaurus of the English Language in Dictionary Form. Rev. and enl. ed. New York: Putnam, 1962. 552 p.
The first revision since 1936 of C. O. Sylvester Mawson's alphabetical arrangement of the Roget system of word classification (see entry on page twenty).

MARCH, FRANCIS ANDREW AND FRANCIS A. MARCH, JR.
March's Thesaurus Dictionary. Issued under the editorial supervision of Norman Cousins. New Supplement by R. A. Goodwin. Garden City: Hanover House, 1958. 1240 p.

The 1925 edition defines over 200,000 words and phrases in the English language; differentiates between those which have found a place in language and those which have not. The New Supplement lists and defines "some 1,800 words and phrases which have come into general use since the turn of the century." The treatment and general format are the same as those employed in the basic volume, and the supplementary material, through the use of symbols and cross references, is integrated with the original.

The 1968 edition has a new title **March's Thesaurus and Dictionary of the English Language,** but is otherwise an unchanged reprint.

MORRIS, WILLIAM AND MARY MORRIS.
Dictionary of Word and Phrase Origins. New York: Harper and Row, Publishers, 1971. Vol. 3.
The third volume contains more than 2,500 additional stories about the origins of everyday words and phrases. Readable and entertaining, not scholarly.

NICHOLSON, MARGARET.
A Dictionary of American-English Usage, Based on Fowler's

Modern English Usage. New York: Oxford University Press, 1957. 671 p.

A simplified version of Fowler's DICTIONARY OF MODERN USAGE, published in 1926. Some of the articles in Fowler's work are omitted, some are shortened, and new entries and illustrations are added. Hence Nicholson's work does not entirely replace the earlier one.

PARTRIDGE, ERIC.
Name Into Word: Proper Names that Have Become Common Property. New York: Macmillan, 1950.

Aims to list the names of persons, places, or things which have become so familiar that they are now accepted as having a symbolic meaning rather than a literal one; and are most likely to be met by the intelligent reader.

A "learned and enchanting work" — (NEW STATESMAN AND NATION, January, 1950).

A "delightful book," with virtually no important omissions — (SATURDAY REVIEW OF LITERATURE, April 15, 1950).

Provides "food for the philosopher and fun for the rest of us. It takes us behind the scenes" — (NEW YORK TIMES, Jan. 15, 1950).

A Dictionary of Clichés. New York: Macmillan Company, 1950.

An alphabetical arrangement of the ordinary cliches arranged into four groups: (1) "idioms that have become cliches"; (2) "Other hackneyed phrases"; (3) "Stock phrases and familiar quotations"; (4) "Quotations from English Literature."

Will "prove a delight to the scholarly reader and a terror to the writer of conscientious English" — (NATION, Nov. 23, 1940).

An "amusing, instructive, and valuable" work — (NEW STATESMAN AND NATION, September 14, 1940).

"Mr. Partridge's . . . dictionary is informative, instructive, and great fun" — (NEW YORK TIMES, October 6, 1940).

A Dictionary of Forces' Slang, 1939–1945. London: Secker and Warburg, 1948. 212 p.

A single alphabet arrangement of navy, army, and air force slang.

A Dictionary of Slang and Unconventional English: colloquialisms and catch-phrases, solecisms and catachreses, nicknames, vulgarisms, and such Americanisms as have been naturalized. Seventh edition revised and enlarged, 2 vols. in 1. New York: Macmillan, 1969. 1528 p.

The main part of the work remains unchanged; the supplement is revised, enlarged, and printed as the second part of the volume. Includes neologisms such as "freakout" and "acid."

An immense work which deals not only with slang, but with foul language as well, such as is found in many modern authors and in very few dictionaries. Many of the terms, in fact, are not even included in many of the slang dictionaries.

PEI, Mario and Frank Gaynor.
A Dictionary of Linguistics. New York: Philosophical Library, 1954. 238 p.

Crisp and authoritative definitions of terms in virtually all fields of language study.

"Medium-sized and large libraries will want to add this useful work to their reference collection of special-purpose dictionaries" — (Library journal, September 15, 1954).

PUGH, Eric.
A Dictionary of Acroynyms and Abbreviations: some abbreviations in management, technology and information science. Hamden, Conn.: Archon Books, 1968. 214 p.

More limited than the Gale Research Company's acronyms and initialisms dictionary, but it includes many entries not found in the larger volume. Classified alphabetically and under subject, with a selective subject index which enables one to locate acronym lists relative to specific subjects, such as chemistry, statisics, water.

RADFORD, Edwin.
Unusual Words and How They Came About. New York: Philosophical Library, 1946. 318 p.

An alphabetical arrangement of the meanings and origins of about 2,500 words and sayings which shed special light on customs and conventions of the age. Words and phrases which have entered the language as slang are excluded. Much of the matter is based, as the author acknowledges, on Brewer's DICTIONARY OF PHRASE AND FABLE.

ROGET, PETER MARK.
Roget's International Thesaurus. 3d. ed. New York: Crowell, 1962. 1258 p.

A complete revision by C. O. S. Mawson of the 1946 edition. Retains the original system of grouping words according to ideas. New categories (mainly scientific and technological) have been added. Quotations, appearing in previous editions, have been elimitated.

Roget's Thesaurus of the English Language in Dictionary Form. Rev. and enl. by C. O. S. Mawson. New York: Garden City Books, 1936. 660 p.

A straight dictionary arrangement, in lieu of Roget's "idea" plan, with synonyms for all entries, but with more extensive lists of synonyms for the principal entries. Also contains a comprehensive group of foreign words and phrases frequently found in English, with their definitions.

SCHWARTZ, ROBERT J.
The Complete Dictionary of Abbreviations. New York: Thomas Y. Crowell Company, 1955. 211 p.

About 25,000 abbreviations employed in virtually every field— business, law, science, music, government; as well as abbreviations of the names of colleges and universities and of the companies used in stock-market quotations. The appendix contains a list of signs and symbols.

SHANKLE, GEORGE EARLIE.
Current Abbreviations. New York: The H. W. Wilson Company, 1944. 207 p.

A fairly comprehensive alphabetical list of abbreviations— music, science, technology, government, and others. The Greek letter fraternities are alphabetized at the end of the appropriate English letter in accordance with the English spelling of the Greek initial.

SHAW, HARRY.
Dictionary of Literary Terms. New York: McGraw-Hill Book Company, 1972. 402 p.

Defines over 2000 literary terms: sophisticated terms; curios of rhetoric (synecdoche, anacoluthon); and random sprinkling of ordinary words (escapism, quibble). Impressive system of cross-references enhances value of the work.

SKEAT, WALTER WILLIAM.
An Etymological Dictionary of the English Language. New ed., rev. and enl. Oxford: Clarendon Press, 1910.

Full histories of more than 14,000 words, with reference to sources. Contents: (1) Dictionary; (2) Appendix: List of Prefixes, Suffixes, Homonyms, Doublets, Indogermanic roots; Distribution of words according to languages from which they are derived. A standard scholarly work.

STEVENSON, HERBERT J.
Abbreviations: A Dictionary of Abbreviations. New York: Macmillan, 1943. 126 p.

Attempts to include the most common abbreviations used. The main division lists alphabetically some 7,500 general abbreviations. A second division lists the abbreviations under special fields,—Books of the Bible; Shakespeare's Works; Legal Literature; Christian Names; Geography, etc.

"Without laughing off the obvious value of Abbreviations to chaps who are thrown for a loss by the other man's shop talk and verbal short cuts, any reviewer should certainly recommend it also for rainy-day reading"—(SPRINGFIELD REPUBLICAN, September 9, 1943).

"Within the limits set the book has been well done, but it is not exhaustive"—(NEW YORK TIMES, November 7, 1943).

Thesaurus of English Words and Phrases. New ed., completely rev. and modernized by Robert A. Dutch. New York: St. Martin's Press, 1965. 1309 p.

The first revision in 26 years of the original Roget's THESAURUS. The text "is entirely rewritten and greatly expanded," and the index is "wholly recompiled, but organically identical with Roget's original."

WALKER, John.
Rhyming Dictionary of the English Language, rev. and enl. by L. H. Dawson. New York: E. P. Dutton & Company, 1924. 549 p.

First compiled in 1775, revised and enlarged by J. Longmuir in 1865, and reprinted many times, the RHYMING DICTIONARY includes over 54,000 entries, arranged according to final vowel sounds. The index lists "allowable rhymes" according to combinations of vowels and consonants.

"Here is a new edition of a standard work as indispensable to poets as Roget's THESAURUS. Here is the whole English language arranged according to its terminations. . . . We welcome this valuable old book in its new spruce dress. It is one of the volumes that are necessary to every complete reference shelf" — (SATURDAY REVIEW OF LITURATURE, January 3, 1929).

WALL, C. EDWARD AND EDWARD PRZEBIENDA.
Words and Phrases Index. Ann Arbor, Michigan: Pierian Press, 1969–70. 4 vols.

Aims to supplement major dictionaries of the English language. Volume one lists unusual words, compound words, and phrases, with citations to pertinent articles or notes appearing in AMERICAN NOTES AND QUERIES (1962–67), AMERICAN SPEECH (1925–66), BRITANNICA BOOK OF THE YEAR (1945–67), and NOTES AND QUERIES (1925–66); volume two indexes materials from the same publications, but in a different arrangement—by key-word nouns, verbs, adjectives, and adverbs; volume three includes some 50,000 references to AMERICAN NOTES AND QUERIES (1941–49), COLLEGE ENGLISH (1939–68), DIALECT NOTES (1890–1939), and the PUBLICATIONS of the American Dialect Society (1944–67); volume four covers material from the same sources as volume three, but in a different arrangement, and includes new entries from CALIFORNIA FOLKLORE QUARTERLY (1942–47) and WESTERN FOLKLORE (1948–67).

WAWRZYSZKO, ALEKSANDRA K.
Bibliography of General Linguistics: English and American. New York: Archon Books, 1971. 120 p.

Focuses on basic linguistics publications of the 1960's. Among the sections are: Theory and Philosophy of Language and Methodology of Language; History of Language and Historical

Linguistics; Phonetics; Phonology; Morphology; Computational Linguistics; and Linguistic Periodicals and Series. The annotations are careful; the classification is thorough.

Webster's New Dictionary of Synonyms. 2d. ed. Springfield, Massachusetts: Merriam, 1968. 909 p.

A revision, updating, and resetting of the earlier edition entitled WEBSTER'S DICTIONARY OF SYNONYMS. The subtitle is: a dictionary of discriminated synonyms, with antonyms and analagous and contrasted words.

WEINGARTEN, JOSEPH ABRAHAM.
An American Dictionary of Slang and Colloquial Speech. New York: Privately printed, 1954. 390 p.

Attempts to give and to authenticate the earliest date for each word and phrase.

WENTWORTH, HAROLD.
American Dialect Dictionary. New York: Crowell, 1944. 747 p.

A comprehensive list of well over 10,000 terms, dealing mainly, as is noted in the "Preface," with "dialect in the sense of localisms, regionalisms, and provincialisms; folk speech, urban as well as rustic New England and Southern United States dialects viewed in their deviations from General Northern or Western. . . ."

"The author is a well known lexicographer and philologist and has lived and studied the subject in all of the regions from which the three main dialect classifications stem. This should prove a valuable reference item" — (KIRKUS, July 1, 1944).

"An excellent dictionary of homely folk speech of America. Mr. Wentworth's editing shows that he is a competent lexicographer. He has brought a mass of loose material into an easily managed order. . . . It will be very useful to students of dialect and to writers of tales and will provide a fine stimulus to further studies" — (NEW YORK TIMES, July 23, 1944).

WHITFIELD, JANE SHAW.
The Improved Rhyming Dictionary. New York: Crowell, 1951. 283 p.

A list of about 115,000 words, arranged under main headings according to general meanings. Particularly useful for the inclusion of recent words, slang, and foreign words.

WOOD, CLEMENT.
Wood's Unabridged Rhyming Dictionary. Cleveland: The World Publishing Company, 1943. 1049 p.

An arrangement of single, double, and triple rhymes according to sound, rather than spelling. The introduction discusses the mechanics and forms of poetry.

ENCYCLOPEDIAS

Chamber's Encyclopedia. Rev. ed. London: Pergamon Press, 1967. 15 vols.

Because it is the only major encyclopedia prepared and produced completely in England, since the BRITANNICA was brought to the United States in 1929, and reflects the British and, to a degree, the European view of the range of human knowledge, it is of unquestionable value to the American scholar and student. Occasional articles are rather long. That on the Papacy, for example, is sixteen pages long; that on Greek art is ten pages long. Typical entries, however, are quite brief, thousands being only a paragraph or two; and the bibliographies are generally skimpy.

Collier's Encyclopedia. New York: P. F. Collier & Son Corporation, 1967. 24 vols.

More advanced than the juvenile encyclopedias, but neither so broad in scope nor so scholarly in treatment as the BRITANNICA and AMERICANA; principally aimed at the junior college level. Articles are contributed by specialists and are initialed, with the full names and positions of the authors given at the beginning of volume 1. A special feature of the encyclopedia is the 140 page briefly annotated bibliography section in the final volume.

THE COLLIER'S YEARBOOK, originally prepared as a supplement to the NATIONAL ENCYCLOPEDIA and called the NATIONAL YEARBOOK, is designed to serve both as a supplement to COLLIER'S ENCYCLOPEDIA, and as an annual survey. Since becoming a supplement to COLLIER'S ENCYCLOPEDIA, it has become increasingly more like it in scope and format.

COLLIER'S was first published in 20 volumes as an entirely new work. In 1962 the set was expanded to 24 volumes. The 1967 edition encompasses changes of a word or sentence to completely rewritten articles. Only about a third of the revisions add significantly to the earlier editions.

Encyclopedia Americana. New York: Encyclopedia Americana Corporation, 30 vols., 1969.

Aims to present "Knowledge with faithfulness and with scholarly impartiality, avoiding the promotion of theories and such discussions and defenses as are entirely foreign to the character and nature of an encyclopedia . . . to present in an intelligent and informing way, the history and nature of the civilization, institutions, systems, activities, and achievements of mankind with sufficient usefulness to furnish the general reader a fair and adequate understanding of the development of man and his social life"—(Pref.).

Although it has a large number of relatively short entries, with special emphasis upon personal and place names, it is notable for the long essay-type treatment of major topics, most of which are followed by comparatively extensive bibliographies; and also for its exceptionally thorough biographical coverage of eminent Americans and Canadians, especially of the nineteenth century and earlier.

The 1918–20 edition was a complete revision, reset throughout with much new material, and is the basis of succeeding editions. "Since 1943 the index volume (v. 30) has been an alphabetical index arranged in dictionary form, instead of the classed index of previous editions. It is kept to date with each printing and should always be consulted in order that pertinent material treated in various parts of the work will not be overlooked." In the 1957 edition, there are more than 58,500 article headings with over 44,000 cross references, 11,500 illustrations, and 185 maps. In the 1969 edition there are approximately 5,500 contributors, some 2,000 of which are new since the 1964 edition. Also added in the 1969 version are 180 black-and-white text maps and 172 color maps, bringing the new totals to 589 and 347 respectively. And significantly evident is the expansion of reference information in science and technology.

Keeping the AMERICANA up-to-date is the AMERICANA ANNUAL: AN ENCYCLOPEDIA OF CURRENT EVENTS, which summarizes the events of the preceding year and, in format, resembles the volumes of the encyclopedia.

Encyclopedia Britannica. Chicago: Encyclopedia Britannica, 1972. 24 vols.

The oldest, largest, and most famous of the English-language encyclopedias, aiming, as is noted in the fourteenth edition, "to provide the fullest, most various digest of universal information."

The first eight editions are now of virtually no use; but the ninth, eleventh, and fourteenth editions and their supplements must still be used: the ninth, "the high-water mark of the Britannica, for subjects where recent information is not of primary importance"; the eleventh, because, though more popular than earlier editions, it is nonetheless a scholarly and carefully edited work, and retains a preference for greater length and comprehensiveness; and the fourteenth because of its up-to-dateness and its greater number of more popular entries.

The 14th edition, first published in 1929, was revised, reset, and reorganized to include short articles on small subjects as well as many long articles. Some of the latter have been carried over from the 9th and 11th editions, sometimes revised and abridged, but still carrying the signature of the original author. After the publication of the 14th edition in 1929, the system of elaborate new editions, which took from three to thirteen years to prepare, was abandoned, and the BRITANNICA is now published under a policy of continuous annual revision.

The main text is comprised by the first 23 volumes; the detailed index, always to be used if one wishes to find all the pertinent material, is embraced by volume 24.

Since 1938, the BRITANNICA has issued a BRITANNICA BOOK OF THE YEAR to cover the events and developments of the preceding year and to keep the work as up-to-date as it can. Each volume contains a cumulative index to that volume and the four preceding ones, as well as a subject index to illustrations.

Speaking of the ninth edition, the reviewer notes that the work, from being a mere compilation, has "become a work of national importance, containing original treatises on science, art, and literature by famous literary and scientific men"— (NATURE, 1875).

The eleventh edition is referred to as a "work of transcendent merit, one unapproached by any similar publication"—(NATION, May 25, 1911).

"The most famous and best reference work in the English language. Complete in every sense"—(SATURDAY REVIEW OF LITERATURE).

Most recent editions follow the continuous revision policy

established in 1932. Although there are over 2,000 fewer entries in the 1972 edition than in the 1967 edition, according to the publisher, the index, inserts, illustrations and number of pages have all increased. And, while many of the older, broad-subject type articles are still found, the tendency seems to be toward the inclusion of more specific articles.

The New Encyclopaedia Britannica. Chicago, Illinois: Encyclopaedia Britannica, 1974. 30 vols.

Wholly different in character from the previous editions of the BRITANNICA. The first ten volumes, called the micropaedia, serve as a book of reference (the traditional concept); but the two parts which are called the propaedia and the macropaedia represent departures from the conventional (or traditional) concept. In these sections the entries "are studies in depth of the subject treated; and all are exercises in *haute vulgarisation* in which the specialist knowledge of experts is made intelligible to laymen, with aid of good pictures and diagrams as well as words." The longest BRITANNICA ever: forty-three million words, twenty-four thousand two hundred and thirty-nine illustrations.

Encyclopedia of Social Sciences. New York: The Macmillan Company, 1930–1935. 15 vols.

Designed to appeal to three groups, scholars, "intelligentsia," and the general public by: (1) providing a synopsis of the progress which has been made in the general areas of the social sciences; (2) assembling those salient facts which will assist those who wish to keep abreast of the most recent investigation and accomplishment; (3) constituting a center of authoritative knowledge for the creation of a sounder and more informed public opinion on problems central to the foundation of social progress and world development.

The first attempt to embrace the entire field of the social sciences. All articles are by specialists, are fully signed, and are followed by bibliographies which are generally adequate.

". . . is another milestone marking the progress of the sciences that seek an understanding of man, and another achievement of American scholarship"—(NATION, Feb. 5, 1930).

". . . a compendium of completed discovery which will for

years remain a standard of information . . ."—(THE NEW RE-
PUBLIC, Aug. 30, 1930).

"Taken as a whole the encyclopedia may be said to represent
the highest standards of scholarship. . . . Viewed in its entirety, the encyclopedia is the best possible refutation of those
who say that the study of man cannot be scientific"—(THE NA-
TION, Sept. 25, 1935).

"Save for minor gaps . . . there seems to be no doubt that
these 15 imposing volumes will hold their place for a long
time as a definitive exhibit of the content and scope of American and international cooperation in a large intellectual field"—
(NEW YORK TIMES, August 11, 1935).

Encyclopedia of World Literature in the 20th Century, edited
by Wolfgang Bernard Fleischmann. New York: Ungar, 1972. 3
vols.

Most of the 1,300 articles in the encyclopedia are bibliographic
in nature, organized in four parts: a headnote brief identification; an article of critical appraisal relative to the author's influence on world literature; a section ("Further Works") listing
titles not mentioned in the main article; and a fourth section
("Bibliography"), a short list of articles and books about the
author's works.

Jewish Encyclopedia: A Descriptive Record of the History,
Religion, Literature, and Customs of the Jewish people from
the earliest times to the present day. New York: Ktav Publishing House, 1964. 12 vols.

A scholarly work which, though somewhat dated, is still valuable for its biographies, its descriptions of the present state of
Jews throughout the world, and for its elucidations of Talmudic
law.

On the one hand it is a true encyclopedia, viewing always
from the Jewish viewpoint; on the other hand, "it is a cyclopaedia as the record of a single branch of knowledge—the civilization of a single race . . ."—(NATION).

The 1964 publication is a photo-offset reproduction of the
early edition, not of the post-World War 1 revision, and hence
lacks some of the death dates and other items found in the later
edition.

McGraw-Hill Encyclopedia of World Drama. New York: McGraw-Hill Book Co., 1972. 4 vols.

The articles generally deal with individual playwrights, rather than with concepts or with terms as such. Of the 910 playwrights listed, 300 are grouped as major playwrights, 610, as minor dramatists. For each major dramatist, the article provides "a factual discussion of the author's life, short synopses of several if not all of his plays, comprehensive listings of his entire body of work, and bibliographic information. . . . Entries on lesser dramatists . . . have been dealt with in the conventional encyclopedic way. Each of these articles traces the dramatist's span of life, touches on significant activities that relate to his dramatic writing, and briefly discusses some of his more prominent plays." ("Introduction")

New Catholic Encyclopedia: An International Work of Reference on the Teachings, History, Organization, and Activities of the Catholic Church, and on All Institutions, Religions, Philosophies, and Scientific and Cultural Developments Affecting the Catholic Church from Its Beginnings to the Present. 15 vols. New York: McGraw, 1967. 15,350 p.

Almost ten years in the making, the NEW CATHOLIC ENCYCLOPEDIA comprises 15,000,000 words; 15,000 pages; 17,000 articles by 4,800 contributors; 7,400 illustrations, including 32 color plates and 300 new maps. Each article is signed and has a select bibliography. The numerous Biblical articles, including seven basic Bible studies which alone cover 140 pages, constitute a complete Biblical encyclopedia. "Every archdiocese in the world, and each diocese and Catholic college and university in the United States has a separate article." The contributors include European scholars and non-Catholics.

New International Encyclopedia. New York: Dodd, Mead & Company, 1902–1930. 23 vols.

Once the first choice of many librarians and bibliographers, it is now, because unfortunately out of date, useful only for articles on subjects which do not require revision. Important articles are by specialists; minor articles, by staff members. Articles are unsigned, but a list of the authors of the main articles appears at the beginning of each volume. A special feature is the inclusion of many biographical articles, some 20,000 in all, principally of Americans of both continents, and its excellent bibliographies.

THE NEW INTERNATIONAL YEARBOOK originally published as INTERNATIONAL YEARBOOK is published as a compendium of the world's progress for the preceding year and also serves as a supplement for the encyclopedia.

Written "throughout by competent persons acting under the direction of a very able editorial staff; it is the result of a critical study of all the famous works of reference which have at any time appeared in Europe or the United States; and it combines the four qualities which are necessary to make up the ideal encyclopedia"—(THE AMERICAN CATHOLIC QUARTERLY REVIEW, July, 1904).

Universal Jewish Encyclopedia: An Authoritative and Popular Presentation of Jews and Judaism since the earliest times. New York: Universal Jewish Encyclopedia, Inc., 1939–1944. 10 vols.

A more popular treatment than the JEWISH ENCYCLOPEDIA covering virtually every phase of Judaism and Jewish life, history, religion, and culture, especially impressive in its treatment of American subjects. Most of the entries are signed by specialists and many of the articles are followed by bibliographies. Admirably supplements, not supersedes the more scholarly work.

LITERARY HANDBOOKS

In addition to the general literary handbooks, the English major should seek familiarity with the many author handbooks, four of the more representative of which are included in this section.

ALDEN, RAYMOND M.
A Shakespeare Handbook. New York: Crofts, 1925. 240 p.

A very useful collection of Shakespeare source material, obviating the need of going to the volumes of Holinshed, Plutarch, Bandillo and the others. Contains the known facts of Shakespeare's life, the chronology of his plays, source material (the main portion of the work), and notes on grammar and versification.

"Shakespeare's lovers and a large number of intelligent readers who wish to join the ranks will find this little volume greatly to their taste"—(EDUCATION REVIEW, October, 1925).

"The book makes available for the student material which will aid him alike in analyzing the structures of the plays and in appreciating the genius with which the dramatist transformed his borrowed plots and characters"—(SPRINGFIELD REPUBLICAN, 1925).

"This useful little book will be helpful to teachers and for self-education. It aims to give students of collegiate grade and other mature, but not learned, readers the materials needed for the study of Shakespeare's principal works"—(WISCONSIN LIBRARY BULLETIN, October, 1925).

ANDERSON, MICHAEL, ET AL.
Crowell's Handbook of Contemporary Drama. New York: Thomas Y. Crowell Co., 1971. 505 p.

Dictionary-arranged entries cover dramatists, outstanding dramatic works, theater companies, and the drama of Europe and

North and South America. Seems to stress in a special way the avant-garde playwrights and their works. A definite aid to all interested in the modern drama.

BARNHART, CLARENCE L. AND WILLIAM HALSEY.
The New Century Handbook of English Literature. New York: Appleton-Century-Crofts, Inc., 1967. 1167 p.

More than 14,000 entries, arranged alphabetically, with pronunciation, and covering Anglo-American, Canadian, Australian, Irish, and South African works of literature. Essentially based upon THE NEW CENTURY CYCLOPEDIA OF NAMES, differing most importantly from it in possessing a greater number of entries dealing with literary forms and other matters not properly falling under the category of "name." A comprehensive collection of data on major literary works, characters, movements, etc., seeking to answer questions most likely to be asked by modern American readers of English literature.

"The publication of a major new reference work is an uncommon event, and especially welcome when that work is of high quality. Clarence Barnhart is an experienced editor of books of reference, and the latest work to bear his name comes well up to expectations" — (BOOKLIST, April 15, 1956).

"Here 'English' means 'not American,' rather than 'English only'. . . . Even American scholars of English literature appear (M. M. Manly of Chicago). But Emerson, Poe, Lowell, and other American men of letters, however influential or active they were in Britain, are out. . . . There is no other reference work which has the same timeliness, scale, and scope as this" — (CHICAGO SUNDAY TRIBUNE, March 18, 1956).

"Throughout the book there is evidence of careful editing and scholarly selection of terms" — (BOOKLIST, October 1, 1956).

New entries have been included in the 1967 edition, and new information has been added to a number of the existing articles; but the overall revision has been accomplished with a minimum of resetting, at the expense, for the most part, of deleting entries or reducing the size of the articles from the 1956 edition.

BARON, JOSEPH L.
A Treasury of Jewish Quotations. New York: Crown Publishers, Inc., 1956. 700 p.

Some 18,000 quotations by or about Jews, in some 1,000 categories, ranging from "Ability" to "Zionism." Many of the quotations are familiar ones, but literally thousands of the striking quotations are from relatively little known persons. Each quotation is identified by author, title of the work, and date. Has an author and subject index.

"Many of the proverbs, maxims, and comments—which cover the secular and religious world of ancient and contemporary Judaism—have never before been translated into English. . . . Of particular value to speakers and students"—(BOOK-LIST, September 8, 1956).

" . . . it will be a useful reference work as well as a fascinating introduction to Jewish thought. 'Of the making of books there is no end,' but this one is recommended for any public or college library"—(LIBRARY JOURNAL, June 1, 1956).

BARTLETT, JOHN.
Familiar Quotations. A Collection of Passages, Phrases and Proverbs Traced to Their Sources in Ancient and Modern Literature. 14th ed. Boston: Little, Brown & Company, 1968. 1750 p.

A standard guide to quotations, containing some 113,500 entries, arranged by authors according to the order of their birth dates. The index is so thorough that often even a vague recollection of the passages is sufficient to reveal the quotation sought after.

The publishers of the eleventh edition noted that for every two quotations added at least one was eliminated. Hence there are times when the tenth edition will still be useful.

"What Bartlett needs now is to have its splendid grab-bag of riches winnowed and put in order by a touch of scholarship"—(TIME, December 13, 1948).

Of the twelfth edition it was noted: The "first half, through Kipling, is unchanged; the remainder is re-edited and enlarged, with quotations of the war years added, as well as more translations from other languages"—(BOOKLIST, December 15, 1948).

"This famous collection of passages, phrases, and proverbs . . . has long been a standby of the library. . . . Bartlett has always been noted for readability; the new edition keeps up to this standard"—(NEW YORK HERALD TRIBUNE, December 19, 1948).

Many new quotations have been added from old and new sources, subject indexing has been expanded, and the earlier edition has been extensively revised. On the other hand, numerous quotations from the 13th edition have been dropped.

BENÉT, WILLIAM ROSE.
The Reader's Encyclopedia. 2d ed. New York: Crowell, 1965. 1118 p.

Brief articles on writers, scientists, philosophers, etc., of all nations and all periods; allusions and literary expressions and terms; literary schools and movements; plots and characters; descriptions of musical compositions and works of art. Emphasizes world literature, especially those areas of growing interest: the Orient, the Soviet Union, Latin America, and the Near East.

BREWER, EBENEZER COBHAM.
Reader's Handbook of Famous Names in Fiction, Allusions, References, Proverbs, Plots, Stories, and Poems. Philadelphia: Lippincott, 1898. 2 vols. Republished by Gale Research Co., Detroit, 1966.

Aims to furnish the reader with a brief and lucid account of the words used in references and allusions by poets and prose writers, as well as to furnish information about plots of dramas, tales, and narrative poems. The appendixes contain: (1) List of English authors and their works; (2) Title list of dramas and operas, giving authors and dates. Later issues of the work lack the appendixes.

"Those readers who remember with affection Brewer's little red READER'S HANDBOOK will relish Mr. Benet's new reference book for readers" — (NEW YORK TIMES, November 7, 1948).

BREWER, EBENEZER COBHAM.
Brewer's Dictionary of Phrase and Fable. Rev. and enl. ed. New York: Harper & Brothers, 1970. 1175 p.

The most recent edition of a work which in England and America has become one of the classic reference works, expanded and brought fully up-to-date by the addition of newer material, those that were fostered by World War II.

The scope of the work is amply indicated by the lengthy subtitle: "giving illustrative quotations from the works of the most famous authors from the earliest time to the present day; a history of the chief figures mentioned in the mythologies of the world; a record of superstitions and customs, ancient and modern; an explanation of phrases commonly in use in the English language, of native origin or borrowed from other tongues; ancient cant and contemporary slang, with their equivalents in others languages of Europe; the stories of well-known characters from novels and romances; local and national legends; a glossary of scientific, historical, political, and archaeological terms and events; references bearing on every description of economic and scientific data; etymological and much other information."

The 1970 edition is based on that of 1963, but, as the editor observes in the Preface, he has patterned the current work upon Dr. Brewer's "original conception by discarding entries . . . which seemed to have little claim to be in a dictionary of 'Phrase and Fable.' Words which have no particular 'tale to tell' have also been deleted . . ."

The present text takes account of more recent scholarship, giving greater attention than in the past to Irish and Welsh fable and to American and Commonwealth expressions.

BRUSSELL, Eugene E.
Dictionary of Quotable Definitions. Englewood Cliffs, New Jersey: Prentice-Hall, 1970. 627 p.

A collection of definitions in which "aphorism and metaphor replace the straight dictionary meaning." Indicates the author of the definition, but does not cite the specific source. Alphabetical arrangement by subject categories.

BURACK, A. S.
The Writer's Handbook: A Complete Reference Library for Free-Lance Writers. Boston: The Writer, Inc., 1957. 650 p.

Contains 79 chapters of instruction by leading authors and editors on every field of writing, craft and commercial phases;

1,000 markets for stories, plays, articles, and other literary productions.

". . . contains a wealth of information of great value to the aspiring writers regardless of what branch of literature he is interested in"—(BOSTON TRANSCRIPT, Jan. 1937).

"Textbook for the literary novice containing articles on various types of professional writing. . . . Most of the articles have appeared in the magazine THE WRITER during the last two years"—(BOOK REVIEW DIGEST, 1937).

BURKE, W. J. AND W. D. HOWE.
American Authors and Books, 1640 to the Present Day. Augmented and revised by Irving R. Weiss. New York: Crown, 1962. 834 p.

The aim is to present "the most useful facts about the writing, illustrating, editing, publishing, reviewing, collecting, selling and preservation of American books from 1640 to 1940"—(Preface).

A quick reference tool, somewhat similar to the OXFORD COMPANION TO AMERICAN LITERATURE with larger coverage but briefer articles. Author, title, fictional characters, magazines, newspapers, places, names, and other entries are alphabetically arranged with cross references. Limited to continental United States.

Omits many of the subject entries of the 1943 edition and updates many author and title entries. New material significantly differentiates the two editions.

"Contains much useful material not hereto readily available . . . . a veritable storehouse of information for journalists, writers, teachers and others actively interested in American literature. Comprehensive and accurate, and includes many hundreds of items which the author does not suggest"—(BOOK WEEK, July, 1949).

CAMPBELL, OSCAR JAMES AND EDWARD G. QUINN, eds.
The Reader's Encyclopedia of Shakespeare. New York: Crowell, 1966. 1014 p.

References to persons, places, literary works, and subjects associated with Shakespeare. Integrates, under one alphabet, studies by scholars, biographers, historians, and critics. Contains summary of plot, characters, sources, stage history, and criticism for each of the 37 major plays; and, for most entries, bibliographic listings.

CLARK, BARRETT HARPER.
Study of the Modern Drama: A Handbook for the Study and Appreciation of the Best Plays, European, English and American, of the Last Century. New ed. New York: Appleton, 1928. 535 p.

Separate chapters on Norwegian, German, French, Italian, English, Irish, and American drama, giving salient facts about the major plays.

"In spite of easily remediable limitations, this book takes its place at once as the best existing survey of modern European and American dramatic movements"—(SPECTATOR, April 18, 1925).

"A student of modern drama would go far to find a more careful and detailed guide book"—(THEATRE ARTS, July, 1925).

"The author's selections are judicious and representative; his treatment impartial"—(CATHOLIC WORLD, June, 1925).

DEUTSCH, BABETTE.
Poetry Handbook: A Dictionary of Terms. 4th ed. New York: Funk and Wagnalls, 1974. 203 p.

Supplementary material from the 2d edition is incorporated into the main body of the work, and new material is added. A useful handbook for the student and practitioner. By and large a reprint of earlier edition.

DeVANE, WILLIAM CLYDE.
Browning Handbook. New York: Appleton, Century-Crofts, Inc., 1955. 590 p.

The main divisions are: Life, Early Poems, Middle Years, and Last Decade. Biography, publication facts, and critical discussions.

"In addition to gathering up the results of Browning's scholarship to date, Mr. DeVane has made contributions of his own, notably in regard to the source of the descriptive passage in

'Childe Roland, in Lairesse's 'The Art of Painting in All Its Branches,' and in the connection between Browning's 'Fifine at the Fair' and Rossetti's 'Jenney' " — (NEW REPUBLIC, December, 935).

"A contribution of exceptional value to Browning study. . . . The new handbook impresses one as a work essential to the student or critical reader" — (SPRINGFIELD REPUBLICAN, July, 1935).

EVANS, BERGEN.
Dictionary of Quotations. New York: Delacorte Press, 1968. 2029 p.

The arrangement is alphabetical; a typical index is followed by the main section of quotations under topical headings arranged in a chronological order to show the development of the idea. The Subject Index is basically a key-word index with the addition of references to names or terms which occur in the explanatory notes rather than in the actual quotations. An author index is also provided. A useful addition to the standard collections; easy to follow.

FREEMAN, WILLIAM.
Dictionary of Fictional Characters. London: Dent, 1963. 458 p.

Lists some 10,000 fictional characters, from approximately 2000 books by some 500 British, Commonwealth, and American authors, written in the last 600 years. Covers novels, short stories, poems, and plays.

GHOSH, JYOTISH CHANDRA.
Annals of English Literature, 1475–1925. The Principal Publications of Each Year with an Alphabetical Index of Authors and Their Works. Oxford: Clarendon Press, 1935. 340 p.

A chronological list, providing year by year the authors and titles of publications, with general descriptions; marginal notes indicate contemporary foreign publications, or events of biographical importance. A detailed author index.

"The book is as practical a small work of reference as has been issued in a long time" — (COMMONWEAL, March 20, 1936).

"Sound in scholarship and admirable in the organization of its vast contents"—(NEW YORK TIMES, March 15, 1936).

"It is not exaggeration to say that the compilers of this little reference book have put every student of English literature in their debt"—(SPECTATOR, February 21, 1936).

"The book can be used equally through the approach of the authors . . . and also through the approach of the years . . . . it can be read straightforward, with both profit and pleasure; and it can be worked backwards from the index in the process of checking dates of authors and of books"—(TIMES LITERARY SUPPLEMENT, February 1, 1936).

GRANGER, EDITH.
Granger's Index to Poetry. 6th ed. completely rev. and enl.; indexing anthologies pub. through Dec. 31, 1970: ed. by William James Smith. New York: Columbia University Press, 1973. 2223 p.

Indexes 514 volumes of anthologized poetry, among which are most of those indexed in the fifth edition and the 1967 supplement. Eliminates a number of out-of-print works and some titles whose popularity has waned. Still one of the best general indexes to poetry.

HALLIDAY, FRANK.
A Shakespeare Companion, 1550–1950. New York: Funk & Wagnalls Company, 1952. 742 p.

Interesting and very readable information about the playwright and his contemporaries. All entries are alphabetically arranged: life, critical studies of Shakespeare, biographical data on his friends, printers, publishers, players, etc.; critical notes on poems, productions. A useful bibliography. For the reader and general student, rather than for the scholar.

HANFORD, JAMES HOLLY.
A Milton Handbook. 5th ed. New York: Appleton, 1970. 374 p.

A companion to Milton studies for the advanced student. The new addition contains a new appendix on Milton in Italy and textual revisions and additions based upon recent research, as well as fuller footnotes and bibliographies.

HARDWICK, Michael and Mollie Hardwick, comps.
The Charles Dickens Encyclopedia. New York: Scribners, 1973.
531 p.

Detailed plot summaries of major and minor works: an alphabetical list of more than 2000 named characters; an extensive
breakdown of the author's life and works; and more than 250
pages of quotations from the works with a full index. Probably
the most extensive and most useful single reference aid to
Dickens study now available.

HARSH, Philip Whaley.
A Handbook of Classical Drama. Stanford, California: Stanford University Press, 1956. 526 p.

Discussions of the structure, purpose, and meaning of 45 Greek
and 36 Latin plays, aiming to constitute "a modern appreciation of the plays as literature and a convenient brief guide to
further critical material." In five parts: GREEK TRAGEDY: Aes-
chylus, Sophocles, Euripides; OLD COMEDY: Aristophanes; NEW
COMEDY: Menander; ROMAN COMEDY: Plautus, Terence;
ROMAN TRAGEDY: Seneca. An extensive bibliography and a very
detailed index.

". . . deserves high praise . . . is a guide that gives relevant
facts accurately and conveniently" — (BOOK WEEK, January 21,
1945).

". . . indispensable for any student of the theater. . . .
Very highly recommended" — (CLASSICAL PHILOLOGY, July,
1945).

". . . is meant for reference and as such will be found useful
to students and to the scholars in the field" — (LIBRARY JOUR-
NAL, July, 1944).

HART, James D.
The Oxford Companion to American Literature. 3d ed. New
York: Oxford University Press, 1956. 890 p.

A chronological arrangement of "short biographies, and bibliographies of American authors, with information regarding their
style and subject matter; nearly 900 summaries and descriptions of the important American novels, stories, essays, poems
and plays; definitions and historical outlines of literary schools
and movements; and information on literary societies, maga-

zines, anthologies, co-operative publications, literary awards, book collectors, printers, etc." — (Preface).

A special feature is the chronological index, a year-by-year outline, giving in parallel columns the literary and social events from 1000 to 1947.

The fourth edition, published in 1965, lacks some of the material found in the third edition, contains substantial additions, retains the format and scope of the third edition.

HART, JAMES D.

The Oxford Companion to American Literature. 4th ed. rev. and enl. New York: Oxford University Press, 1966. 991 p.

HARTNOLL, PHYLLIS.

The Oxford Companion to the Theatre. London: Oxford University Press, 1965. 1088 p.

The new edition (3rd) greatly expands the 2d edition, incorporating numerous articles and adding much new material. International in scope and comprehensively historical. Emphasizes the popular, rather than the literary theater, and the actor, rather than the playwright. Devotes one article to opera and one to ballet; does not cover the cinema. Includes information to the end of 1964.

HARVEY, SIR PAUL.

The Oxford Companion to English Literature. 4th ed. Oxford: Clarendon Press, 1967. 961 p.

An alphabetical arrangement of brief articles on authors' lives, pseudonyms, characters in fiction, plots of novels and plays, famous works, places in literature, allusions. Includes a small number of American authors; many bibliographies. New entries are added for a number of 20th-century writers and works.

HARVEY, SIR PAUL.

The Oxford Companion to Classical Literature. 4th ed. rev. by Dorothy Eagle. Oxford: Clarendon Press, 1967. 961 p.

Entries for the twentieth century are updated, new entries are made for new writers, and articles on established writers are expanded.

A useful handbook of concise information on the principal classical authors and their works, with as much background data as is necessary to render the works intelligible.

HOBSBAUM, Philip.
A Reader's Guide to Charles Dickens. New York: Farrar, Straus and Giroux, 1973. 319 p.

The introduction briefly surveys Dickens' political reportage and his pamphleteering for prison reform and describes the earliest works. The main part of the work provides neat and well-informed summaries on all the books, from SKETCHES BY BOZ to EDWIN DROOD. A long and very useful bibliography with indispensable items indicated by asterisks.

HOLMAN, C. Hugh.
A Handbook to Literature: Based on the Original by William Flint Thrall and Addison Hibbard. 3d. ed. New York: Odyssey, 1972. 646 p.

In this latest edition, more than 600 entries have been added and most of the others have been revised. There has also "been some effort to include Eastern Literature."

MALKOFF, Karl.
Crowell's Handbook of Contemporary American Poetry. New York: Crowell, 1973. 338 p.

A more comprehensive collection of essays on the subject than any recent comparable collection, with twenty-one poets receiving extended commentary. ". . . an energetic, accomplished and useful guide which does justice to the excitement and diversity of contemporary American poetry." (AMERICAN SCHOLAR, Summer, 1974).

MARTIN, Michael Rheta and Richard C. Harrier.
The Concise Encyclopedic Guide to Shakespeare. New York: Horizon Press, 1972. 450 p.

Synopses of Shakespeare's plays and characters; quotations and explanations of words and phrases from the plays. Eight useful appendixes contain biographical sketches of critics, scholars, actors and others associated with the playwright's work; charts of historical characters; discography; bibliography.

MOSSE, FERNAND.
Handbook of Middle English. Baltimore: The Johns Hopkins Press, 1952.

"This admirable work (long introductions, texts, notes, glossary and reproductions of manuscripts) should . . . greatly benefit medieval English studies in French universities. The author insists on 'phonetic reality,' cites originals where and when they are known, assumes a knowledge of Old English, verifies all the texts, and omits diacritics save in the earliest. . . . There are however serious blemishes. Many misprints, wrongly numbered references, and wavering punctuation must be added to the already lengthy errata though some mis-spellings will not deceive the student . . ."—(REVIEW OF ENGLISH STUDIES, January, 1951).

MYERS, ROBIN, ed.
A Dictionary of Literature in the English Language from Chaucer to 1940. Pergamon, 1970. 2 vols., 1497 p.

A bibliographical and biographical guide to some 2,500 authors who have used English as their medium of expression over a period of 600 years. The first volume is arranged alphabetically by author's last name. Volume II is a title-author index to some 60,000 works cited in Volume I. A sequel which will cover the period 1940–1970 is planned for future publication.

New Oxford Book of English Verse, 1250–1950. Edited by Helen Gardner. New York: Oxford University Press, 1972. 974 p.

Encompasses seven centuries of verse: private and personal poems; poems dealing with public events, historic occasions; religious, moral, and political convictions; satire; and light verse. The level of poetry is uniformly high; the choices are generous.

Oxford Dictionary of English Proverbs. 3d ed. rev. by F. P. Wilson. Oxford: Clarendon Press, 1970. 930 p.

Planned on the lines of the O.E.D., with each proverb illustrated by dated quotations. The first edition (1935) contained approximately 10,000 proverbs, arranged alphabetically by first word, including the article. The second edition contains about 11,000 proverbs, arranged alphabetically according to the first significant word, with preceding words, if any, generally transferred to the end. The third edition follows that of the previous edition. Many new proverbs have been added, and the number of cross-references increased. A much improved version.

PATRICK, David.
Chamber's Cyclopedia of English Literature. rev. by J. L. Geddie. Philadelphia: Lippincott, 1922–38. 3 vols.

A chronological arrangement, containing many articles on individual writers, some on literary forms, periods, and subjects. For each author treated, gives brief biography, comment on, and specimens of, his writings, a bibliography, and, in some instances, a portrait. Volume 3 consists of an author-title index.

"The revision of the material covering the late 19th and 20th centuries seems, in proportion to the broad scope of the work, sufficient to bring the set up to date, although more comprehensive discussion of the contemporary literature of the British overseas dominions and of the United States would have been desirable . . . . is recommended" — (SUBSCRIPTION BOOKS BULLETIN, April, 1939).

"The new edition . . . is the result of a conservative revision which has left unchanged the size, proportion, and special characteristics of the work while changing articles for essential accuracy and up-to-dateness. . . . The large library should find it useful" — (LIBRARY JOURNAL, 49:17).

The Reader's Adviser: A Guide to the Best in Literature. Edited by Winifred F. Courtney. 11th edition revised and enlarged. New York: Bowker, 1969. 2 vols.

Designed primarily for use by booksellers and librarians, but is of value to anyone as a general guide to basic works in a wide variety of fields, frequently with useful annotations.

The ninth edition is entitled BESSIE GRAHAM'S BOOKMAN'S MANUAL. The tenth edition published in 1964 and edited by Hester Rosalyn Hoffman, is entitled THE READER'S ADVISER. The first volume of the eleventh edition deals with literature. The second volume deals with: General biography and autobiography; Reference Books; Bibles and related texts; World Religions; Philosophy; Psychology; Science; The Social Sciences, etc. An alphabetical arrangement of brief articles on authors' lives, pseudonyms, characters in fiction, plots of novels and plays, famous works, places in literature, allusions. Includes a small numbr of American authors; many bibliographies.

"For here is collected a vast amount of information which should, but all too rarely does, form the equipment of the cultured reader, conveniently arranged, and catholic enough in scope to meet a wide variety of needs"—(SATURDAY REVIEW, April 18, 1933).

"Published as a literary reference book, it will be of service to editors, teachers, and librarians"—(NEW REPUBLIC, March 8, 1933).

"The content of the book has been updated, enlarged, and changed to reflect current opinion. . . . an indispensable tool. . . . Highly recommended for all libraries."—(LIBRARY JOURNAL, 94:1601 Ap. 15, 1969.)

The Reader's Encyclopedia of World Drama. Edited by John Gassner and Edward Quinn. New York: Thomas Y. Crowell Co., 1969. 1030 p.

The entries focus on plays, their authors, and their historical background, ranging from such diverse manifestations of Theater as the Japanese Kabuki, the Javanese shadow-puppet shows, the much neglected Jesuit theater of the baroque period to the world renowned playwrights themselves. It is an extraordinary one-volume work, a veritable hoard of riches on and about drama, illustrated with some 350 photographs and engravings.

ROSE, HERBERT JENNINGS.
Handbook of Greek Literature: From Homer to the Age of Lucian. 2d. ed. New York: E. P. Dutton, Inc., 1942. 454 p.
Aims to survey the entire field of Greek literature and to embrace the findings of the latest investigations on the subject. Social backgrounds and influences, as well as writers and their works are analyzed. In chapter form, with a very detailed index.

Professor Rose has covered Greek literature "not only comprehensively but with a wealth of criticism that will prove richly rewarding to the reader. . . . Because it is not a mere summary of literary trends and attainments, but embodies a penetrating commentary, Professor Rose's new volume is certain to recommend itself highly to students"—(NEW YORK TIMES, December 15, 1935).

". . . a brief but inclusive survey of developments from Homer to Lucian"—(BOOK REVIEW DIGEST, 1935).

SIMPSON, James Beasley.
Contemporary Quotations. New York: Crowell, 1964. 500 p.

Quotations (since 1950) are gleaned from newspapers, magazines, speeches, sermons, radio, television, the theater, etc., and are grouped in broad categories with subheadings. The source and subject indexes are helpful.

SOBEL, Bernard.
The Theater Handbook and Digest of Plays. New York: Crown Publishers, 1948. 897 p.

A single alphabet arrangement of theatrical terms, biographical notices, synopsis of almost 1,000 plays, playwrights, producers, and brief essays, many of them signed, by specialists on specific phases of drama or theater. The addenda includes a bibliography and a subject index of plays.

"Should prove extremely useful despite the fact that it is not clear just what principles of inclusion and exclusion were adopted in compiling a 900-page encyclopedia of the theater of all time"—(NATION, Jan. 13, 1940).

"Mistakes are inevitable in an undertaking of this kind, and omissions as well . . . but the book has a breezy, theatrical quality of its own, combining the casual and the eternal, . . . and it serves well its double purpose of providing information and entertainment"—(THEATER ART, Feb., 1940).

"At last a revised edition in compact and handy form of one of the most useful theatre handbooks available. The biographies have been rewritten and brought up to date and are of considerable value. . . ."—(LIBRARY JOURNAL, December, 1948).

"An excellent reference compiled by a distinguished laborer in the Broadway vineyard"—(SATURDAY REVIEW OF LITERATURE, October 30, 1948).

"The style is lively, the facts are accurate and well-indexed as anybody could hope for"—(THEATRE ARTS, October, 1948).

TAVENNER, Blair.
Brief Facts: A Concise Handbook of Useful Information for the Student, Traveler, Writer, Teacher, Librarian, Speaker, Business Man and General Reader. New York: Putnam's Sons, 1936. 941 p.

Partial contents: Battles; Bible Characters; Colleges and Universities; First Aid Rules; Geologic History of the Earth; Inventions and Discoveries; Mathematical Tables; Mountain Ranges; Mythological Characters; Natural Wonders; Operas; Rulers of England; Sport Records; Stars and Constellations; State Flowers and Birds; Weights and Measures and World War Outlines.

"The facts filling this book are indeed briefly stated, but there is such an outstanding number and variety of them that as the reader looks through the pages he feels more and more overwhelmed, almost awed. By the herculean labor of collecting, sorting, and arranging them, Mr. Tavenner has done a big job very efficiently, and has provided a book that ought to prove extremely useful to anybody"—(BOOK REVIEW DIGEST, 1936).

TRIPP, RHODA THOMAS.
The International Thesaurus of Quotations. New York: Crowell, 1970. 1,088 p.

An attempt to adapt the basic principles of Roget's THESAURUS to the classification of quotations; hence intended more for the user of quotations than for the reader of them. The entries are alphabetically grouped under "idea categories." Thorough cross-referencing.

WALCUTT, CHARLES CHILD AND J. EDWIN WHITESELL, eds.
The Explicator. Chicago: Quadrangle Books, 1966. 366 p.

A selection of over 200 of the best analyses of outstanding modern British and American poems from THE EXPLICATOR. A second volume to cover earlier poetry, and a third volume to cover prose works are expected to be published in the future. Critical selections are alphabetically arranged by poet, and the date, source, and critic are indicated.

WALDHORN, ARTHUR.
A Reader's Guide to Ernest Hemingway. New York: Farrar, Straus and Giraux, 1972. 284 p.

A guide to Hemingway, the man and his art; a synthesis of his work and that of his critics. Part I presents his life and style; Part II follows the patterns his writing took. The Appendixes include a filmography and a chronology of Nick Adams' development.

WALSH, William S.
Handy Book of Literary Curiosities. Philadelphia: J. B. Lippincott Company, 1893, 1925. 1104 p.

A useful and entertaining collection of items generally not found in the usual reference work,—plagiarisms, literary forgeries, puns, riddles, and others.

"The tracing of analogies or finding of parallelisms for familiar quotations has especially engaged the author's zeal, and proverbs and slang have next received his attention, while under a large number of general titles he has stored away a mass of anecdote, fact and fancy beyond the reach of his index of cross references." Some of the material we "could easily have dispensed with, but we preferred to have it rather than to part with it for occasional reference"—(THE NATION, January 5, 1893).

WESSEN, Maurice H.
Crowell's Dictionary of English Grammar: A Handbook of American Usage. New York: Thomas Y. Crowell Company, 1928. 703 p.

Essentially a guide to variations between English and American idiom. All entries are alphabetically arranged and treated briefly—parts of speech and their uses, syntax, synonyms, idioms, homonyms, slang, colloquialisms, errors of speech and of grammatical constructions.

"The principal virtues of the volume are simplicity and completeness." The book is "simultaneously a guide to grammatical correctness, a dictionary of grammatical terms, a list of words and constructions to avoid, a compendium of current slang, and a stylebook of contemporary usage. His work should prove of great service to students, editors, proofreaders and young writers"—(BOOKLIST, July, 1928).

WHITING, Bartlett Jere.
Proverbs, Sentences, and Proverbial Phrases: From English Writings Mainly Before 1500. Cambridge: Harvard University Press, 1968. 733 p.

A common form of the proverb or saying (entered alphabetically by key-word) is followed by variants, with reference to printed sources and date of usage. Index of important words.

ANTHOLOGIES AND HISTORIES

Anthologies

ALDERMAN, E. A. AND J. C. HARRIS.
Library of Southern Literature. New Orleans: Martin and Hoyt, 1908–1923. 17 vols.

The first thirteen volumes contain the biographical and critical sketches, and selected extracts arranged alphabetically according to the authors covered. The fourteenth volume comprises miscellanea, — poems, anecdotes, letters, epitaphs, and inscriptions, quotations, bibliography. Volume fifteen is a biographical dictionary, containing 3800 sketches. Volume sixteen constitutes a handbook of supplementary historical reading, as well as references to the bibliographies in the first thirteen volumes, and the supplementary lists; index of authors, titles, and subjects. Volume seventeen is a Supplement.

BENET, W. R. AND H. N. PEARSON.
Oxford Anthology of American Literature: An Historical Selection of Verse and Prose Arranged Chronologically. New York: Oxford University Press, 1938. 2 vols.

Volume One, John Smith to Abraham Lincoln; Volume Two, Walt Whitman to the Present.

Contains an alphabetical index of authors, first lines, and titles, as well as biographical and bibliographical data. The separate bibliography following the Commentary is divided into two parts: Historical, Social and Intellectual Background; and Literary History and Criticism.

"The worth of such a volume is entirely dependent upon the conscience and literary taste of its editors"; whence the work "is most fortunate, for William Rose Benet and Norman Holmes Pearson planned and executed it with great care and intelligence. . . . Their judgment was admirable, and the most essential examples of creative writing have been fitted into the general pattern of our intellectual development"—(NEW YORK TIMES, December 25, 1938).

"Arguing with a pair of anthologists who admit everything beforehand makes little sense. Fortunately, their volume represents so Catholic a taste that probably a few specialists will find much to carp at and most readers will find much to delight them"—(YALE REVIEW, Spring, 1939).

"This book provides ample evidence of the usefulness of intelligence and sound scholarship in making an anthology. Principles guided the construction of this book, though the statement of these principles in the preface is much fuzzier than that made by the selections themselves and in the commentaries"—(YALE REVIEW, Spring, 1939).

BRYANT, WILLIAM CULLEN.
New Library of Poetry and Song; rev. and enl. with recent authors and containing a dictionary of poetical quotations. New York: Baker, 1903. 1100 p.

"The marked success of A LIBRARY OF POETRY AND SONG, as issued in the year 1870, showed that the work supplied a real popular need. Since the date of its publication, between seventy and eighty thousand copies of the book have been taken by the public whose confidence in the name of Mr. Bryant, as its editor, has been borne out by the work itself. . . . Great pains have been taken to insure the correctness of the text with a view to making it a standard for reference, as well as to give an ample provision for general or special reading. . . . And the chief object of the collections—to present an array of good poetry so widely representative and so varied in its tone as to offer an answering chord to every mood and phase of human feeling—has been carefully kept in view, both in the selection and the arrangement of its contents. So that, in all senses, the realization of its significant title has been an objective point"—(Preface).

Useful for bibliography even though an older standard collection. Material is arranged topically. There is an alphabetical list of authors in the beginning of the volume and an alphabetical index of titles at the end.

"When the book appeared in 1870, it met with an instant and remarkably popular welcome, selling more than twenty thousand copies during the first six months"—(J. G. Wilson, MEMOIRS OF WILLIAM C. BRYANT).

CUNLIFFE, J. W. AND A. H. THORNDIKE.
Warner's Library of the World's Best Literature. New York: Warner Library Co., 1917. 30 vols.

First edited by Charles Dudley Warner, Hamilton Wright Mable, Brander Mathews, W. P. Trent and others, and reissued in 1917 under the editorship of Cunliffe and Thorndike, this long famous literary encyclopedia-anthology has also appeared as the Columbia University Course in Literature, Based on the World's Best Literature.

The entries are arranged alphabetically by authors, movements, and source topics, providing for each author included a brief biographical sketch, followed by excerpts from his principal works. Biographical sketches are signed; references are made to the best available biography; and a list of important works by the author is indicated.

The general contents are as follows: volume one to twenty-six, an alphabetical arrangement of the world's best literature (sketches and selections); volume twenty-seven, songs and lyrics; volume twenty-eight, dictionary of authors; volume twenty-nine, digest of books; volume thirty, students course in literature, and a general index of authors, titles, subjects, national literature.

ELIOT, CHARLES W.
The Harvard Classics. New York: Collier, 1909. 50 vols.

The "Five Foot Shelf," as the collection is sometimes called, is a set of extracts from all those authors, ancient and modern, who have contributed to the cultural tradition of the Western

World,—English, European, Greek, Latin, and Oriental. Selections vary in length from several pages to hundreds of pages and are representative of over seventy authors.

Volume 50 contains an analytical author, subject, and title index to all of the material contained in the set, and an index to the first lines of poems, songs, hymns, and psalms.

"This library seems truly to reflect the mind that assembled it. It is large, wise, serene, sure and contemplative. . . . We should imagine that the doctor's opinion about it is quite sound and true: that any man can have the essentials of a liberal education if he and these books become familiar friends"— (CURRENT OPINION, April, 1909).

"In its complete form it will inevitably illustrate the inability of individual taste, however cultivated, to prescribe a rigid course in the world's best literature which serves all readers" — (NEW YORK WORLD, April, 1909).

KENMODE, FRANK AND JOHN HOLLANDER, GEN. EDS.
The Oxford Anthology of English Literature. 2 vols. Vol. 1, The Middle Ages Through the Eighteenth Century; vol. 2, 1800 to the present. New York: Oxford University Press, 1973.

Some of the sections are quite impressive—the Medieval and (excepting perhaps the coverage of Shakespeare) the Renaissance, and the Eighteenth Century. Other sections, most notably the Victorian, are something less than adequate. Useful components are the: Glossary, Annotated Bibliography, Author and Title Index, and First Line Index.

MACK, M. AND W. FROST AND L. DEAN.
English Masterpieces: An Anthology of Imaginative Literature from Chaucer to T. S. Eliot. New York: Prentice-Hall, 1950–1951. 8 vols.

Contents: Volume I, AGE OF CHAUCER; Volume II; ELIZABETHAN DRAMA; Volume III, RENAISSANCE POETRY; Volume IV, MIL-

TON; Volume V, THE AUGUSTANS; Volume VI, ROMANTIC AND
VICTORIAN POETRY; Volume VII, MODERN POETRY; Volume
VIII, SELECTED PROSE.

MOULTON, CHARLES WELLS.
**Library of Literary Criticism of English and American Authors.
Through the Beginning of the Twentieth Century.** Abr. rev. and
with add. by Martin Tucker. New York: Ungar, 1967. 4 vols.

The general format follows that of the 1905 edition; but some
of the Moulton material has been abridged and new material,
including eleven authors, has been added. The section on Melville has been wholly replaced.

For each author included, there is given a brief biographical
sketch and then selected quotations from criticisms of his work
arranged as follows: (1) personal criticisms; (2) criticisms of
individual works; (3) general criticisms. Volume eight contains two indexes: (1) authors criticized; (2) authors of
the criticisms.

NYREN, DOROTHY.
A Library of Literary Criticism: Modern American Literature.
4th enl. edition. New Yok: Ungar, 1969. 3 vols.

The third edition was planned as a successor, for American
Literature, to Moulton's LIBRARY OF LITERARY CRITICISM. It provided excerpts from critical material found in popular and
scholarly journals and books on Americans who wrote or became prominent after 1904. The fourth edition enlarges and
updates the 1964 publication, adding one hundred and fifteen
authors and more recent excerpts on two-thirds of the authors
treated in the third edition. Volume three contains an index of
critics.

SISAM, CELIA, ed.
The Oxford Book of Medieval English Verse. Oxford: Clarendon
Press, 1971. 617 p.

A collection of miscellaneous medieval verse from about 1150
to 1500. Difficult words and passages are glossed on the same
pages as the texts. While designed for the general reader, the
wide scope of subjects and verse forms should also appeal to

the scholar; and, although familiar verses are included, many works not commonly anthologized before are present in graceful abundance. A monument to sound learning and taste.

STEDMAN, E. C. AND E. M. HUTCHINSON.
Library of American Literature. New York: Charles L. Webster and Company, 1890. 11 vols.

Representative selections of the work of principal American Authors, 1607–1889, chronologically arranged according to authors. A biographical dictionary of the writers included is contained in volume eleven (pp. 467–614), as is also a general index of persons, subjects, and, in some instances, titles.

"This work . . . has increased in usefulness with each successive issue and now in its total of eleven large volumes opens as complete a survey of the history and character of the American mind as is possible by the method followed . . . a remarkable execution . . . soundness of judgment in selection . . . extraordinary breadth and variety of acquaintance with forgotten books and . . . impartiality and justice of . . . choice of authors" — (ATLANTIC, 66:707).

STEVENSON, BURTON E.
Home Book of Verse: American and English, 1580–1918. New York: Henry Holt and Company, 1915. 4009 p.

A collection of the familiar English and American poems from 1580–1922, with an appendix containing a few well-known poems in other languages, aiming, as the introduction states, to include nothing which did not seem to ring true; to recognize the validity of popular taste as well as of classical taste; to lay emphasis upon the lighter forms of verse; and to especially stress the work of living English and American poets, "particularly of the younger generation." Remarkable for its range and inclusiveness.

"Mr. Stevenson's selective power is shown perhaps to best advantage in his omissions, in his ability to remain unswayed by a more or less meretricious vogue. His striking and admirable discriminations against every influence that tends to impair the practice of poetry will appear upon examination of his work" — (THE NATION, November 9, 1918).

STEVENSON, Burton Egbert.
Home Book of Quotations, Classical and Modern. 9th ed. New York: Dodd, 1964, 2817 p.

More than 50,000 quotations, arranged alphabetically by subject with a subordinate arrangement by smaller topics. Includes an index of authors ("giving full name, identifying phrase, and dates of birth and death, with references to all quotations cited") and a word index. The ninth edition adds over 500 new entries to the previous edition and contains many additional clarifications.

TEMPLE, Ruth and Martin Tucker, eds.
A Library of Literary Criticism: Modern British Literature. New York: Ungar, 1966. 3 vols.

Planned as a sequel to Moulton's LIBRARY OF LITERARY CRITICISM, and follows a similar plan for over 400 British and Commonwealth authors who wrote in or made their reputations in the twentieth century. The excerpts are drawn from British and American periodicals, newspapers, book reviews, and books. There is a bibliography of each author's work, an index to critics, and cross-references of authors.

WINSLOW, Ola Elizabeth.
Harper's Literary Museum. New York: Harper and Brothers, 1927.

The subtitle is: A Compendium of Instructive, Entertaining and Useful Matter Selected from Early American Writings Being the First of a Series of Volumes Covering Also Other Literatures and Times.

Since literary merit was not a principle of inclusion, preference, in fact, being evidenced for the odd, unfamiliar, and ordinary material, the work has definite usefulness for an understanding of the background of the times.

"A particularly amusing and revealing collection of American tidbits, including in a final section, representative advertisements from newspapers and handbills from the earliest time well on into the last century"—(THE NATION, January, 1927).

"The items that comprise it are in a large measure fresh

discoveries, the arrangement modeled on that of the literary annual of the early 19th Century has a delightful miscellaneity of an old curio shop, and text and type both preserve in flavor the atmosphere of antiquity" — (NEW YORK HERALD TRIBUNE, January 28, 1927).

"The work of selecting and compiling the contents has been admirably done by Miss Winslow, for she has shown a notable discrimination in choosing extracts that are representative of the spirit of the time from which they are taken. The result is a volume especially colorful and flavory of ancient days" — (NEW YORK TIMES, December 11, 1927).

Histories of English Literature

BAUGH, ALBERT C. ed.
A Literary History of England. New York: Appleton-Century-Crofts, Inc., 1948.

A comprehensive history of the literature of England, scholarly and readable, suited to the needs of mature students of literature and to cultivated readers generally. The Old English section provides a noteworthy emphasis upon philological material; the Modern English section gives acceptable treatment to economics, politics, and sociology.

"One might carp and cavil endlessly about details of interpretation and emphasis . . . . but to do so would be to obscure the authors' positive achievement. They have not produced just another classroom textbook; they have furnished a comprehensive guide to their subject. . . . If the student or layman wants a particular piece of information, he may not always find it in this book. But if it isn't there, he can be fairly sure that the author will tell him precisely where to go next in his search" — (NEW YORK HERALD TRIBUNE, May 2, 1948).

"Since practically every writer of any importance is discussed, the references to each are necessarily brief, and sometimes, especially in the latter chapters, the judgments seem a little perfunctory. But all four sections are so crisply written that the book can be read for pleasure as well as for information" — (NEW YORKER, March 27, 1949).

GARNETT, R. AND E. GOSSE.
English Literature: An Illustrated Record. London: Heinemann; New York: Macmillan, 1903. 4 vols. Reprinted, 4 vols. in 2, 1935.

Aims to "stimulate and gratify curiosity concerning the leading authors of" England; to tell who the author was, what he looked like and wrote; "where he lived . . . what his handwriting was . . . and how he appeared in caricature to his contemporaries" — (Pref.)

The special reference value of the work resides in the many illustrations, largely derived from contemporary prints, illuminations, portraits, etc. The revised edition of 1923 adds a section on literature from 1902–1922. Beyond this, it does not differ from the original edition.

Referring to volume two a reviewer has noted: "While all the literature of this extraordinary period is reviewed with appreciative judgment, and as fully as the design of the work admits, most stress is naturally laid on those two great, and we might say mutually complementary, personages, Bacon and Shakespeare." Of volume four, the same reviewer wrote: "The writers of the last quarter of the eighteenth century and virtually the whole of the nineteenth will probably be to most readers the most attractive of all. . . . For the lives of these writers abundant details were at hand, and the editors have used them so as to seize the illuminating points." Of the complete work, the reviewer concluded: "it is a worthy history of the grandest body of literature in any modern language" — (THE NATION, March 3, 1904).

"The pictorial is the unique feature of this work, and it may be said at the outset that the publishers have amply fulfilled their promise to enforce this story of a nation's letters by a larger appeal to the eye than has ever before been attempted. . . . Mr. Garnett's scholarship has the calm, judicial comprehensiveness of the learned and the painstaking, but his language moves along with the lumbering dignity of an elephant." This history of literature is, "except for minor reservations . . . the most complete that has yet appeared, and as such it can justly claim to supersede its predecessors in the field of popular exposition" — (THE OUTLOOK, May 14, 1904).

WARD, A. W. AND A. R. WALLER.
Cambridge History of English Literature. London: Cambridge University Press, 1907–1927. 15 vols. A reprint, published in 1931 by Macmillan, lacks the bibliographies. The cheaper edition was also published by Cambridge in 1954.

An authoritative account of the successive movements of English literature, major and secondary. Each chapter is by a specialist and has a relatively full and useful bibliography. The bibliographies, the detailed index in the fifteenth volume, and the eminence of the contributors constitute the special features of the work. The standard book.

Among the representative reviews of the individual volumes of the work are the following:

Vol. I. "The volume has an interest as well as a value, only the interest is rather linguistic than literary" — (NEW YORK TIMES, December 28, 1907).

Vol. II. "To the reader of ordinary culture, the second volume seems vastly more interesting and instructive in the right sense, rather than the first volume" — (NEW YORK TIMES, June 20, 1908).

Vol. III. "The absence of any dominating names renders this volume even more useful for the student of English literature, since it is the second and third rate little masters about whom it is difficult to get full and accurate information such as is afforded in the present volume. Apart from a few defects the present volume seems to be fully up to the standard of the two preceding" — (NEW YORK TIMES, February 27, 1909).

"This rich composite history of English literature is a real service to English scholarship" — (SATURDAY REVIEW OF LITERATURE, May 1, 1909).

Vol. IV. "Taken as a whole, the volume is rather a disappointment; but it must be remembered that it is intended more as a book of reference than a readable and connected history of literature; and if this is borne in mind the present, as the preceding volumes, amply fulfills its purpose" — (NEW YORK TIMES, May 14, 1910).

Vols. V. & VI. "An admirable book of reference, but it is somewhat straining the use of words to call it a history of English literature. The bibliographical apparatus is on the same scale as in the previous volumes, and will probably form the useful portion of the whole series, though in the present section the work of Prof. Schelling has anticipated most of the special details" — (NEW YORK TIMES, January 29, 1911).

Vol. VIII. "The selection is remarkably comprehensive, and the arrangement is generally admirable. In general character the eighth volume possesses the scholarly sanity and thoroughness of its predecessors" — (NEW YORK TIMES, May 12, 1912).

"It was a happy thought to engage a leading authority on the Elizabethan Drama, like Professor Schelling, for this subject, inasmuch as one of the chief problems in the study of the Restoration Drama is its relation to that of the earlier years of the century . . . — (THE NATION, May 9, 1912).

Vol. IX. "If the greater portion of the present volume of the Cambridge history leaves much to be desired in the way of close characterization and philosophic grasp, it is, like its predecessors, an invaluable treasure house to the student of English literature" — (ATHENAEUM, December 20, 1913).

"The bibliographies make up about one-fourth of the entire volume, and in some sections have an exceptional value. For example, the list of Defoe's writings, compiled by Professor Trent, is the fullest and most accurate in existence" — (THE NATION, Feb. 27, 1913).

Vol. X. "We cannot conclude without offering those concerned our warmest congratulations on the bibliographies in this volume. They are marked by exceptional complete-ness and accuracy, and will be of the greatest value to students of the period" — (ATHENAEUM, November 21, 1913).

Vol. XI. "Taken as a whole, the volume quite sustains the high reputation of the series, while the value and bulk of the bibliographical studies at the end increases as modern times are approached" — (ATHENAEUM, November 21, 1914).

Vol. XII. "Some sixty pages are given to elaborate bibliog-raphies, including an excellent one on the 'Relations of English and continental literatures in the romantic period'" — (NEW YORK TIMES, March 5, 1916).

Vols. XIII. & XIV. "The chapters devoted to the literature of all the Dominions from the freshness of their matter and their treatment are among the most enthralling in the book" — (SATURDAY REVIEW OF LITERATURE, May 12, 1917).

SAMPSON, GEORGE.
The Concise Cambridge History of English Literature. 3d rev. & enl. ed. by R.C. Churchill. London: Cambridge University Press, 1969. 938 p.
Based on the 1907 13-volume edition of the CAMBRIDGE HISTORY OF ENGLISH LITERATURE. Generally reworked in the light of con-temporary scholarship, with added chapters on the literature of the United States (from the Colonial period to Henry James).

WILSON, PERCY AND BONAMY DOBREE.
Oxford History of English Literature. London: Oxford Univer-sity Press, 1945—.

When completed the work will consist of twelve volumes, cover-ing the entire field of English literature from its earliest begin-nings to the present. Each volume or partial volume will be an independent part of the series, written by an acknowledged authority and containing extensive bibliographies.

". . . . Now it is obvious enough that any literary history must discuss a great deal of work possessing little intrinsic merit, and that much of the historian's activity will necessarily be cultural sociology rather than criticism. But unless the primary concern is with that in literature which is alive for us as part of the "mind of Europe," the social and cultural history will lack power and significance. Unrelated to any clear system of value of judgments, it will tend to become a dull and academic recital of facts contributing nothing to the understanding of the relation between literary modes and ways of thinking and feeling, between quality of writing and quality of living.

. . . It cannot be said that Mr. Bennett has altogether succeeded in avoiding this danger. . . .

". . . . In all fairness it must be said that there is little satisfying analysis of Chaucer to be found anywhere. . . .

". . . . As a whole the book is valuable chiefly as a scholarly summary of factual information. It cannot be said to have the same unity and organizing sections of Courthope's HISTORY OF ENGLISH POETRY" — (TIMES LITERARY SUPPLEMENT, April 17, 1948).

"Sir Edmund Chambers has here produced a most learned compendium of knowledge, but it is not among the most urbane and attractive of his great achievements, and even the scholar, apart from the mere student of literature may find the ample fare provided a little difficult to assimilate. . . .

"It is, no doubt, ungracious to ask for more when we have been given much, but it is . . . a matter for regret that Sir Edmund has not been given or has not taken the opportunity to write in the fulness of his wide scholarship a more complete account of English literature at the close of the Middle Ages" — (MODERN LANGUAGE REVIEW, XL 1).

". . . . Mr. Lewis's volume was certainly worth waiting for. Learned, vivacious, individual, this nine-years-pondered handbook is a notable performance.

"This book has so many virtues that we may be forgiven for calling attention to two particulars in which it is tiresome . . . giving his references, when he quotes, in the body of the text.

. . . The other fault is a defective table of contents. . . . The same tiresomeness is found in the other volumes of the Oxford

History"—(TIMES LITERARY SUPPLEMENT, September 17, 1954).

"Crammed as the book is, it is eminently readable. . . .
"One third of the whole book is occupied by Chronological Tables and an important . . . Bibliography under six headings covering the field with reasonable exhaustiveness. They give ample evidence of Professor Bush's accuracy and of his watchful eye for everything in print concerning his subject and his authors"—(MODERN LANGUAGE REVIEW, XL 1).

"Two difficulties which arise from Bush's method will occur to any reader, but they certainly cannot be called weaknesses of the book. The first is that in treating a topic such as "The Literature of France" the number of titles is so great and Bush's learning so imposing that the ordinary mortal will wish the eleven pages expanded into a monograph . . . a second difficulty inherent in the method of the volume is that the topical arrangement forces the historian to treat parts of the work of certain authors in one chapter and parts in other chapters"—(Modern Language QUARTERLY, IX).

Histories of American Literature

PARRINGTON, VERNON L.
Main Currents in American Thought. New York: Harcourt, Brace & Company, 1927–30. 2 vols.
A scholarly interpretation of American literature from the viewpoint of the main political and religious ideas that have influenced her from the beginning of her history. The first volume, THE COLONIAL MIND covers the period from 1620 to 1800; the second volume, THE ROMANTIC REVOLUTION IN AMERICA, covers the period, 1800 to 1860. Each volume contains an extensive bibliography.

"Technically the book is a piece of literary history. The evidence in the book is drawn largely from written sources; the influential American writings are individually considered with freshness and brilliance. But the treatment as a whole goes beyond most literary history"—(NEW YORK HERALD TRIBUNE, May 1, 1927).

QUINN, Arthur Hobson.
The Literature of the American People: An Historical and
Critical Survey. New York: Appleton-Century-Crofts, Inc.,
1951.

A scholarly and readable treatment of literature, stressing its
relation to the allied arts of painting, sculpture, architecture,
politics, and social thought.

"Although it is obvious that no single book treating such a
vast subject can hope to please everyone, this one seems to fall
short of what might be hoped for in the way of over-all organization and integration. . . . On the whole, and in spite of
some of the faults suggested, the book is very competent and
deserves wide use in the kind of courses for which it was prepared"—(UNITED STATES QUARTERLY BOOK REVIEW, Sept.,
1951).

"Throughout the book there are many afterthoughts and
many interpolations; the reader's attention is too often dragged
from the consideration of development to the consideration of
detail. . . . Many of the errors of detail and distortion of
emphasis spring from an earnest patriotism which is prepared
to twist all historical standards in order to create the illusion
that literary progress in America has been constantly in alliance
with the development of an American way of life . . . . chauvinism is seldom scholarly, and when chauvinism is designed for
classroom reading, its fallacies take on proportions that are at
times terrifying"—(LONDON TIMES, June 29, 1951).

SPILLER, R. E., W. Thorp (and others).
Literary History of the United States. New York: The Macmillan Company, 1948. 3 vols.

The first two volumes constitute a survey of American literature
from colonial times to the present. The third volume is a comprehensive bibliography. The chapters are not signed, but a list
of the contributors is given in volume two (pp. 1393–1396).

"Nothing so good in the general presentation of American
Literary History has yet appeared. Inclusive in scope, and
judicious in its acumen, the history is a landmark and itself
becomes a part of our growing tradition and an influence for
the future. We have waited a long time for such a book; now
that it has come, there can be nothing but gratification, con-

gratulation and a sense of indebtedness to the group who are responsible for this highly significant work of criticism and scholarship"—(SATURDAY REVIEW OF LITERATURE, November 27, 1948).

". . . considers the development of American literature from both the critical and historical vantage point, and is written to read like a prolonged and freely flowing narrative"—(NEW YORKER, February, 1949).

"By banishing by-lines without going in for sufficiently sharp and unsparing editing, the designers of the LITERARY HISTORY have sacrificed what advantages there may be to a frank miscellany without achieving the impact of a homogeneous work"—(THE NATION, January 22, 1949).

STEWART, J.I.M.
Eight Modern Writers. London: Oxford University Press, 1963. 704. p.

Represents the twelfth volume of the OXFORD HISTORY OF ENGLISH LITERATURE; covers, in eight separate essays: Hardy, James, Shaw, Conrad, Kipling, Yeats, Joyce, and Lawrence. Chronological Table, Bibliography, Index.

TRENT, W. P., J. ERSKINE (and others).
Cambridge History of American Literature. New York: Putnam, 1917–1921. 4 vols.

The 1954 reissue by Macmillan in three volumes is textually complete, but lacks the bibliographies (indexed in Northup's REGISTER) which are an important feature of the original edition.

Volume one covers colonial and revolutionary literature; volume two, early and later national literature; volumes three and four, later national literature. In its time, and perhaps at present, the most important history of American literature.

"A valuable, comprehensive, and from beginning to end, a more interesting book. Emphasis must be laid upon the care and detail which the authors and editors have devoted to the early literature of our land . . . . is of the utmost importance"—(NEW YORK TIMES, November 25, 1917).

"This history brings to our notice writers whom we should otherwise have overlooked; fills up gaps in our knowledge of the literary history of the country, and supplies accurate data as to the various activities of the press and the biographies of writers" — (SATURDAY REVIEW OF LITERATURE, May 31, 1919).

"On the whole, the history is a treasure house of information exhibited to the curious by intelligent guides. Not the least important part of these two volumes is the vast bibliographic index, covering 237 pages of small but clear types. Every important author has his detailed and dated list of works; and the word "important" is used generously. Then there is an immense list of critical books and articles invaluable to anyone who wishes to "work-up" an author or movement" — (NEW YORK TIMES, November 5, 1921).

". . . supersedes all earlier attempts to tell the story and appraise the achievement of our national literature" — (THE NATION, April 13, 1921).

"This lack of balance, together with the lack of contagious enthusiasm in the writing, and the dearth of comparative estimates constitute in our view faults which prevent us from extending such a cordial reception to the second volume as we did to the first" — (THE TIMES LITERARY SUPPLEMENT, July 17, 1919).

BIOGRAPHICAL DICTIONARIES

Indexes

Biography Index: A Cumulative Index to Biographical Material in Books and Magazines. New York: The H. W. Wilson Company, 1947—.

Appears quarterly (September, December and March), with annual cumulations in June. The first volume covers material published after January 1, 1946. The two sections of the index are: (1) Name alphabet, giving for each entry, full name, date, nationality, occupation; (2) Index by occupation.

"It includes current books in the English language wherever published; biographical material from the 1500 periodicals now regularly indexed in the Wilson indexes, plus a selected list of professional journals in the fields of law and medicine; obituaries of national and international interest from the NEW YORK TIMES. All types of biographical material are covered; pure biography, critical material of biographical significance, autobiography, letters, diaries, memoirs, journals, genealogies, fiction, drama, poetry, bibliographies, obituaries, pictorial works and juvenile literature. Works of collective biography are fully analyzed. Incidental biographical material such as prefaces and chapters in otherwise non-biographical books is included. Portraits are indicated when they appear in conjunction with indexed material . . ."—(Preface).

"It appears that the BIOGRAPHY INDEX will provide an up-to-date, well-organized service which should be valuable in all kinds of reference works"—(SUBSCRIPTION BOOKS BULLETIN, VOL. 18, NO. 2).

"The coverage of biographical material offered by this well-organized index is comprehensive and reliable. The BIOGRAPHY INDEX will be a useful and time-saving reference service for all types of libraries"—(SUBSCRIPTION BOOKS BULLETIN VOL. 18, NO. 4).

HEFLING, HELEN AND EVA RICHARDS.
Index to Contemporary Biography and Criticism. New ed. rev.
and enl. by Helen Hefling and Jessie W. Dyde . . . introd. by
M. E. Hazeltine. Boston: Faxon, 1934. 229 p.

Supplements BIOGRAPHY INDEX for the period before 1936.
The original work indexes some 200 collections of biography
and criticism; the enlarged edition indexes 417 collections of
biography and criticism. The alphabetical arrangement is by
author and by title.

"It supplies a ready reference key to biography and criticism
of figures important in the modern world—the word contemporary being defined as referring to persons whose birth oc-
curred around the year 1850 or later; 417 book titles have been
indexed in this edition, more than twice as many as for the
first edition"—(WISCONSIN LIBRARY BULLETIN).

O'NEIL, EDWARD HAYES.
Biography by Americans, 1658–1936: A Subject Bibliography.
Philadelphia: University of Pennsylvania Press; London: Mil-
ford, 1939. 465 p.

An alphabetical listing of all the known biographies authored
by Americans. For the more famous men only the more important works are given. The arrangement is by biographical
subject. Locates copies in eight libraries, but does not have an
author index.

PHILLIPS, LAWRENCE BARNETT.
Dictionary of Biographical Reference: Containing over 100,000
Names, Together with a Classed Index of the biographical
literature of Europe and America. New ed. rev., cor. and augm.
with supplements to date, by Frank Weitenkampf. Philadelphia: Gebbie, 1889. 1038 p.

Covers all periods; provides full name, identifying phrase, dates,
and reference to collections containing biographical data.

RICHES, PHYLLIS.
Analytical Bibliography of Universal Collected Biography:
Comprising Books Published in the English Tongue in Great
Britain and Ireland, America and the British Dominions . . .

with an Introduction by Sir Frederic Kenyon. London: Library Association, 1934. 709 p.

Divided into three parts: (1) index of people written about, set up in an alphabetical order, following which are arranged short biographies alphabetically grouped by authors' names; (2) bibliography of the works dealt with, some evaluation being supplied from standard bibliographies, while others are added by the compiler; (3) indexes, chronologically listed according to centuries and arranged alphabetically.

"It is one of those long needed works of reference which few would lightly undertake and fewer could have completed as efficiently as Miss Riches has completed this" — (TIMES LITERARY SUPPLEMENT, Dec. 6, 1934).

". . . . It is remarkable that she used neither the two sets of the Peabody Institute of Baltimore Catalog or the splendid Catalog of the Boston Athenaeum Library. . . . Some of the short titles, too, are misleading.

"Nevertheless, the work has been performed, seemingly, in a painstaking manner and deserves praise rather than blame. It surely fills a gap in our bibliographical handbooks and makes available many of out-of-the-way biographical treatments. As such it merits a place in every reference department in the country, for, in addition to its other values, it may well be used as a purchasing guide for libraries or bookstores" — (LIBRARY JOURNAL, July 15, 1935).

". . . but it might have been made more complete, accurate and up-to-date by checking such obvious sources as Minto's REFERENCE BOOKS, Mudge's GUIDE and the entry "Biographic Dictionaries" in the Subject Index of the London Library. These biographical dictionaries are not analyzed. . . .

"And so the book has its weaknesses, but it is a good book, and it has already proved its worth. All those who are interested in the problem which gives occasion to the book, and all those who make good use of it will be grateful to Miss Riches" — (LIBRARY QUARTERLY, January, 1936).

SLOCUM, ROBERT B.
Biographical Dictionaries and Related Works. Detroit: Gale Research, 1968. 1056 p.

Subtitle: An international bibliography of collective biographies, bio-biographies, collection of epitaphs, selected genealogical works, dictionaries of anonyms and pseudonyms, historical and specialized dictionaries . . . bibliographies of biographers, biographical indexes, and selected portrait catalogs. Author, title, and subject indexes. Aims to embrace all languages and cultures.

STAUFFER, DONALD ALFRED.
English Biography Before 1700. Massachusetts: Cambridge University Press, 1930.

Aims to consider historically and critically the art of biography from the earliest time to 1700. The principal purpose is to present new facts in the history of biography; the method is to give bibliographies of all the extant pieces of English biography and to describe the more important ones. The first part of the bibliography is a subject and author index of English biography before 1700.

The author "has a large sympathy with the men whose biographical efforts he interprets, and a quick eye for all their charm and their merit . . . The bibliography with which he concludes his work is a splendid example of what such a bibliography ought to be"—(SATURDAY REVIEW OF LITERATURE, November 29, 1930).

"The story which Dr. Stauffer tells with faithful weaving of a great many threads, thick and thin (and the whole guaranteed and much increased in value by some eighty pages of bibliography), is the growth of biography into recognition and practice as a literary art"—(TIMES LITERARY SUPPLEMENT, December 11, 1930).

STAUFFER, DONALD ALFRED.
The Art of Biography in 18th Century England: Bibliographical Supplement. Princeton, New Jersey: Princeton University Press, 1941. 293 p. 2 vols.

An attempt "to present as historically comprehensive a picture as possible of 18th Century biography."

Volume I: the initial parts of the chapters contain analytical discussions; the concluding parts are devoted to the most significant biographies, those that best illustrate the main positions of the chapter. Chapter VI considers individually the best-known biographies of the century.

Volume II: an alphabetical list of biographies read in connection with the study; descriptions of important biographies not taken up in the main text.

The pages of this work reveal "a microcosm, little mirrors of the times reflecting from a thousand facets the variety and vitality of life itself." However, the author "devotes many pages to discussing the social currents reflected in the biography of the period and the social forces that affected its development, without throwing any searching light upon them. . . . Professor Stauffer seizes upon the best critical comments of the eighteenth-century biographies, but he is less a critic himself than a journalist-antiquary with a lively nose for news and an enjoyment of human nature"—(NEW REPUBLIC, May 26, 1931).

"Mr. Stauffer would have been better advised not to attempt to make such a big book. His material needs pruning and knitting more closely together. It would have been an additional advantage if the fortuitous element in the bibliography had been more decisively subordinated to the selective. The book bears everywhere the marks of enthusiasm and industry: it is unfortunately lacking in form"—(SPECTATOR, October 10, 1941).

"I feel strongly that this admirable book on English biography deserves to be ranked as a work of scholarship. . . . It would be an injustice to say that Mr. Stauffer has written a Baedeker's guide to his subject, although he is equally compendious. His book is altogether on a higher level. It has a good but unpretentious style, written with a gusto which unconsciously and most pleasantly reveals the author's genuine enthusiasm for letters. The writing of this book, one feels, was not a task but a pleasure"—(SATURDAY REVIEW OF LITERATURE, April 19, 1941).

International Dictionaries of Biography

Chamber's Biographical Dictionary. J. O. Thorne, ed. New York: St. Martin's Press, 1969. 1432 p.

The new edition evidences considerable revision and contains many new listings, especially of contemporaries. Each entry is a meaningful commentary, not a simple listing of facts. Pronunciation of difficult names is indicated. The subject index locates "authors through their books, artists through their paintings, historical personalities through associated places and events."

A useful updating of the 1961–62 edition, but by no means an extensive revision of the latter.

Contemporary Authors: A Bio-Bibliographical Guide to Current Authors and Their Works. 1st rev. Detroit: Gale Research, 1967–.

An updating and a cumulation of the first four volumes of the original series, with none of the earlier sketches omitted. "Plans call for revision and cumulation of all the earlier volumes in yearly units, simultaneously with publication of new volumes in the original series."

Current Biography: Who's News and Why. New York: The H. W. Wilson Company, 1940 –.

A monthly publication, cumulated annually in a single alphabet and including all biographical sketches and obituary notices, featuring national and international names in the news of the day. The 1956 edition, the 17th annual cumulation with index, 1951–1956, includes biographies of 335 persons prominent in the news during 1956. Each issue generally provides: full name, pronunciation, dates of birth and death, occupation and reason for prominence, address, biographical sketch with portrait, and reference to further sources of information. Probably the most useful single source of biographical data on contemporary American and foreign persons of prominence.

HOEHN, Matthew.
Catholic Authors: Contemporary biographical sketches, 1930–1947. Newark, New Jersey: St. Mary's Abbey, 1952. 2 vols.

Aims simply to introduce the reader to contemporary Catholic writers. Does not attempt critical appraisal of the authors; affects no judgment of the catholicity of doctrine or thought.

Foreign authors are included if at least one of their works appears in translation. Of the 1,600 authors screened, 620 were selected. A Supplement, which bears a 1952 copyright, includes 374 additional entries.

"No really representative library, personal or institutional, is complete without CATHOLIC AUTHORS. . . . A prodigious and invaluable work"—(CATHOLIC WORLD, December, 1948).

"Father Hoehn can rest after a labor well done. It is a much-needed volume and arranged for the greater convenience of the majority of readers. . . . The author cannot hope to satisfy every conceivable taste or opinion. Suffice it to say that the selection of authors is good and that the biographical material is comprehensive and as up-to-date as could be expected in such a work.

"If you cannot find what you are looking for in these 620 biographies, it's either inconsequential or it doesn't exist"—(CATHOLIC WORLD, August, 1948).

HYAMSON, ALBERT M.
Dictionary of Universal Biography. New York: E. P. Dutton & Co., Inc., 1951. 679 p.

Supplies brief information (dates of birth and death, nationality, profession) of about 110,000 famous persons who died before 1950. Also indicates sources where further information is contained. "The great change, an improvement I hope that will be received by all who consult the book is that every entry of this new edition contains an indication of the principal works of reference in which biographies of the subjects of the entries are found."

"One person, one line," the stated goal of the compiler, is generally achieved.

"A sampling of pages throughout the main section of the book reveals comparatively few entries where the date of death is later than 1930, and none later than 1947 were noted. There is, however, an Addenda of 86 names taken from the Annual Register 1948 and 1949. This edition features a Key to References, a list of twenty-four reference works in which full biographies of the subject can be found. . . . It is a scholarly, accurate work, compiled by an experienced editor"—(SUBSCRIPTION BOOKS BULLETIN, July, 1952).

International Who's Who. London: Europe Publications, 1935—.

An annual compilation of very brief biographies, often only three or four lines, of living internationally prominent persons of all countries. Especially valuable for the inclusion of representatives of smaller nations who are seldom cited elsewhere.

". . . aims to supplement and coordinate the national biographical reference books, not to supersede them. The editors are anonymous. According to the Forward, the editors have gone directly to the subjects themselves for their biographical data, as well as to the usual sources . . . omitting but few biographies of international significance in the fields they have sought to cover, namely, economics, banking, mineralogy, diplomacy, music, authorship, art, science, criminology, history, medicine, industry, law, education, the judiciary, anthropology, the church, insurance, and sociology" — (SUBSCRIPTION BOOKS BULLETIN, 1948).

"Much work has been put into it, and to secure accuracy a questionnaire has been sent to the hundreds of people whose names appear. The value of the work consists in the fact that although many, perhaps most, of the names can be found in the national Who's Who, the task of searching innumerable volumes in many languages is quite impossible to all but a few" — (MANCHESTER GUARDIAN, December, 1936).

KUNITZ, STANLEY J.
Living Authors: A Book of Biographies. New York: H. W. Wilson Company, 1931. 466 p.

Concise and very readable biographical sketches of 371 living authors of many different nationalities, with portraits and brief lists of their principal works. As stated in the WILSON BULLETIN, these are "lively and unconventional in tone but frequently useful for estimates and biographical data, not easily found elsewhere."

"Many of the writers are so recently arrived at fame . . . that they will not be found in any other work of reference. . . . The descriptions are catholic, and there seems to be few notable exceptions from contemporary eminence.

". . . . The defect of the compilation is its desire to be an entertainment as well as a work of reference. . . . Yet the book is better than its tone might imply" — (TIMES LITERARY SUPPLEMENT, August 13, 1931).

"This compilation may be called a new and useful kind of reference book, interesting enough for casual conning . . . equally well-planned for what we believe to be a more general though lower-browed comment in the personalities of public performers" — (BOSTON TRANSCRIPT, June, 1931).

"Whatever other reference book you have, you can still use this" — (SATURDAY REVIEW OF LITERATURE, July 27, 1931).

"A volume for days of pleasant browsing, as well as for the perennial reference shelf" — (CATHOLIC WORLD, September, 1931).

KUNITZ, STANLEY J.
Authors Today and Yesterday. New York: H. W. Wilson Co., 1933.

Brief and readable biographical sketches of 320 authors whose works appeared mainly since 1900. The biographies in the companion volume, LIVING AUTHORS, are not repeated, but a Joint Index to biographies in both volumes is contained in AUTHORS TODAY AND YESTERDAY.

Generally speaking, the biographies in this volume are about twice the length of those in the earlier work; the number of foreign authors is larger.

"Many of the writers have contributed short autobiographies and others have supplied information. Each of the biographies is accompanied by a portrait and bibliography. To a person interested in contemporary and recent literature, the book is fascinating" — (COMMONWEAL, Feb. 23, 1934).

"Either one of these two books is useful and fascinating alone. Together they form a lively dictionary of contemporary literary biography" — (NEW YORK TIMES, March 11, 1934).

"An effective supplement to LIVING AUTHORS. . . . Together, the two books provide a convenient and fairly complete library of general information about contemporary writers" — (NEW REPUBLIC, April 11, 1934).

KUNITZ, STANLEY J. AND H. HAYCRAFT.
Twentieth Century Authors: A Biographical Dictionary of Modern Literature, Complete in One Volume with 1850 biographies and 1700 portraits. New York: The H. W. Wilson Co., 1942. 1577 p.

Differs somewhat from the earlier volumes in offering critical comment. As the authors state in the Preface, the "editorial policy in offering a descriptive comment has not been to attempt an independent appraisal, but to give a few summations of reliable critical comments."

The 1955 edition, TWENTIETH CENTURY AUTHORS: First Supplement, edited by Stanley J. Kunitz, assisted by Vineta Colby, "brings the original biographies and bibliographies up-to-date and contains some 700 new biographies, 670 with portraits, mostly of authors who have come into prominence since 1942, though with the inclusion of a small number of older authors whose omission from the earlier volumes it has seemed advisable to rectify. The total listing of approximately 2,550 names is to be found . . . incorporated into a single alphabet"—

"It kept us waiting four years and is worth it. . . . LIVING AUTHORS set a standard back in 1931; AUTHORS TODAY AND YESTERDAY maintained it; this surpasses them both"—(BOOKS, January 24, 1943).

"Invaluable for reference libraries, interesting to everyone who wishes to be informed about the person behind the book he reads"—(CHRISTIAN SCIENCE MONITOR, March 13, 1943).

". . . an indispensable tool for any library that boasts even a modest reference department. It will also prove invaluable to anyone with a modicum of curiosity concerning the men and women who have done, or are doing, the imaginative and non-imaginative writing of our times.

". . . more than doubles the usefulness of the earlier books.

"The editors have been generous in their conception of what authorship in the twentieth century means"—(LIBRARY QUARTERLY, October, 1943).

ROMIG, WALTER.
Book of Catholic Authors: Informal self-portraits of famous modern Catholic writers, with preface and notes. Detroit: W. Romig and Co., Inc., 1942. 6 volumes.

Some fifty sketches of "famous modern Catholic writers,—poets, essayists, novelists, sociologists, historians, editors, and lecturers, with portraits and a list of the author's writings.

"It is of course far from complete, but we are promised a second and third series if this first volume receives a hearty welcome. We are confident that it will" — (CATHOLIC WORLD, January, 1943).

SHARP, ROBERT F.
Short Biographical Dictionary of Foreign Literature. New York: Dutton, 1933. 302 p.

A concise biographical dictionary of some 550 authors, with short biographical notes and a list as practicable as possible of first editions of author's works. "Where an English translation of a work exists, the title of the translation is inserted after that of the original."

THOMAS, JOSEPH.
Universal Pronouncing Dictionary of Biography and Mythology. Philadelphia: Lippincott, 1930. 1550 p.

More popularly known as LIPPINCOTT'S BIOGRAPHICAL DICTIONARY, this work has long been a standard reference source and, though now long out of print (the 1930 printing being actually the third edition of the 1901 edition, revised and brought up to date), is still very useful as a ready reference. Includes persons of all nations and times, and names from many mythologies, —Greek, Roman, Teutonic, Sanskrit, and others. Some articles are fairly long, but most are quite brief.

The Appendixes comprise: (1) Vocabulary of Christian (or first) names, with pronunciations and equivalents in the principal foreign languages; (2) Disputed or doubtful pronunciations.

Webster's Biographical Dictionary: A Dictionary of Names of Noteworthy Persons, with Pronunciations and Concise Biographies. Springfield, Massachusetts: G. & C. Merriam Company, 1969. 1697 p.

Contains approximately 40,000 entries, not restricted by period, nationality, race, religion, or occupation, about one-third of which are of living men and women. The sketches are generally at least several lines in length, often reaching twenty lines, and not infrequently forty lines or more. Among the special features are: the effort which is made to give syllabic division and pronunciation of all names; the tables of United States presidents, vice-presidents, justices of the Supreme Court, and sovereigns of foreign nations.

Although the entries are unsigned, and one must still resort to such monumental biographical dictionaries as the DNB and the DAB for more extended treatment and for critical evaluation, the facts given in this work for each person are generally trustworthy and sufficiently full for the great majority of inquirers.

"The nineteen pages of "A Guide to Pronunciation" of words in each of the languages concerned is a marvel of composition and clarity for so complex a subject. William Allen Deilson . . . and . . . staff . . . deserve our thanks for producing such a handy volume" — (LIBRARY JOURNAL, 69:1944, 164).

"The biographies are competent, succinct and remarkably informative for the space they cover" — (THE COMMONWEAL, October 29, 1943).

"Particular pains have been taken with respect to the correct pronunciation and syllabic division of the names; and for this information, as well as for the dates and other main facts concerning the persons included, the volume is an invaluable reference tool" — (LIBRARY QUARTERLY, January, 1944).

The 1969 printing remains basically the same work as the original; hence it is not useful for information on contemporary personalities.

Who's Who Among Living Authors of Older Nations: Covering the Literary Activities of Living Authors and Writers of All Countries of the World except the United States of America, Canada, Mexico, Alaska, Hawaii, Newfoundland, the Philippines, the West Indies and Central America. Vol. 1, 1931–32, ed. by A. Lawrence. Los Angeles, California: Golden Syndicate Publishing Co., 1932. 482 p.

Three principal sections: (1) an alphabetical arrangement of authors; (2) a press section comprising biographies of editors, magazine and press writers, with names of periodicals in which their writings appear; (3) supplement, containing a list of authors and writers by countries, a list of poets by countries, a list of authors showing pen names, a list of pen names showing real names.

"Recommended for the library able to afford this somewhat expensive addition to its reference resources" — (SUBSCRIPTION BOOKS BULLETIN, July, 1932).

World Biography. New York: Institute for Research in Biography, Inc., 1940.

The first three editions appeared as: BIOGRAPHICAL ENCYCLO-

PEDIA OF THE WORLD. The fourth edition, which appeared in 1948 in two volumes (5,120 p.), contains about 40,000 "who's who" type sketches of important living persons of over sixty nations of the world. The fifth edition appeared in 1954.

". . . there are twice as many names in WORLD BIOGRAPHY as in any other international work, and the proportion is even greater. WORLD BIOGRAPHY is a very useful library tool"— (SUBSCRIPTION BOOKS BULLETIN, April, 1949).

English Biographical Dictionaries

BOASE, FREDERICK.

Modern English Biography: Containing Many Thousand Concise Memoirs of Persons Who Have Died Between the Years 1851–1900, With an Index of the Most Interesting Matter; 2d. ed. New York: Barnes & Noble, 1965. 6 vols.

Aims to give the essential facts of each life and, in the case of authors, brief but accurate titles of their principal work and references to books where longer accounts may be found. Especially useful for minor nineteenth century names not included in the DNB. The first three volumes (A-Z, Index) appeared between 1892–1901; the last three (suppl. vols. 1–3, A-Z) appeared between 1908–1921. Contains a useful subject index, providing lists of pseudonyms, fancy names, class lists, et cetera.

". . . there is no service which any serious student can rank higher than that of the good guide who will prevent waste of precious time by giving what we may call basic facts, and offering the first clues for further study"—(NOTES AND QUERIES, November 5, 1921).

The second edition represents a reprinting of the basic set published during the years 1892–1901 and of the supplement in three volumes, spread over the years 1908–21.

Catholic Who's Who. London: Burns, Oates & Washburne, Ltd. 1908—.

Originally published as an annual, the title until 1935 being CATHOLIC WHO'S WHO AND YEARBOOK, the 34th edition appeared in 1941, the 35th edition, in 1952.

"After eleven years the CATHOLIC WHO'S WHO has again come

out. It contains 5,500 biographies of Catholics in Great Britain, the Commonwealth and Ireland, and 'is the most substantial book of reference about Catholic personalities, ecclesiastical and lay, in the language.'

"It has been well edited and does not, as used to be the case, concentrate mainly on the aristocracy and the government services. The arts are excellently represented" — (AMERICA, August 9, 1952).

"For all who are engaged in Catholic (or indeed any) journalism, publishing or bookselling, this is a reference book of immense value which will save hours of valuable time; all reference libraries will want a copy" — (BOOKS ON TRIAL, June, 1952).

KUNITZ, S. J. AND H. HAYCRAFT.
British Authors Before 1800: A Biographical Dictionary. New York: The H. W. Wilson Company, 1952. 584 p.

Contains 650 biographies and 220 portraits of English authors, major and minor, from the dawn of English literature to Cowper and Burns. The sketches, which range in length from 300 to 1,500 words — roughly proportionate to the importance of the subject — are followed by a list of the principal works of the biographee, with dates of the original publication and selected source material.

"The information is attractively presented and is generally correct and abreast of current scholarly research. As a reference work it seems to be directed to the beginning student or to the general reader and to be designed for the small library which does not possess the DICTIONARY OF NATIONAL BIOGRAPHY, the CAMBRIDGE BIBLIOGRAPHY OF ENGLISH LITERATURE, or the BRITANNICA — although in several instances it corrects information in some of these standard sources. . . . When the editors have checked with modern scholarly research, their summaries are accurate and informed (e.g., Boswell and Pope). When they have omitted to do so, they perpetuate old errors" — (LIBRARY QUARTERLY, October, 1953).

". . . brief, careful, factual reporting characterizes the sketches of the book . . . but one wonders about a decision to include Mary Godwin and not William" — (SATURDAY REVIEW OF LITERATURE, March 21, 1953).

"This latest volume of the Wilson 'author books' will be welcomed for every reference collection" — (WISCONSIN LIBRARY BULLETIN, November, 1952).

KUNITZ, S. J. AND H. HAYCRAFT.
British Authors of the Nineteenth Century. New York: The H. W. Wilson Company, 1936. 677 p.

Contains some 1,000 biographies and 350 portraits of the non-living major and minor British authors of the nineteenth century. The sketches, which range in length from 100 to 2,500 words, depending upon the importance of the subject, are followed by a list of the principal works of the author, with dates of the original publication and selected source material.

". . . the salient facts . . . are so chosen and pointed that the men and women presented emerge as personalities, products of their ancestry, impressed by their times and leaving their own impress on those times in turn. . . . Some of the Catholic sketches—for example, that of Lord Acton—are guilty of wrong emphasis"—(COMMONWEAL, January 15, 1937).

"Students of English literature who have had to get their information about authors' lives from the usual encyclopedias of biography with their bone-dry listings of dates and titles will be grateful for the book. . . . Not only are the characterizations more than ordinarily vivid; the literary quality of the various sketches is well above the average to be found in such collections; the book should be widely used"—(NEW REPUBLIC, January 27, 1937).

"An invaluable reference book. Contains brief but competent biographies of at least 1,000 persons . . . should prove indispensable to all those whose work or interest demands information on writers"—(SATURDAY REVIEW OF LITERATURE, December 19, 1936).

KUNITZ, STANLEY J. AND VINETA COLBY, eds.
European Authors, 1000–1900: a Biographical Dictionary of European Literature. New York: The H. W. Wilson Company, 1967. 1016 p.

Contains 967 biographies, 309 portraits, and includes continental European writers born after 1000 A.D. and dead before 1925. Authors of 31 different nations are treated. The appended bibliographies emphasize English translations and studies of the works and authors. "This book will find its place beside the other volumes in this series and be indispensable to every type of library."

Dictionary of National Biography. Leslie Stephen and Sir Sidney Lee, eds. London: Smith, Elder, and Company and Oxford University Press, 1885—.

The most complete and the most authoritative work of its kind, containing more than 30,000 biographies of deceased Britons. First published in 63 volumes, it was reissued in 22 volumes in 1908–1909, the 22nd volume being the supplement of persons who had been omitted in the first selection either because they were still alive at the time or because their importance had been originally underestimated. The second supplement (ed. Sir Sidney Lee) added 1,660 articles about individuals who died up to January 1, 1912. The third supplement (eds. H. W. C. Davis and J. R. H. Weaver) covered the period 1912 to 1921. The fourth supplement (ed. L. G. W. Weaver) covered the period 1922 to 1930 and contained an Index covering all supplements 1901–1930. The fifth supplement (ed. L. G. W. Legg) covered the period 1931 to 1940 and contained an Index covering all supplements 1901–1940. THE CONCISE DICTIONARY OF NATIONAL BIOGRAPHY is an epitome volume which lists all the persons included in the foundation work and its supplements. The articles, however, are reduced to about one fourteenth of the original work.

The foundation work, its supplements, and the concise D.N.B. include biographies of virtually every prominent Briton whose life-period falls within the date-lines of D.N.B. publications.

"A competent and representational review of the greats of England. A must for every well-organized library. The D.N.B. is unsurpassed for all-around balance and or authority. Recommended"—(SUBSCRIPTION BOOKS BULLETIN, April, 1932).

"The language of commendation becomes almost monotonous in dealing with the successive volumes of the Dictionary of National Biography"—(LONDON TIMES, October 2, 1891).

Dictionary of National Biography. The Concise Dictionary. Part II, 1901–1950. Oxford, England: Oxford University Press, 1961. 528 p.

Brief biographies of outstanding Englishmen who have died during the period covered. Supplements Part I (from beginning to 1900). A new feature is the select subject index. Future revisions are expected to up-date Part II every ten years in order that Part I will remain the basic volume.

Who's Who: An Annual Biographical Dictionary, with which is Incorporated Men and Women of the Time. New York: Macmillan, 1849—.

An annual publication—the pioneer work of its kind—giving brief biographical facts about living men and women and, in the case of writers, a chronological list of publications. Principally British, but not completely so, since it also includes a number of internationally famous names (e.g., Franklin Delano Roosevelt, Mussolini, Hitler, Stalin).

The content order of the typical WHO'S WHO is generally: (1) A list of abbreviations; (2) Obituary; (3) The Royal Family, with portraits, all in the preliminary pages spaced between advertisements; (4) Biographies, in alphabetical order, with each sketch containing full names, degrees, honors, present position, birth, parents' names, education, publications, present address.

WHO'S WHO is supplemented by editions of WHO WAS WHO, which contains the biographies of those who died during the period. Each volume contains the final biographical sketches of deceased persons previously listed in WHO'S WHO, generally only with the date of death added,—in a few instances, with some additional information.

"Because of the scope and accuracy and because it continues to be the standard reference tool of its type in the British market, WHO'S WHO is highly recommended"—(SUBSCRIPTION BOOKS BULLETIN, April, 1950).

American Biographical Dictionaries

American Catholic Who's Who. Detroit, Michigan: Walter Romig, 1934—.

An earlier edition, published by B. Herder in St. Louis, 1911, was edited by G. P. Curtis. Short biographical sketches of outstanding American Catholic churchmen and persons prominent in all fields and professions.

Appleton's Cyclopedia of American Biography. J. G. Wilson and John Fiske, eds. New York: D. G. Appleton & Company, 1887–1900. 7 vols.

Fairly long biographical sketches of the native and adopted citizens of the United States; as well as of eminent individuals of Canada, Mexico, and other countries of North and South America; and persons of foreign birth closely connected with American history. Contains many portraits, facsimiles of autographs, but little bibliography.

Contains, according to several sources, many utterly fictitious biographies; yet the accuracy rating of its other entries is said to be impressive. Practically superseded by the DAB, but still useful for names and information (e.g., illustrations, facsimiles of autographs), not included in the later work.

The edition entitled CYCLOPEDIA OF AMERICAN BIOGRAPHY (New York Press Association Compilers, Inc.), published in 1915, represents a slight revision of the Appleton. Six non-alphabetical supplementary volumes (VII–XII) were released by the same publisher between 1918 and 1931.

Concise Dictionary of American Biography. New York: Scribner, 1964. 1273 p.

A condensation of every article in the DAB. As in the main work, no subject who died later than 1940 is included; in a few instances, however, where recent scholarship has revealed new information, some revisions have been made by the writers of the original articles.

Dictionary of American Biography. Allen Johnson, ed. New York: Charles Scribner's Sons. 1928–1937. 21 vols. (Revised edition with Index and Supplement 1, 1943–45, 22 vols.)

The title-page verso of each volume contains the following statement: "Prompted solely by a desire for public service the New York Times Company and its President, Mr. Adolph S. Ochs, have made possible the preparation of the manuscript of the DICTIONARY OF AMERICAN BIOGRAPHY through a subvention of more than $500.000 and with the understanding that the entire responsibility for the contents of the volumes rests with the American Council of Learned Societies."

Incorporates three restrictions in the definition of "American biography": (1) no living persons; (2) no persons who had not lived in the territory now known as the United States; (3) no British officer serving in America after the Colonies had declared their independence.

Although the DAB is narrower in scope than APPLETON'S CYCLOPEDIA OF AMERICAN BIOGRAPHY, which includes Canadian and Latin-American names, and is less inclusive than the NATIONAL CYCLOPAEDIA OF AMERICAN BIOGRAPHY, which includes many more minor names, it possesses more distinctive articles than either and far better bibliographies. The biographies range in length from 500 to 16,000 words, depending upon the importance of the subject.

Dictionary of American Biography. Published under the Auspices of the American Council of Learned Societies. Supplement 2, Robert Livingston Schuyler, ed.; Edward T. James, assoc. ed. New York: Scribner, 1958. 745 p.

Supplement 1 is volume 21 of the main work. Supplement 2, volume 22, contains 585 biographies of persons who died during the period 1936–40 inclusive, and follows the general pattern of the basic volumes.

JAMES, EDWARD T., ed.
Dictionary of American Biography: Supplement Three, 1941–1945. New York: Scribner's, 1973. 879 p.

Biographies of 573 important American personalities who died between 1941 and 1945. Numerous references to primary and secondary sources. A combined index to all three supplements.

KUNITZ, S. J. AND H. HAYCRAFT.
American Authors, 1600–1900: A Biographical Dictionary of American Literature, Complete in one Volume with 1300 biographies, 400 portraits. New York: The H. W. Wilson Company, 1938. 846 p.

Includes major and minor authors who contributed to the making of our literary history from the time of the first English settlement in Jamestown in 1607 to the close of the nineteenth century. Excludes living authors. The sketches, which range from 150 to 250 words, roughly proportionate to the importance of the subject, are followed by a list of the printed works of the biographee, original dates of publication, and a list of biographical and critical sources.

". . . in spite of occasional straining for freshness, the compilation has literary merit and the virtue of inclusiveness"— (BOOK REVIEW DIGEST, 1939).

". . . an invaluable reference book for literary students, librarians, writers, and just plain readers"—(NEW YORKER, October 29, 1938).

Lamb's Biographical Dictionary of the United States. J. H. Brown, ed. Boston: Federal Book Company, 1900–1903. 7 vols.

An alphabetical arrangement of short sketches. Useful because of the inclusion of some names not found in APPLETON'S CYCLOPAEDIA OF AMERICAN BIOGRAPHY or in the NATIONAL CYCLOPAEDIA OF AMERICAN BIOGRAPHY.

Also published in ten volumes by the Biographical Society (Boston, 1904) as TWENTIETH CENTURY BIOGRAPHICAL DICTIONARY OF NOTABLE AMERICANS (Rossiter Johnson, ed.).

National Cyclopaedia of American Biography. New York: James T. White & Company, Inc., 1892–. 41 vols.

Biographical sketches of all persons who are prominently connected with the history of the nation,—rulers, statesmen, soldiers, clergymen, lawyers, artists, literary men, scientists, representatives of professions generally, and even those who have contributed to the industrial and commercial progress and growth of the country. The arrangement is by period, field or profession, and by reference to important events or movements. An Index at the end of each volume lists alphabetically: (1) biographies of persons included; (2) general categories under which the names are arranged, with cross-indexing to the names connected with the categories. More comprehensive than the DAB; more current than APPLETON'S or LAMB'S.

Supplementary volumes keep the NATIONAL current, and all volumes are indexed in a special locked binder, which is divided into three parts: I, volumes 1–30; II, volumes 31–41 (present permanent volume); III, current volumes.

Of volumes I–XX, a reviewer noted: "The current volumes are useful. Biographies of men and women living at the time the volumes were issued are included and the material is valuable because these men are important enough to have their biographies used frequently but not sufficiently important to have the material accessible elsewhere. . . . The current volumes only are recommended as useful in large reference collections"—(SUBSCRIPTION BOOKS BULLETIN, January, 1918).

"Like the earlier volumes, they include information on some persons about whom little or nothing else is available in most libraries. At the same time, much of this material is not likely to be ofen needed, except where there is local interest in certain individuals. Volumes XXI–XXVI are recommended as an auxiliary source for American biography in libraries with large reference collections"—(SUBSCRIPTION BOOKS BULLETIN, April, 1938).

PRESTON, WHEELER.
American Biographies. New York and London: Harper, 1940. 1147 p.

Very brief sketches, two or three item bibliographies, of names which are virtually all found more fully treated in the DAB; hence mainly of value in the small library which lacks the larger work.

"The rather short sketches emphasize accomplishment rather than details of personal life and are briskly concise and informative. A special feature is the bibliography supplied for further reference under every name"—(NEW YORK TIMES, November 10, 1940).

"More than 5,000 compact biographical sketches of Americans, from Colonial times to the present. The names of living people have been expressly omitted . . . with this exception, every man or woman from Colonial times onward who has played a noteworthy part in the making of the United States finds a place . . . including non-Americans who had a share in the history of the nation"—(BOOKLIST, December 15, 1940).

White's Conspectus of American Biography: A Tabulated Record of American History and Biography. 2d ed. New York: James T. White & Company, Inc., 1937. 455 p.

A revision and modernization of A CONSPECTUS OF AMERICAN BIOGRAPHY, which was published in 1906 in combination with the indexes to the NATIONAL CYCLOPAEDIA OF AMERICAN BIOGRAPHY. Useful both as a classified index to the NATIONAL CYCLOPAEDIA and as an independent tool of information.

"The chief merit of this work is that it affords a chronological survey of Americans active in government affairs, letters, and the arts. It is possible to learn from these lists at once who were Presidents, vice-presidents, cabinet officers, senators, congressmen, American ministers and ambassadors, heads of bureaus, governors, and chief justices of the states in any year since the establishment of the governmental unit concerned" — (SPRINGFIELD REPUBLICAN, April 11, 1938).

"Though part of the matter which makes up WHITE'S CONSPECTUS is available in almanacs or other volumes found in most libraries, some of it is not so easily located. It is brought together here in a convenient form which makes it, in spite of certain flaws, useful for quick reference. The CONSPECTUS is recommended for large libraries and also for smaller libraries whose need for this type of material might justify the expenditure" — (SUBSCRIPTION BOOKS BULLETIN, April 1938).

WILLARD, F. AND M. LIVERMORE.
A Woman of the Century: 1470 biographical sketches accompanied by portraits of leading American women in all walks of life.

A useful supplement insofar as it contains sketches of important women of the nineteenth century whose biographies appear in no other reference work.

Who's Who in America: A Biographical Dictionary of Notable Living Men and Women. Chicago: The A. N. Marquis Company, 1949—.

The best known and the most generally useful dictionary of contemporary biography. Aims to include the names of the best known men and women in all lines of useful and reputable achievement. The standards of admission are: "(1) those selected on account of special prominence in creditable lines of effort making them subjects of extensive interest, inquiry or discussion; and (2) those included arbitrarily on account of position—civil, military, educational, corporate or organizational."

For those who are not listed in WHO'S WHO IN AMERICA, or for whom additional information is desired, one should refer to the more specialized dictionaries of the "WHO'S WHO" type: local (e.g., WHO'S WHO IN THE MIDWEST); professional (e.g., WHO'S WHO IN COMMERCE AND INDUSTRY); foreign-American (e.g., WHO'S WHO IN POLISH AMERICA); religious or social (WHO'S WHO IN AMERICAN JEWRY).

"It is the standard reference work in its field and has no serious competitors . . . Because of its accuracy, breadth of scope, and general reference utility, it is a recommended reference work"—(SUBSCRIPTION BOOKS BULLETIN, July, 1950).

INDEXES

To Indexes

HASKELL, Daniel C.
A Checklist of Cumulative Indexes to Individual Periodicals in the New York Public Library. New York: Library, 1942. 1946 p.

An alphabetical list of thousands of cumulative indexes available in the New York Public Library.

IRELAND, Norma Olin.
An Index to Indexes: A Subject Bibliography of Published Indexes. Boston: Faxon, 1942. 107 p.

Aims to assemble into one volume a selection of published indexes which will aid librarians, students, and scholars who need to locate quickly the index source of various subject fields. Characteristically, five types of indexes are used: (1) Special Indexes; (2) Indexes to sets of books; (3) Periodical Indexes; (4) Cumulative indexes to individual periodicals; (5) Government document indexes. Embraces 1,000 separate indexes listed under 280 different subjects.

"The book is neither comprehensive nor consistent, and it does not bring all the indexes mentioned down to date" — (AMERICAN HISTORICAL REVIEW, January, 1943).

"Mrs. Ireland by her broad and somewhat loose definition of 'index' permits the inclusion of indexes to periodicals, documents, and books, bibliographies, and check lists, and related publications. It is obvious that she had to limit herself to a selection. Foreign indexes are A PRIORI excluded. The result is somewhat discouraging" — (LIBRARY JOURNAL, March, 1943).

IRELAND, Norma Olin.
Local Indexes in American Libraries: A Union List of Unpublished Indexes. Boston: Faxon, 1947. 221 p.

A companion to Ireland's AN INDEX TO INDEXES.

To Ephemeral Materials

Vertical File Index. New York: The H. W. Wilson Company, 1935—. 640 p.

Formerly called, THE VERTICAL FILE SERVICE CATALOG; this publication is issued every month (except August), with an annual cumulation in December, and, for material listed, provides title, author, paging, publisher, and price.

"An annotated subject list of pamphlets, booklets, brochures, leaflets, circulars, folders, maps, posters, charts, mimeographed bulletins and other inexpensive material which falls outside the classification of books, but still has a place in the library . . . Some of the pamphlets are frankly propaganda or advertising, often biased in viewpoint but, like the other titles in the catalogue, they are listed in the belief that they may prove to be of some reference value"—(Preface).

To Newspapers and Serials

AYER, N. W. AND SONS.
Directory of Newspapers and Periodicals: Guide to Publications Printed in the United States and its Possessions, the Dominion of Canada, Bermuda, Cuba and Republic of the Philippines; Descriptions of the States, Provinces, Cities and Towns in which They Are Published; Classified Lists; 70 Maps. Philadelphia: Ayer, 1880—.

The stated purpose of the work is, "to provide, first, facts about those publications that are essential in the promotion of commercial and other interests through advertising." Hence the primary reference value of Ayer's is for current information about newspapers and periodicals such as: names of publishers and editors; frequency of publications; special leanings and interests; format; price and circulations. It is also useful for information of a geographical nature, such as: location, population, chief industries, distances to places of importance. "The standard list."

KELLER, Dean H.
Index to Plays in Periodicals. New York: Scarecrow, 1972. 558 p.

Serves as an index to 103 selected periodicals which, generally, have been indexed to 1969. The work is in two parts: the Author Index, which is the main entry, and the Title Index. Each entry includes the author's full name, dates, the title of the play, the number of acts, a brief description of the play, the name of the periodical in which the play appears, the volume and the date, the pages, the language in which it is printed if other than English, and the names of the translators or adapters.

Modern Language Association of America. Directory of Journals and Series in the Humanities. Compiled by Harrison T. Meserole and Carolyn James Bishop. New York: M.L.A., 1970. 135 p.

Subtitle: A data list of the periodical sources on the master list of the MLA INTERNATIONAL BIBLIOGRAPHY. Aims to give fuller information on the journals represented on the MLA master list in the annual bibliography; does not include all the journals found on the master list.

New York Daily Tribune Index, 1875–1906. New York: Tribune Association, 1876–1907. 31 vols.

More limited in scope than the NEW YORK TIMES INDEX, but still useful for the period covered. No longer published.

New York Times Index, 1913–. New York: New York Times Index, 1913–.

Appeared as a quarterly until 1929; as a monthly until 1948; as a semimonthly, with a cumulative annual, since 1948. It is today also available in microfilm. The scope of this carefully constructed work is evident from a description of the 1949 issue which contains 20,000 personal names separately indexed; 18,000 additional names of institutions and associations; 940 geographical headings; 175 listings of educational institutions; and 3,500 more subjects given under separate headings.

"Besides being primarily an index to the NEW YORK TIMES, the INDEX is also an independent reference work in that the entries give a synopsis of the newspaper articles. It serves as a guide to the publication of news in other newspapers"— (PUBLISHERS WEEKLY, 158:671, August 12, 1950).

Palmer's Index to the Times Newspaper, 1790–. Palmer's Index to the TIMES Newspaper, 1790–. London: Palmer, 1868–.

Considerably briefer than the official index of the TIMES of London, but still useful because of the length of time covered. "The indexing of obituary, death and funeral notices under the heading "Deaths" in each volume frequently supplies biographical material difficult to find elsewhere."

SEVERANCE, HENRY O.
A Guide to the Current Periodicals and Series of the United States and Canada. Michigan: Michigan University Press, 1931.

The first edition appeared in 1907; the second, in 1909; the third, in 1913; the fourth, in 1920; the fifth, in 1931. Includes fewer titles than the AYER AND SONS DIRECTORY, but is handier and more convenient mainly because of its alphabetical arrangement.

"... an accessible and reliable source of information regarding American periodicals, society publications, and society transactions"—(THE LIBRARY JOURNAL, July, 1907, 334–335).

The Standard Periodical Directory, 1964–65. New York: Oxbridge Publishing Co. 1964. 544 p.

An annual directory of magazines, journals, government publications, newsletters, house organs, etc., except local newspapers. Five parts: Preface, Table of Contents, Subject Guide (with key word index), Periodical List by Subject, Alphabetical List by Title. A handy work, since it includes items which the Ayer and Ulrich works do not and excludes works which the Ayer and Ulrich contain.

Times Official Index, 1906–. London: Times Office, 1907–.

A valuable reference tool; contains a detailed alphabetical index referring to date, page, and column. Originally published as a monthly, with annual cumulations for 1906–1913, it has been published, since 1914, in quarterly cumulations.

Ulrich's Periodical Directory: A Classified Guide to a Selected List of Current Periodicals, Foreign and Domestic. 13th ed. New York: R. R. Bowker Company, 1969–70. 2 vols.

The first edition appeared in 1932; the second, in 1935; the third, in 1938; the fourth, in 1943; the fifth, in 1947; the sixth, in 1951; the seventh, in 1953; the eighth, in 1956. Different editions have special features. Thus the fourth edition was an Inter-American edition, covering North, Central, and South America, the West Indies, and Hawaii; the fifth edition emphasized the publications of North and South America and the British Empire; the sixth edition includes many foreign titles which were left out during the war years.

"An outstanding feature, added in 1956 by Graves, is the notation of the many indexing and abstracting services: it indicates in which general periodical index each is indexed or abstracted . . . every user . . . will be grateful to the compiler for bringing together in convenient compass so many titles, especially those less easily accessible to the searcher, such as Slavic Publications. By the aid of the UNION LIST OF SERIALS the student may now easily locate, in some American libraries, sets of periodicals brought to his notice by this directory" — (LIBRARY QUARTERLY, 1932, 432–435).

More than 40,000 periodicals are included in the various entries which include title, subtitle, supplements, date of origin, frequency, price, size, publisher, place of publication, and indexes, if any. Perhaps the most useful guide to magazines, especially of the Americas and the British Empire.

With this edition the work reverts to the plan of the 10th edition; instead of separate volumes for science and technology and for humanities and social sciences being published in alternate years, editions will appear biennially using a single alphabetical arrangement of all subject classes, with title and subject index.

To Periodicals and Learned Journals

Annual Library Index, 1905–1910. Including Periodicals, American and English; Essays, Book-Chapters, Bibliographies, Necrology, and an Index to Dates of Principal Events. New York: Publishers' Weekly, 1906–1911. 6 vols. o.p.

Differs from its predecessor, the ANNUAL LITERARY INDEX, mainly in this, that its index to periodicals contained authors, titles, and subjects in one alphabet, instead of two distinct subject and author lists. For author entries, superseded in 1911 by the AMERICAN LIBRARY ANNUAL; for subject entries, it is now virtually superseded by READERS' GUIDE and the INTERNATIONAL INDEX. Still useful for some author entries for 1905–1906.

"The field of periodical literature has been very efficiently cared for, these many years by first the CUMULATIVE INDEX which, later combined with the READERS' GUIDE, is now furnishing all the help that any library could ask along the lines of periodical literature"—(PUBLIC LIBRARY, VOL. 10, March, 1905, 127).

Annual Literary Index, 1892–1904: Including Periodicals, American and English; Essays, Book-Chapters, etc. New York: Publishers' Weekly, 1893–1905. 13 vols.

Each volume contains: (1) subject index to periodicals; (2) subject index to general literature; (3) author index to periodical and other literature; (4) bibliographies; (5) necrology; (6) index to dates of main events.

The composite annual index comprehends among the six divisions of the work four distinct indexes: a subject index, an annual continuation of POOLE'S INDEX, which indexes the same periodicals in the same way and forms the basis for the five-year supplements; (2) a subject index to essays, a continuation of the A.L.A. Index; (3) a needed author index, lacking in POOLE'S INDEX; and (4) an index to dates, serving practically as an index to newspapers.

"Undoubtedly this index will be found a necessity in even the smaller libraries. . . . Nothing could do more to enable a librarian to make the most of a small library"—(LIBRARY JOURNAL, VOL. 17, 1892, 7).

Annual Magazine Subject Index. Boston: F. W. Faxon Co., Inc., 1908–52. 43 vols.

The first volume, entitled MAGAZINE SUBJECT INDEX, indexed 79 periodicals (44 from their first issue to Dec. 31, 1907; 35, for the year 1907). The subsequent volumes, entitled ANNUAL

MAGAZINE SUBJECT INDEX, are annual supplements.

Provides abbreviated title of periodical, volume, date, inclusive paging, and indication of illustrations, portraits, maps, and plans.

". . . opens a new field of research because it indexes nothing included in POOLE'S INDEX, THE LIBRARY INDEX, or the READER'S GUIDE. Originally intended to be simply a cumulation in one alphabet of the four quarterly installments in the BULLETIN OF BIBLIOGRAPHY for 1907, it has been broadened to include the back years of many periodicals and those which heretofore were not included in the BULLETIN"— (LIBRARY JOURNAL, XXXIII, July, 1908, 164).

The entries in the 43 volumes are cumulated into one alphabet.

Book Review Digest, 1905–. New York: The H. W. Wilson Company, 1905–.

An index of selected book reviews in seventy or more English and American periodicals (principally the latter), providing in many cases brief excerpts from the reviews, indicating the length of the review in number of words, and the negative or positive tone of the review. For each book entered, it gives the author, title, paging, publisher, price, a brief descriptive note, and exact references to the periodicals in which the notices or reviews appeared.

Primarily useful for the general layman and the undergraduate, because of the character of the book listed and the character of the periodical from which the review is derived— learned journals being only occasionally the sources.

Cumulated subject and title indexes for the previous 5-year period are included in the annual volumes for 1921, 1926, 1931, 1936, 1941, 1946, 1951, 1961, 1966.

"The summaries are well done, though a tendency toward the favorable point of view is perhaps to be observed"— (LIBRARY JOURNAL, XXX, April, 1905, 245).

Catholic Periodical Index: A Cumulative Author and Subject Index to a Selected List of Catholic Periodicals. New York: Catholic Library Association, 1939–.

The 1930–1933 publication forms the first permanent volume

and supersedes the earlier two volumes for 1930–1931. The 1939–1943 volume, published in 1945, represents the second cumulation. The 1943–1948 cumulation appeared in 1955. The 1934–1938 cumulation remains unpublished.

"This service . . . is one for which we cannot be too grateful. A pioneer in its field, it is indeed an event in American Catholic literature. If librarians have realized its need, research and editorial workers have been no less hampered for lack of it, and it is already proving itself of inestimable value to them. Modeled mainly on that excellent prototype, H. W. Wilson's READERS' GUIDE TO PERIODICAL LITERATURE, it is a difficult task well done"—(CATHOLIC WORLD, VOL. 131, June, 1930, 378).

"The uses of the index are many and varied. Aside from constant use and research workers' attention, it is copiously useful in enabling educators to keep abreast of all current literature on subjects on which they are interested"—(ECCLESIASTICAL REVIEW, VOL. 82, April, 1930, 445).

Catholic Periodical and Literature Index. Haverford, P.: Catholic Library Association, 1968–. Vol. 14.

Bimonthly with biennial cumulation. Beginning July 1968, THE CATHOLIC PERIODICAL INDEX and THE GUIDE TO CATHOLIC LITERATURE were combined in a single publication under this new title, which continues the volume numbering of the INDEX. The 1967–68 cumulation includes about 60,000 entries from 123 periodicals, and listings for some 2,100 books. Book review citations appear in a separate section at the end of the cumulated volume.

Nineteenth Century Readers' Guide to Periodical Literature, 1890–1899. Supplementary indexing, 1900–1901. Helen Grant Cushing and Adah V. Morris, eds. New York: The H. W. Wilson Company, 1944. 2 vols.

An author, subject, and illustrator index to the contents of fifty-one periodicals principally—for thirty-seven, actually—for the years 1890–1899. The other periodicals are carried forward as far as 1922.

The periodicals indexed are mainly general and literary. Short stories, novels, and plays are indexed under author and title; reviews of books are listed under author entry only; more

than 13,000 poems are listed by title, with a full entry under
the author's name. A retrospective supplement to READERS'
GUIDE.

Poole's Index to Periodical Literature, 1802–1821. Rev. Ed.
Boston: Houghton Mifflin Company, 1891. 2 vols. Supplements.
1887–1908, 5 vols.

The pioneer index to American and English periodicals and,
though now discontinued, still significantly useful, covering as it
does the longest period (105 years) and constituting the largest
index of its kind—including the greatest number of items (590,-
000 articles; 12,241 volumes; 470 English and American periodicals).

Users of the index should remember that: (1) it has no
author entries; (2) articles which have a distinct subject are
entered under that subject; (3) articles which have no subject are entered under the first word of the title (excepting
articles); (4) book reviews are entered either under subject,
if the book has a definite subject, or under the author's name,
if it does not have a distinct subject. Specific references are
made to maps, portraits, and other illustrations, as well as to
bibliographies.

"It is hardly necessary to urge upon the attention of . . .
colleges and academies the utility of making POOLE'S INDEX
available for their senior students"—(CATHOLIC WORLD, January, 1890, 558).

"As is truly said in nearly every article, there is no need to
enlarge upon its importance; it is something eagerly desired
by every librarian, and something we have been looking for
every year, only to be constantly disappointed"—(THE AMERICAN
LIBRARY JOURNAL, April 30, 1877, 279–287).

Readers' Guide to Periodical Literature, 1900—. New York:
The H. W. Wilson Company, 1905—.

The major guide to general periodicals. Initially, it indexed a
small group of popular periodicals. But by 1903 it had ab-
sorbed the CUMULATIVE INDEX; and by 1911 it had taken over
the function of the ANNUAL LIBRARY INDEX. Today it indexes
as many as 125 periodicals, mostly general and popular, although a few scientific and scholarly publications are included.

Among its basic features are: (1) full dictionary cataloguing of all articles (author, subject, and, when necessary, title; (2) uniformity of entries; (3) catalog subject headings, instead of catchword subject; (4) full reference information (volume and page, and to exact date and inclusive paging); (5) cumulative features designed to keep the index up to date; (6) indexing of book reviews through 1904, after which they are to be found in the BOOK REVIEW DIGEST.

"Poetry, which is ignored by POOLE'S except as a subject treated of, is carefully recorded by the new index. And another point: each entry of poetry or other articles gives not only the volume and page of the magazine, but also the date" — (NEW YORK TIMES, February 3, 1906, 72).

Review of Reviews: Index to the Periodicals of 1890–1902. London and New York: Review of Reviews, 1891–1903. 13 vols. o.p.

The title of the first volume is, ANNUAL INDEX OF PERIODICALS AND PHOTOGRAPHS FOR 1890. The title of the second, third, and fourth volumes is, INDEX TO THE PERIODICAL LITERATURE OF THE WORLD.

While it contains some author entries, it is essentially a broad subject index, providing for each entry a brief title, periodical, volume, month, and page reference, and an exact reference to the REVIEW OF REVIEWS where a summary or other notice of the article is to be found. Since it covers a number of periodicals, especially British ones, that are not indexed in Poole's, it serves as a supplement to the latter work.

"The present volume is estimated to contain about 12,000 articles, and is as useful, practical, and detailed as could be expected" — (LIBRARY JOURNAL, XXIX, 1904, 102).

"The overall arrangement is good and its inclusions comprehensive. The work is a 'must' for any American library, although its speciality seems to be that of British periodicals" — (LIBRARY JOURNAL, XXVII, 1902, 1029).

Saturday Review of Literature.

The REVIEW is the most embracive American weekly devoted primarily to the review of books. General and semi-popular works are reviewed by professional reviewers; the scholarly

books are reviewed by specialists. In addition, the SATURDAY
REVIEW contains feature articles on many subjects; (in the first
issue), a section devoted to science reports, research developments, social aspects, etc.; (in the final issue) a lengthy recording section with popular and classical record reviews, as
well as articles on artists, music, and composers.

"Its success, however, should not be experimental in view
of the extraordinary increase of popular interest in the field of
literary discussion and combat"—(NEW YORK TIMES, August
1, 1934, 5).

Social Sciences and Humanities Index: formerly International
Index. New York: Wilson, 1916–. Vol. 1–.
The subtitle of this index, when first published in 1907, was:
"Devoted Chiefly to the Humanities and Science." The first
volume indexed only seventy-four periodicals, but the subsequent volumes were enlarged by the inclusion of forty-five
serials, mainly foreign, previously indexed by the analytic cards
issued by the American Library Association Publishing Board.
Beginning with volume forty-three, scientific, psychological, and
foreign language periodicals were dropped, and fifty-three new
periodicals, in the fields of the humanities and social sciences
in the English language were added. Among the subjects now
emphasized are language, literature, anthropology, archaeology,
geography, and history; and economics, sociology, political
science, labor, public opinion, philosophy, religion, musicology,
and the theater arts. The title varies: volumes one and two,
READERS' GUIDE TO PERIODICAL LITERATURE SUPPLEMENTS;
volume three, INTERNATIONAL INDEX TO PERIODICALS.

"Of these, the one of most interest, perhaps, in the large
library, is the new permanent volume of the INTERNATIONAL
INDEX which appears with the imprint date of 1924, though
not ready until 1925. It is much larger than the preceding
cumulation of 1916–1919, containing 600 more pages than the
earlier issue and indexing some 275 periodicals as against 126
in 1916–1919. Of these 275 periodicals, 185 are in English,
33 in French, 49 in German, while a few titles in Dutch,
Spanish, Italian, and Swedish complete the list. . . . The indispensable index for the university library"—(LIBRARY JOUR-
NAL, January 1, 1925, 13).

Title varies: the first two volumes, READERS' GUIDE TO PERI-

ODICAL LITERATURE SUPPLEMENT; volumes 3 to 52, INTERNATIONAL INDEX TO PERIODICALS; volumes 53, no. 1, June, 1965, SOCIAL SCIENCES AND HUMANITIES INDEX.

A cumulative index made up of three forms: (1) permanent cumulated volumes covering four, three, or two years; (a) annual volumes; and (3) current numbers issued quarterly, June, Sept., Dec., and March (frequency varies). Covers the more scholarly journals in the humanities and social sciences. Since the war, foreign titles have been dropped, as well as psychological and scientific periodicals. Now indexes about 175 American and English periodicals.

Subject Index to Periodicals. 1915 — . London: Library Association, 1919 — .

An English index which was first issued as the ATHENAEUM SUBJECT INDEX, the outcome of a resolution passed at a meeting of the Library Association in 1913, advocating the resumption of an index to periodicals on the lines of POOLE'S. Until 1922, the indexes were divided into classified lists according to broad subjects (e.g., theology and philosophy; historical, political, and economic sciences; education and child welfare). Since 1926, when the publication was revived, there has been a single alphabetical indexing, principally by subjects.

"The index is not altogether inclusive, but perhaps it was not intended to be so. There are many insertions referring to subjects in American periodicals, which perhaps could not be otherwise, for the language of America is of the Modern European" — (PUBLIC LIBRARIES, VOL. XXVI, 1921).

To Books

American Catalogue of Books, 1876–1910. New York: Publisher's Weekly, 1876–1910. Reprinted in 1941 by Peter Smith.

The 1938 publication of the AMERICAN CATALOGUE reprints and continues the BIBLIOTHECA AMERICANA of Roorbach, and brings the work down to 1861; the 1941 publication was compiled by Lynds E. Jones and published in reprint form by Peter Smith in 1941.

The standard American list for the period covered. Aims to include all books published in the United States which were in print and for sale to the general public on July 1, 1876, excepting: local directories, periodicals, sheet music, unbound maps, tracts, and miscellaneous cheap pamphlets.

"Reference librarians are particularly grateful for the reprint of POOLE'S INDEX now available complete except for the annual library service of 1907–1910, but an even greater debt of gratitude is due the publishers for helping to make available the complete chain of American national bibliography. Already Kelly's AMERICAN CATALOG, previously unobtainable for love or money, is available in two volumes at a price of $7.50 a volume. Roorbach's BIBLIOTHECA AMERICANA, four volumes, is listed at a total cost of $20.00, and now comes a most welcome P.S. from Peter Smith: 'We expect to announce shortly our project for a reprint of the AMERICAN CATALOG OF BOOKS, 1876–1910 — the whole blessed business'" — (WILSON LIBRARY BULLETIN, XIII, 482).

"The AMERICAN CATALOGUE, that monumental undertaking begun by Frederick Leypoldt in the 1870's . . . is being reissued in photographic reprint by Peter Smith. . . . The availability of this 13-volume series will be a boon to any number of librarians and their users, and to the rare book trade. The volumes have long been out of print, and though very substantially printed with wide margins for rebinding they have been difficult to pick up for many years" — (PUBLISHER'S WEEKLY, May 24, 1941, 2070).

"If we do not praise the linotype for its mechanical beauty in this instance, its aid to bibliography ensures full devotion" — (THE NATION, January–June, 1905, 501).

American Library Association Catalog: An Annotated Basic List of 10,000 Books. Chicago: American Library Association, 1926–. 1295 p. o.p.

First published in 1893, followed by a second edition in 1904, and then by supplements covering the period 1904–1911 and 1912–1921. A classified list, arranged in the main according to the Dewey Decimal System, and providing, for United States publications since 1893, author, title, date, paging, publisher's name, Library of Congress card number, and an annotation to indicate scope and value. Its two main limitations are perhaps: (1) omission of materials published outside of the United

States; (2) annotations, though often quotations from other comment, are given without an exact indication of source. Contains separate lists for biography and fiction and for children's books.

"For the reference worker the full author, title, and subject index is an excellent tool. It is a valuable for all libraries, book stores, schools, and to anyone wanting an authoritative survey" —(BOOKLIST, 23:60, November, 1926).

"Is well indexed with reference to author, title, subject. Well printed and bound. Will be the standard of selection for many years to come"—(WISCONSIN LIBRARY BULLETIN, 22:239, December, 1926).

"The biography section is a treasure house of good reading. It is impossible to criticize it. . . . A curious omission is a statement of policy with regard to the inclusion of out-of-print books. . . ."—(LIBRARY JOURNAL, December 1, 1926).

"The A.L.A. CATALOGUE is in a class by itself as an aid to book selections for the American library. For this purpose it is indispensable and invaluable. Its use as a reference tool would have been increased, however, by the giving of authorities for the quoted or adapted annotations, and by a more frequent indication of dates of first publication where recent reprints are chosen for inclusion"—(LIBRARY JOURNAL, VOL. LII, 82).

American Library Association Index to General Literature. 2d ed. Chicago: American Library Association Publications Board, 1901. 679 p. Supplement, 1914, 223 p.

The basic volume deals with books in English published before 1900; the supplement deals with works published between 1900 and 1910. The predecessor to the current ESSAY AND GENERAL LITERATURE INDEX, it aims to do for books of essays and general literature what POOLE'S INDEX does for periodicals. The works indexed belong to the following groups: (1) historical, literary, and biographical essays; (2) books of travel; (3) reports and publications of literary, historical, and sociological societies; miscellaneous works. Its two most serious shortcomings: includes only works in English; indexes by catchword subject, rather than, as its successor does, by a combination of entries.

Annals of English Literature, 1475–1925: The Principal Publications of Each Year with an Alphabetical Index of Authors and Their Works. Oxford: Clarendon Press, 1935. 345 p.

"Sound in scholarship and admirable in organization of its vast contents, this reference volume increasingly stirs the reader as he turns the pages with thoughts of the endless patience, care and hard work that went into the making. . . . As a reference work for any one interested in literature and a handbook for literary students, the volume will be invaluable" — (COMMONWEAL, March 20, 1936).

"No more useful work on English literature than this has been produced for a considerable time" — (SPECULUM, 156:320, Feb. 21, 1936).

"It can be read straightforward, with both profit and pleasure, a conspectus of the expansion of English literature . . . and it can be worked backwards from the index in the process of checking dates of author and of books" — (TIMES, London, Feb., 1936, 97).

Essay and General Literature Index, 1900–1933: An Index to about 40,000 Essays and Articles in 2,144 Volumes of Collections of Essays and Miscellaneous Works. New York: The H. W. Wilson Company, 1934. 1952 p.

1934–1940: An Index to 23,090 Essays and Articles in 1,241 Volumes of Collections of Essays and Miscellaneous Works. New York: The H. W. Wilson Company, 1941. 1362 p.

1941–1947; An Index to 32,226 Essays and Articles in 2,023 Volumes of Collections of Essays and Miscellaneous Works. New York: The H. W. Wilson Company, 1948. 1908 p.

The 1948–1954 cumulation was published in 1955.

An author, subject, and, occasionally, title index to collections of essays in all fields, as well as an index to some miscellaneous works which have reference value, such as collective biography. Provides: (1) list of essays by given author; (2) authorship of an essay when only the title is known; (3) analytical material on a given subject, particularly in areas in which there exist no solid treatments; (4) biographical and critical material; (5) criticisms of individual books; (6) different works in which an essay may be found.

A reviewer of the basic volume notes that: "While only books published since 1900 are included, the material to be found in collections by various authors includes not only the work of modern essayists but also a great many essays by the earlier standard essayists, such as Addison, Bacon, Carlyle, Emerson, Hazlitt, and Lamb" — (BOOK REVIEW DIGEST, 1935, 295).

Essay and General Literature Index: Works Indexed 1900–1969. New York: The H.W. Wilson Company, 1972. 437 p.

Lists 9917 titles in cumulations covering 70 years, with authors in alphabetical order, and with cross references from titles, pseudonyms and other forms of the name, translators, and joint authors and editors.

Guide to Catholic Literature, 1888–1940. Detroit: Romig, 1940. 1240 p.

Volume two covers the years 1940–1944; volume three, the years, 1944–1948; volume four, the years 1948–1951. The work now appears annually with four-year cumulations.

An author-subject-title index in one alphabet of books and booklets, in all languages and in all subjects by Catholics and of particular interest to Catholics.

"The format does not make for legibility or for quick reference use. The main entries are in bold type, but the items appearing under each entry are not adequately spaced. . . . While some cross references are used, they are neither consistent nor adequate. While some foreign language publications are included, the list is by no means complete. . . . In spite of the numerous inaccuracies and its incompleteness, as an index to works on general subjects it is recommended for Catholics and for large public libraries" — (SUBSCRIPTION BOOKS BULLETIN, April, 1941).

SERIALS

Ephemeral Materials

Pamphlets, booklets, brochures, circulars, bulletins, charts, posters, and similar materials at times constitute a significant supplement to book, periodical, and newspaper content. The basic index to such information is the VERTICAL FILE SERVICE CATALOG; an annotated subject list (issued monthly except August) of inexpensively published materials, which gives title, author, page, reference, publisher, and price.

Newspapers

The New York Times, 1851 —. New York: New Times Company.

The most comprehensive newspaper in America. Originally a four-page, handset sheet, its Sunday issue now exceeds three hundred pages. It is supplemented by the SUNDAY TIMES BOOK REVIEW and the TIMES MAGAZINE. Among its special features are: reproductions of full texts of treatises and pronouncements, speeches, and other significant documents; and departments devoted to book reviews, education, art, music, theater, and industrial activities.

". . . learned, but not pedantic; objective, but never indifferent; detailed and painstaking, but not intolerant; forthright in politics, but rarely partisan; world-wide in vision, coverage, and influence, but always American"—(MEYER BERGER, THE STORY OF THE NEW YORK TIMES, 565).

Its hundred years of success are "proof of the soundness of the theory of responsible journalism"—(THE CHRISTIAN CENTURY, October 3, 1951, 115–116).

The TIMES continues to be an example of devotion to the reporting of news almost as a "public service to the world community"—(THE SATURDAY REVIEW OF LITERATURE, October 6, 1951, 26).

London Times, 1788 —. London: The Times.

The LONDON TIMES was founded in 1788 by the Walter family. In 1906 there was added a literary supplement, similar in appearance to a representative American Sunday supplement. The TIMES is generally considered to be the foremost newspaper published in the English language.

"It has written the history of the British Empire and of the modern world with a breadth of view and a sense of perspective which its keenest critics must concede and admire. The TIMES foreign correspondents have always been men with ability and much training. . . . it has so long risen above the level of partisanship and has so clearly and successfully interpreted British opinion, that it has come to be regarded as a national institution"—(THE OUTLOOK, Vol. 88, 66).

In recent years the paper's influence has visibly declined. "Still, it retains a prestige greater than any other newspaper. . . . its supreme reputation was won by its unexampled corps of foreign correspondents. . . . Above and beyond all these titles to distinction, there was for years a quality in the TIMES which really gained for it the name of 'The Thunderer.' This was its ability to hit English public opinion between wind and water. When it spoke, its voice was really the voice of England" —(NATION, VOL. 86, 18–25).

Learned Journals

American Literature, 1929 —. North Carolina: Duke University Press, 1929—.

AMERICAN LITERATURE, the only research organ exclusively devoted to the study of the literature of the United States, first appeared in March, 1929. It is published by the Duke University Press; editorially sponsored by the American Literature Group of the MLA; and is indexed in the BIOGRAPHY INDEX and the INTERNATIONAL INDEX. It publishes only original papers of a critical, historical, or bibliographical nature, as well as a checklist of articles in the area of its special interest and a list of dissertations in progress or completed.

'There could be no better evidence of the new life that has recently come into the scholarly study of the literature of our own country than the establishment of AMERICAN LITERATURE, A Journal of Literary History, Criticism, and Bibliography. If we may judge by the 111 pages of this first number (33 of which are given to reviews by distinguished scholars), the new quarterly will not only stimulate investigation and offer it a needed outlet, but will also maintain standards of accuracy, thoroughness, and good writing, together with breadth of outlook, in a field where these qualities have sometimes been to seek"— (MODERN LANGUAGE NOTES, VOL. 44, 420).

American Notes & Queries. New Haven, Conn.: Lee Ash, 1962–.

Generally comprises several well-defined sections: three or four short items on literature; queries, replies to questions regarding research and bibliography; editor's comments and readings; reviews of recent foreign reference books; shorter book notes. Especially useful to students of research and bibliography.

Chaucer Review: A Journal of Medieval Studies and Literary Criticism. University Park, Pa.: Modern Language Association, 1966–.

The articles, generally of substantial length, are on all phases of Chaucer studies and other literature of the medieval period. Carries the annual report of the Committee on Chaucer Research and Bibliography CHAUCER RESEARCH, which lists current research and completed projects, published books and articles that appeared or were announced during the year.

Contemporary Literature. Madison, Wisconsin: University of Wisconsin Press, 1960–.

Known, until 1968, as WISCONSIN STUDIES IN CONTEMPORARY LITERATURE. Publishes articles on poetry, fiction, drama, and, in recent years, mainly criticism (English and American fiction). Issue generally contains six to eight articles, of short to moderate length, frequently revolving around a single subject or theme. Reviews a number of books, almost always in clusters; issues two basic bibliographies annually: "Criticism: A Review," and "Poetry." An important journal for the student interested in modern literature.

Criticism: A Quarterly for Literature and the Arts. Detroit, Michigan: Wayne State University Press, 1959–.

Its stated purpose is to examine "the arts and literatures of all periods and nations, either individually or in their interrelationships, and critical theory regarding them." Generally concentrates on English and American authors. A typical issue contains five or six reviews, rarely less than one thousand words, often two or three times that.

Critique: Studies in Modern Fiction. Atlanta, Georgia: Georgia Institute of Technology, 1956–.

Comprises fairly brief essays devoted mainly to American writers, with frequent issues limited to one or two contemporary authors and containing a comprehensive checklist or bibliography on the author or authors covered. Each issue averages six or seven articles (5000–6000 words) and reviews which, though few in number, are frequently quite long. Tone is scholarly, but not overly academic.

English Language Notes. Boulder, Colorado: University of Colorado Press, 1963–.

A scholarly, specialized journal (its notes being rarely more than five or six pages, often just one or two pages) which treats all periods and genres of English, and occasionally American, literature. Articles cover incidents in authors' lives, literary sources and parallels, word usage, and corrupt texts. Beginning with 1964, it has carried as a supplement to the September issue the Romantic Movement bibliography (previously carried in *Philological Quarterly* and *ELH*).

English Literary History: A Journal of English Literary History. Baltimore: The Tudor and Stuart Club, The Johns Hopkins University, 1934–.

Not detailed in its treatment of literary backgrounds, but provides a well-balanced, unbiased, and scholarly handling of literary personnages. Publishes no reviews. From 1934 to 1950, it provided in its March issue a critical bibliography of the Romantic movement. In 1950, "The Romantic Movement: A Selective and Critical Bibliography," began to appear in the April issue of PHILOLOGICAL QUARTERLY.

"This attractively printed periodical is unique in several respects: it is edited by young men, it is sponsored by a university literary club, it contains no reviews, it appears three times a year, it costs only $1.50. The length of time that a learned article dealing with English literature must wait before publication makes clear the need of another magazine in this field. The first two issues of ELH promise a journal of high standards which should be supported by all those interested in the scholarly study of English literature"—(MODERN LANGUAGE NOTES, VOL. 49, 551).

English Literary Renaissance. Amherst, Mass.: University of Massachusetts, 1971.

Emphasizes publication of literary texts, studies, and bibliographies of Tudor and early Stuart England. A fairly typical issue contained, in addition to standard material, the texts of two previously unpublished letters of Sir Philip Sidney and an annotated bibliography of Sidney scholarship covering twenty-seven years.

English Literature in Transition, 1880–1920. Tempe, Arizona: Arizona State University Press, 1957–.

Scholarly articles, mostly brief, and containing, in almost every issue, annotated bibliographies of writers of the period, as well as a few signed and critical reviews (sometimes fairly long, usually 500–1000 words). A regular feature is "Critical Forum," devoted to discussion (in a short "Letters-to-the-Editor" format).

English Studies. A Publication of the English Association. London: John Murray, 1948–.

A journal of English letters and philology (not to be confused with ENGLISCHE STUDIEN, which has been published at Leipzig since 1877 and is sometimes abbreviated EST or ENG STUD). Publishes no reviews. ENGLISH STUDIES replaces ESSAYS AND STUDIES, which was published annually from 1910 to 1948.

"Two articles which have little or nothing to do with English studies fill rather more than a quarter of this volume. In 'The Character and Private Life of Edmund Burke' Sir Philip Magnus writes interestingly and at length of the politician and his finances, mentioning the author and his works only briefly and by the way. The other five contributions are genuine English studies, although of varying merit. But taken as a whole the volume does not illustrate any clear conception of the characteristic preoccupations and necessary limits of English studies. It is regrettable that its apparently aimless eclecticism should have the official approval of the English Association"—(NEW SERIES, 2, 1951, 294–296).

Essays in Criticism. Oxford: Blackwell Press, 1951—.

The basic sections of this quarterly—it appears in January, April, July, and October—are: "Feature Articles," "Book Reviews," and "The Critical Forum." A representative issue (April, 1960) ranged from Shakespeare and Coleridge to James Joyce. "The Critical Forum" is a kind of free court in which scholars and would-be scholars exchange volleys of opinion.

"ESSAYS IN CRITICISM resembles SCRUTINY more than any other English periodical, but it is a less unified magazine, with a less distinctive tone of voice. . . . The flavor of the magazine as a whole is that of a 'new' academicism rather too spryly conscious of not being the 'old' academicism"—(TIMES LITERARY SUPPLEMENT, 1953, 353).

"If the admirably high standard and variety of critical writing manifest in this first number should be maintained, the new journal will deserve a much longer life than the probationary three years. An editorial board representative of English studies both at Oxford and other universities seems to give assurance that it will be maintained"—(THE TIMES LITERARY SUPPLEMENT, Feb. 16, 1951, 105).

Folklore, 1890—. London: William Glaisher, Ltd., 1890—.

FOLKLORE is the result of the merging in 1890 of the ARCHAEOLOGICAL REVIEW and the FOLKLORE JOURNAL. It publishes reviews and notes of interesting events in the field of folklore, as well as news of meetings. It is indexed in the MAGAZINE SUBJECT INDEX. Its articles lack the scholarly tone of its American counterpart.

"It appears to us, so far as the present issue may be considered a fair sample, that the Folklore Society has got the best of the bargain, and there is not much room left for archaeology proper. We are no doubt promised the revival of some of the special features of the ARCHAEOLOGICAL REVIEW, and we hope that the promise will be kept"—(NOTES AND QUERIES, VOL. 9, April 19, 1890, 320).

Huntington Library Bulletin. Cambridge, Massachusetts, 1931–1937. 11 vols.

The Huntington Library was required by trust indentures to render its possessions accessible to scholars and students engaged in research or creative work, and to this end the HUNTINGTON BULLETIN was published. Specifically, the BULLETIN aimed: to particularize the resources of the Library; to give bibliographies and other information about its collections, especially texts of rare unpublished manuscripts; list the research articles which resulted from the studies made from bibliographic material; include short notes of interest to the library and its staff. The BULLETIN was at first intended to be an occasional number, rather than a periodical publication.

"In communion with bibliographers and students of English and American culture everywhere, we are glad to welcome the HUNTINGTON LIBRARY BULLETIN. . . . If we may judge from the contents of the first number, the execution of this program will be followed with the keenest interest by scholars"— (MODERN PHILOLOGY, Vol. 29, 375).

"The publication of the HUNTINGTON LIBRARY BULLETIN is therefore a notable event in American librarianship. More than 100 pages, approximately one-half of the first number, are given over to matter which should form a part of the working data of every advanced reference worker"—(LIBRARY QUARTERLY, 1932, 87).

The HUNTINGTON LIBRARY BULLETIN was succeeded by the HUNTINGTON LIBRARY QUARTERLY, published at San Marino, California, 1937—.

Journal of American Folklore, 1888—. Philadelphia: The University of Pennsylvania, 1888—.

The JOURNAL OF AMERICAN FOLKLORE was founded mainly to collect and preserve the fast—vanishing memoirs of American folklore (of the English, the Negroes in the South, and the Indian tribes in the north as well as that of Mexico and French Canada), and to publish the special studies of them.

"The Society is to be congratulated upon the substantial and diversfied contents and attractive appearance of the two numbers which have already appeared. It is understood that the American Society's membership has already outstripped that of its much older English sister" — (MODERN LANGUAGE NOTES, VOL. 3, 1888, 471).

Journal of English and Germanic Philology. Urbana, Illinois: The University of Illinois Press, 1897—.

As the JOURNAL OF GERMANIC PHILOLOGY, Volumes I to IV were published at Bloomington, Indiana, and Volume V at Evanston, Illinois, between the years 1903 to 1905. Since 1906 it has been published by the University of Illinois, at Urbana, Illinois, as the JOURNAL OF ENGLISH AND GERMANIC PHILOLOGY. Contains articles on English, German, and Scandinavian languages and literatures, books reviewed and received (April issue), and comments of the reviewers.

Although it is issued as a quarterly, there are occasional supplements containing more extensive contributions which the journal deems worthy of publication. The contributions are received from international scholars, and the subject matter often varies and extends to all of the languages and the fields of the humanities.

"This new periodical begins its career on a well-founded plan . . . none but trained and competent experts will be solicited as contributors, but the journal will be made beneficial for the progressive teacher of any level and for all students of Germanics. . . . The JOURNAL will have a purely pedagogical purpose, and will establish a relation between pure and applied philology. . . . It will also give American investigators a hearing before the whole Germanic world" — (THE CRITIC, VOL. 30, January–June, 1897).

Journal of Modern Literature. Philadelphia, Pa.: Temple University Press, 1970–.

Features solid articles on major literary figures and important currents and extensive book reviews. The annual review number surveys in more than 300 pages critical scholarship on modern literature published from 1970 to the present. When expedient, incorporates special coverage of important professional events in twentieth-century literature.

Modern Fiction Studies: A Critical Quarterly Devoted to Criticism, Scholarship and Bibliography of American, English, and European Fiction since about 1880. Lafayette, Indiana: Purdue University Press, 1955–.

Two of the issues are devoted to works of fiction, writers, or problems in fictional technique. The Summer and Winter issues comprise a series of articles on individual writers and include a checklist of criticism relating to the writer and his works. These numbers carried (through 1968) the "'Modern Fiction Newsletter'" which commented informally on recent critical works and listed recently published books and articles about the writers of recognized stature. In 1969 this was changed to the review section "Recent Books on Modern Fiction," which covers about fifty titles, mostly on British and American fiction. The reviews average five hundred words in length.

Modern Language Notes. Baltimore: The Johns Hopkins University Press, 1886–.

Cumulative indexes to volumes 1–50, 51–60, beginning in 1962, limited to Romance and German languages and literatures.

Modern Language Quarterly. Seattle, Washington: University of Washington Press, 1940–.

A scholarly journal devoted to the perpetuation of philology and the modern languages through the encouragement of research in all the areas of the humanities. As an illustration of its scope, one might note that a typical issue contains a cultural interpretation of Beowulf, an offering of the Folger Shakespeare Library, and a study of Herman Melville's stories. Publishes book reviews and indexes books received. Articles are not signed. An Arthurian Bibliography beginning with the years 1936–1939 was inaugurated with the first edition and continues to the present.

"A new journal to which STUDIES IN PHILOLOGY extends a welcome is MODERN LANGUAGE QUARTERLY, published by the University of Washington Press and edited by Ray Heffner. The unusual range and policy of this journal is doubtless suggested by the contents of its first issue. . . . Its one hundred twenty-six pages contain ten articles and four reviews"— (STUDIES IN PHILOLOGY, VOLUME 37, 563–564).

Modern Language Review. Cambridge, England: 1905—. Supersedes MODERN LANGUAGE QUARTERLY, London, 1897–1904. 7 vols.

Devoted to the study of medieval and of modern literature and philology. Volumes I to X are indexed in Volume X; Volumes XI to XX are indexed in Volume XX; and Volumes XXI to XXX are indexed in Volume XXX. "It is part of the justification of the REVIEW that it has sought to be an organ of international scholarship and thought. . . (and the growth of it) in its fifty years service has accompanied and closely reflected the growth of organized modern language study in British universities." Publishes reviews.

Modern Philology: A Journal Devoted to Research in Modern Languages and Literatures. Chicago: The University of Chicago Press, 1903—.

A quarterly journal interested in all significant developments in the fields of literary study. It ordinarily does not treat of linguistics, but articles of general interest in this field are sometimes accepted. From 1933 to 1957 it published an annual Victorian bibliography, listing American and foreign publication in the period, and frequently citing and quoting from reviews of more significant works. In 1957 the bibliography was taken over by VICTORIAN STUDIES and its coverage expanded.

Since each volume begins in one year and carries over into the next, it is necessary to give a double-year date. In citing a particular article, however, it is quite proper to give only the year in which the particular article appeared.

Notes and Queries. London, 1849—.

A weekly publication devoted to the presentation of notes—little articles submitted by readers and scholars—and queries—questions sent in by readers.

From November, 1849 to December, 1923, there were twelve series, comprising twelve half-year volumes each, with an index for every series. Beginning in January, 1924, the series number was dropped. An index to Volumes CXLV to CLVI (July, 1923 to June, 1929) was followed by one to Volumes CLXII to CLXVIII. Publishes reviews.

Novel: A Forum on Fiction. Providence, Rhode Island: Brown University, 1967–.

Devoted to the novel of all periods and countries. Issues usually contain five to seven articles, a few review essays, and six to ten excellent reviews (1000 to 2000 words) on all aspects of fiction. The reviews are divided into two sections: those built around a single theme; and those concerned with, or related to, perceptive notes on recent fiction.

Philological Quarterly: A Journal Devoted to Scholarly Investigation in the Classical and Modern Languages and Literatures. Iowa City: State University of Iowa Press, 1922–.

Embraces Greek and Latin as well as the modern European languages, but it does not publish articles which are primarily concerned with non-European languages or their literatures. In general, it leans toward articles on specific problems or interpretations in language or literature.

The July issue features a bibliography of current English literature for the period 1660–1800, and since 1950 the April issue contains a bibliography of the Romantic Movement, a feature taken over from the March issue of ENGLISH LITERARY HISTORY. In recent issues, book reviews appear to have been eliminated.

"Under the competent editorial management of Professor Hardin Craig, its scholarly character is abundantly assured; and the cooperation of the chosen associate editors . . . strongly ratify that assurance. The uniting of classical and modern language studies has a fresh significance at this time. This will enable the new periodical to assume the attractive and no less important function of expounding and contributing to the illumination of one of the principal chapters in present-day educational and cultural problems"—(MODERN LANGUAGE NOTES, VOLUME 37, 254).

Publications of the Modern Language Association of America. Baltimore, 1884–.

The first issue in 1884 comprised fifty pages. Current issues frequently exceed three hundred pages. The first three volumes contained articles on pedagogy, but the emphasis since then has been in the areas of modern languages and literature.

Since 1921, the March issue has carried a bibliography; this is now carried in the Supplement. Until 1956 the bibliography was limited to American writers of books and articles in the field of modern languages; in 1957 the bibliography was broadened to include English, Dutch, French, German, Spanish, Italian, Portuguese, and Scandinavian. It does not publish reviews.

"Volume I, TRANSACTIONS OF THE MODERN LANGUAGE ASSOCIATION OF AMERICA, covered the years 1884–1885. Volumes II–III, called TRANSACTIONS AND PROCEEDINGS, covered the years 1886–1887. Volume IV, called PUBLICATIONS OF THE MODERN LANGUAGE ASSOCIATION OF AMERICA, was divided into four numbers for 1888–1889. Thereafter the serial was a regular quarterly under the title PUBLICATIONS OF THE MODERN LANGUAGE ASSOCIATION OF AMERICA, with a cover title PMLA in recent years. There has been a distinguished editorship: A. Marshall Elliott, founder of MLA and its first secretary, James W. Bright, Charles H. Grandgent, William Guild Howard, Charton Brown, and Percy Waldron Long"—(MOTT, A HISTORY OF AMERICAN MAGAZINES, 1865–1885, Volume 3, 236).

Renaissance Quarterly. New York, N.Y.: Renaissance Society of America, 1954–.

First issued as a section of the JOURNAL OF RENAISSANCE AND BAROQUE MUSIC, then as a separate publication RENAISSANCE NEWS. It assumed its present title in 1967. Scholarly articles range from art and music to literature and history. Each issue contains a few short articles (three or four), but extensive (twenty-five or more) book reviews, signed and critical, averaging about one thousand words; also, a bibliography of publications in the field, arranged by subject.

Review of English Studies: A Quarterly Journal of English Literature and Language. Oxford: Clarendon Press, 1925–.

A typical issue contains: notes and short notices, book reviews, a summary of periodical literature, and a list of publications received.

Southern Review. Baton Rouge, Louisiana: Louisiana State University Press, 1965–.

The only connection between this and the original SOUTHERN
REVIEW which, edited by Cleanth Brooks and Robert Penn Warren, ran from 1935 to 1942, is the title and the place of publication. Features outstanding articles on literary criticism, superior
short stories and poetry, and fine, essay-length book reviews,
covering fifty books or more.

Speculum: A Quarterly Journal of Mediaeval Studies. Cambridge, Massachusetts: The Mediaeval Academy of America,
1926—.

Each issue contains a bibliography of the periodical literature
in the mediaeval period that appeared during the preceding
quarter; and it often publishes articles intended to illuminate
neglected areas and to open up new fields of research. It is
indexed by the ART INDEX and the INTERNATIONAL INDEX;
publishes reviews.

In addition to articles such as "The Ancient Classics in the
Medieval Libraries," a typical number might contain: book
reviews; a bibliography of periodical literature organized by
subjects, such as fine arts, Dante, language, folklore, philosophy,
religion, books received, sometimes with a few words of description; publications of the Medieval Academy.

"Its intention is to stimulate further researches and more
extensive publication in the medieval field, to serve as a co-
ordinating bureau for all activities in America concerning life
and thought of the Middle Ages, and to foster international
cooperation in the same field. . . . This initial number of
SPECULUM is of high quality and admirable appearance"—
(AMERICAN HISTORICAL REVIEW, VOLUME 31, NUMBER 3, 609).

"The officers of the Academy and the editors of the journal
are men who have won distinction in the classics, in history, in
architecture, and in modern languages. This is a heartening
fact, since one great need of modern scholarship is collaboration
among workers whose fields have much in common, but who
are kept apart by the artificial 'departments' of college catalogues. There is also reason for congratulation in the fact that
both medieval specialists and scholars whose primary interests
lie outside the Middle Ages may find, in SPECULUM, monographs, notes, and reviews which deal with a single great period
of human culture"—(MODERN LANGUAGE NOTES, VOLUME 41,
271).

Studies in English Literature 1500–1900. Houston, Texas: Rice University 1961–.

A scholarly journal which devotes each issue to a particular period and genre of English Literature: "Nondramatic Prose and Poetry of the English Renaissance" (Winter); "Elizabethan and Jacobean Drama" (Spring); "Restoration and Eighteenth Century" (Summer); "Nineteenth Century" (Autumn). Each issue carries ten to twelve articles, of moderate length, ranging over all aspects of the literature of the period covered; and, while there are no book reviews as such, the last number of each issue represents a review of the scholarship of the year in the area of the issue's concentration.

Studies in Philology. Chapel Hill, North Carolina: University of North Carolina Press, 1906–.

A journal of special interest to students of the Renaissance period. From 1023 to 1969 it carried (as the May number in recent years) the extensive bibliography LITERATURE OF THE RENAISSANCE, which covers articles and monographs, citing reviews of the books listed. Does not publish book reviews.

"STUDIES IN PHILOLOGY attracted the attention of scholars all over the country from its beginning . . . gained new importance and became recognized as one of the leading scholarly journals, internationally as well as nationally"—(STUDIES IN PHILOLOGY, VOLUME 42, 1945).

The annual bibliography "Literature of the Renaissance" (also called in some issues "Recent Literature of the Renaissance"), appeared for the last time in 1969 "because of the relatively heavy expense involved in publishing . . . and because other bibliographies now duplicate most of the information that has been given in "Recent Literature of the Renaissance."—STUDIES IN PHILOLOGY, May, 1969, prelim. note.

Studies in Romanticism. Boston, Mass.: W.H. Stevenson, 1961.

Published by the Graduate School of Boston University, it was designed to present articles on literature, society, and art of the romantic period in all countries. In practice, the dominant emphasis is on the standard figures in English literature. A typical issue has three to five articles (averaging about 5000 words each). Since 1971 the journal has carried book reviews (two or three an issue), usually several thousand words in length.

Studies in Short Fiction. Newberry, South Carolina: Newberry College, 1963–.

Exclusively concerned with "serious commentary on short fiction;" a typical issue contains: six to ten articles (5000 words or less); some shorter notes (*explication de text*, textual criticism, unpublished letters, etc.); eight to twelve reviews (500 to 1000 words in length) of books.

Times Literary Supplement. London, 1902–.

A weekly publication, with an annual index. The "Correspondence" columns contain many items of interest to scholars. It publishes reviews.

Twentieth Century Literature: A Scholarly and Critical Journal. Los Angeles, California: IHC Press, 1955.

Contains "articles on all aspects of modern and contemporary literature, including articles in English on writers in other languages." Each issue comprises three or four articles, rarely more than 5000 words in length, and, in recent years, frequent bibliographies of individual writers. Its "Current Bibliography" is an abstract of periodical articles on twentieth century literature which have appeared in American, British, and European journals, a valuable complement to the annual MLA BIBLIOGRAPHY.

Victorian Studies

The annotated annual bibliography of studies on this period appears in the June issue. The annotations, fairly brief, are appended to about a third of the entries; book reviews are recorded. The bibliography for the Victorian period first began to appear in VS in 1958; from 1933 through 1957 it was printed in Modern Philology (MP).

BIBLIOGRAPHY

Guides and Manuals of Theory and History

Bibliographical Services Throughout The World. Paris: UNESCO, 1955—. Vol. I. Annual.

Embraces two separate reports on the development and bibliographical services throughout the world. Principal arrangement is by continent; subordinate arrangement is by country. Describes "the national bibliography, official publication lists, union catalogs, bibliographical publications, bibliographical committees and institutes.

BINNS, Norman E.
An Introduction to Historical Bibliography. London: Association of Assistant Librarians, 1953. 370 p.

A history of bookmaking, including chapters on publishing and bookselling, copyright, and development of book trade bibliography. Bibliographies are appended to each chapter; contains an index.

BOWERS, Fredson.
Principles of Bibliographical Description. Princeton: Princeton University Press, 1949. 505 p.

Aims to expound a system of bibliography based upon what is considered to be the most acceptable current practice. Not a survey of methods and procedures, but a comprehensive treatment of analytical bibliography as applied to the description of books. Includes the principles of describing incunabula, as well as those which relate to the description of English and American books of the sixteenth through the twentieth centuries. Complements McKerrow's INTRODUCTION TO BIBLIOGRAPHY. The Appendices contain samples of bibliographical description, a digest of formulary, and the applications of the formulary notation to incunabula.

"Professor Bowers has written a formidable work . . . one that deserves careful study by those producing detailed bibliographies. . . . Notwithstanding some faults, the book will be of great value to bibliographers if it is borne in mind that their first aim is to describe editions, issues, etc., as well as they can, rather than to elaborate a system of symbols not easily understood"—(LONDON TIMES LITERARY SUPPLEMENT, Sept. 29, 1950).

"It is regretable that the index is not more comprehensive . . . a completed list of abbreviations and symbols . . . would have been desirable"—(LIBRARY JOURNAL, VOLUME 75, 1040).

BUHLER, CURT F.
Standards of Bibliographical Description. Philadelphia: University of Pennsylvania Press, 1949. 120 p.

A series of lectures presented under the Rosenthal Fellowship by three distinguished bibliographers, each of whom sets forth a distinct approach to a common problem: Curt Buhler, "Incunabula"; James McManaway, "Early English Literature"; Lawrence C. Wroth, "Early American Literature." The lectures constitute the 1946–1947 presentations under the A.S.W. Rosenbach Fellowship in Bibliography.

"Careful proofreading adds to the attractiveness of this well designed volume. And since it is a volume of theory not primarily of reference, the lack of an index is perhaps endurable. . . . The first and longest lecture, by Dr. Buhler, is possibly the most stimulating and satisfying"—(LIBRARY QUARTERLY, VOLUME 21, 1951, 65–66).

"Some of the most distinguished bibliographical essays published in North America in recent years were originally delivered as Rosenbach Lectures in Bibliography at the University of Pennsylvania. The three studies in the current volume . . . are no exception to this statement. . . . The wealth of ideas in STANDARDS OF BIBLIOGRAPHICAL DESCRIPTION will form the basis for important studies in the immediate future"—(INTERNATIONAL LIBRARY REVIEW, 1952–1953, 176–177).

Chicago University Press: A Manual of Style for Authors, Editors, and Copywriters. 12th ed. Chicago: Chicago University Press, 1969. 546 p.

Contents have been rearranged, and much of the text is new or completely rewritten, taking cognizance of changing practices and procedures in editing and bookmaking. Principles are enunciated as fully as possible and aptly illustrated.

ESDAILE, ARUNDELL.

A Student's Manual of Bibliography. (4th ed.) rev. by Roy Stokes. London: Allen and Unwin and The Library Association, 1967.

A revision of the basic manual published in 1954 covering the history of manuscripts and of printing (type faces, illustration, binding, collation). Two chapters deal with bibliographies and their arrangement.

In addition to the updating of reading lists, there has been considerable rearrangement of the content of the work.

"Esdaile, wisely avoiding detail, discusses the various aspects of bookmaking, collation, and description in a skilfully clear exposition. . . . In the discussion on the history of printing there is no additional material on fine printing since 1930. A list of type designers is added, but there is no mention of the recent and excellent typography at the Curwen Shakespeare Head, or the university presses. Some errors remain, others appear for the first time" — (LIBRARY JOURNAL, January, 1955, 58).

"Real errors in fact or in type are few and insignificant, and the occasional errors of dogmatism which we have noted are inevitable in such a condensed and elementary book and are more than offset by the general accuracy of statement, sanity of opinion, and clearness of exposition" — (THE LIBRARY QUARTERLY, April, 1932, 157–159).

MCKERROW, RONALD B.
An Introduction to Bibliography for Literary Students. Oxford: The Clarendon Press, 1927. 359 p.

An excellent and thorough exposition of the mechanical production of books — formats, paper, printing presses, and bibliographical techniques — from the beginning to 1800, with special emphasis upon the fifteenth and sixteenth centuries.

"The first part considers book production from the point of view of the producers, the compositor, and the pressman. The second part discusses the completed book in relation to the processes previously discussed; the final part compares the

book . . . with the author's manuscript. . . . In its present
enlarged state, the book will find readers among students of
printing and bibliography, and will be valuable to amateur librarians and collectors" — (BOOKLIST, 24:167).

"It is not too much to say that the publication of this substantial volume is a real landmark in the development of bibliography of the critical kind" — (LONDON TIMES LITERARY
SUPPLEMENT, November 3, 1927, 787).

SANDERS, CHAUNCEY.
An Introduction to Research in English Literary History: With
a Chapter on Research in Folklore by Stith Thompson. New
York: Macmillan, 1952. 423 p.

A manual and textbook designed as an introduction to bibliography and method for graduate students. The four major divisions are: "The Materials of Research"; "The Tools of Research"; "The Methods of Research"; and "Suggestions on
Thesis-Writing." The subordinate divisions of the third section
are: the problems of — editing, biography, authenticity and attribution, source study, chronology, success and influence, interpretation, technique, ideas, folklore.

"Unfortunately this valuable material is marred by the author's confused objectives and his lack of awareness of current
developments in the field. He gives seven pages to book bind-
ings and only twenty lines to cancels; he does not mention Professor Hinman's revolutionary machine for collating texts; he
gives only a seven page summary to such a central subject as
literary techniques, and nearly twice as many to such ancillary
subjects as biography and the history of ideas. He presents in
Part IV a method of documentation that has been obsolete
since the MLA Style Sheet in April, 1951" — (LIBRARY JOURNAL,
December, 1952, 58).

SCHNEIDER, GEORG.
Theory and History of Bibliography. New York: Columbia University Press, 1934, 306 p.

A translation by R. R. Shaw of a portion of a basic and comprehensive work, HANDBUCH DER BIBLIOGRAPHIE, first published
at Leipzig in 1923, and covering, in addition to the theoretical-

historical treatment (translated by Shaw) general bibliography, national bibliography, bibliographies of incunabula, newspapers, society publications, and, in addition to other data, lists of biographical dictionaries.

"It will no doubt be widely adopted as a textbook for classes in bibliography; but in this the teacher must not forget that it is, after all, only textual translation and that there is an idiom of thought as well as an idiom of language in any German writing that is not easily turned into English. If Schneider's ideas are to be assimilated by American students and his teachings adopted at their true value, the instructor will have to supply a great deal of running comment and interpretation to supplement Mr. Shaw's excellent translation" — (LIB. QUARTERLY, 5:240).

"Mr. Shaw has rendered a twofold service to American bibliographers — he has republished Schneider's treatise on the theory of their science which is no longer easily available, and he has done this in a readable English translation. . . . The scientific aspects of bibliography are quite as important as the practical. But these are matters that are not adequately treated by any of our own writers" — (LIBRARY JOURNAL, v, April, 1935).

"Written by a librarian, primarily for librarians, Schneider's discussions of the bounds, uses, and value of bibliography, as well as his consideration of more detailed matters, such as bibliographical entries and the Brussels classification, are of interest likewise, to bookmakers, scholars, and bibliographers" — (BOOKS ABROAD, VOLUME IX, 340).

SHERA, J. H. AND M. E. EGAN, eds.
Bibliographical Organization. Chicago: University of Chicago Press, 1951. 275 p.

A series of lectures treating of the role of bibliographic organization in contemporary civilization, the history of attempts to organize bibliography internationally, the approaches to bibliographic organization and problems, and a synthesis and summary of all that transpired at the Fifteenth annual conference of the Graduate Library School.

"The fifteenth annual conference of The Graduate Library

School rendered a great service to the world of learning by assembling a group of specialists to discuss the vexing and critical problems of bibliographic organization. The papers presented before this conference now constitute, in this ably edited volume, one of the most distinguished contributions to American Library Literature. . . . The book is so charged with information and stimulative ideas that it merits careful and prolonged examination and discussion"—(THE LIBRARY QUARTERLY, XXI, 229–230).

THOMSON, SARAH KATHARINE.
Interlibrary Loan Procedure Manual. Chicago: Interlibrary Loan Committee, American Library Association, 1970. 116 p.

Aims to interpret the policy stated in the "National Interlibrary Loan Code, 1968: "the presentation of standardized, efficient methods of transacting interlibrary loan; and the explanation of details of procedure to be followed."—Preface.

VAN HOESEN, H. B. AND W. F. KELLER.
Bibliography, Practical, Enumerative, Historical: An Introductory Manual. New York: Scribner, 1928. 519 p.

Designed, as the "Preface" indicates, as a textbook for upperclassmen and graduate students. Aims "to indicate the scope, functions, and methods of bibliographical work of all kinds and topics," and to "describe or enumerate the fundamental works through which the student may most advantageously approach the selection of books." The basic substance of the work is adapted from a series of lectures delivered at Princeton University in 1923.

"In most cases the compilers write with first hand knowledge of the books they record, and they have supplemented their own judgment by recourse to the specialist"—(LONDON TIMES LITERARY SUPPLEMENT, September 27, 1928, 688).

"The person whose needs the authors have tried especially to keep in mind and provide for is the student, say, in the field of political science, who has begun to specialize and needs to know how to proceed in order to make a survey of the literature of his field"—(POLITICAL SCIENCE QUARTERLY, March, 1929, 124–126).

Guides and Manuals of Reference Works and Bibliographies

ALTICK, RICHARD DANIEL AND ANDREW WRIGHT.
Selective Bibliography for the Study of English and American Literature. 2d ed. New York: Macmillan, 1963. 149 p.

A highly selective guide to research materials; classified arrangement, with author, title, and subject index.

BOND, DONALD FREDERICK.
A Reference Guide to English Studies. Chicago: University of Chicago Press, 1962. 171 p.

A successor to Tom Peete Cross's BIBLIOGRAPHICAL GUIDE TO ENGLISH STUDIES; follows the same plan, with slight variations, but almost doubles the number of entries. Includes many rarely used items and foreign language works.

COLLISON, ROBERT L.
Bibliographies, Subject and National: A Guide to Their Contents, Arrangement, and Use. 3rd ed. rev. & enl. London Crosby Lockwood, 1968. 203 p.

Serves as an informal bibliography of bibliographies. Part one covers subject bibliographies; part two covers national and universal bibliographies.

"A ready reference handbook, an excellent beginning text in the field. It seems essential for all reference and cataloguing collections. The compiler suggests that bibliographies make excellent reading. This one certainly does"—(LIBRARY JOURNAL, October, 1951).

"In spite of its readability and other attractive features, it is somewhat too narrowly British in point of view to serve as anything but a supplementary text in this country"—(LIBRARY QUARTERLY, April, 1952).

CROSS, TOM PEETE.
Bibliographical Guide to English Studies. Chicago: University

of Chicago Press, 1947. 10th ed., with an index, 1951. 81 p.

Compiled as a guide to graduate students in the Department of
English of the University of Chicago. Generally restricted to
books and articles which are exclusively bibliographical or contain bibliographical features.

"A list of books and articles, chiefly bibliographical, designed
to serve as an introduction to the bibliography and methods of
English literary history. Librarians may find valuable suggestions as to available reference materials. Publishers are not
indicated"— (BOOKLIST, XVI).

Works "such as Heyl's CURRENT NATIONAL BIBLIOGRAPHY,
Baker's DRAMATIC BIBLIOGRAPHY, and Jaggard's famed (however faulty) bibliography of Shakespeare" are omitted, whereas
items of lesser import, "many in periodicals" are included—
(LIBRARY QUARTERLY, IX).

DOWNS, ROBERT B.
American Library Resources: A Bibliographical Guide. Chicago:
American Library Association, 1951. 428 p.

A compilation of bibliographical holdings in American libraries.

Approximately 6,000 titles: bibliographies, union lists, surveys,
check lists, catalogs of particular libraries, special collections,
whether published as separate pamphlets or books or in periodicals. In some instances, unpublished bibliographies are listed.
Entries are listed according to the Dewey Decimal classification.

A 226 page Supplement, covering the years 1950–1961, was
published by the American Library Association in 1962.

DOWNS, ROBERT B.
American Library Resources: A Bibliographical Guide. Supplement 1961–70. Chicago: American Library Association, 1972.
244 p.

Uses same pattern and scope as the original volume; lists some
3400 bibliographical aids to finding materials in a large number
of libraries. Includes citations to printed library catalogs, union
lists, descriptions of special collections, and calendars of archival
collections.

ESDAILE, ARUNDELL.

The Sources of English Literature. Cambridge: Cambridge University Press, 1928. 131 p.

Contains the lectures given by the author as the Sandars Reader in Bibliography for 1926. Includes sections on: "Lists of the Works of Members of Religious Bodies"; "Bibliographies of Literary Forms"; "Lists of Bibliographies of English Literature"; "Catalogues of Private Libraries to 1887"; "Some Private Libraries"; "Booksellers and Collectors Guides."

"The ground is well covered and only specialists may perhaps complain of omissions. This is a book to be referred to rather than read. Fortunately it has an adequate index"—(NEW STATESMEN, May 26, 1928).

"Any student who reads this book carefully, and having made from it a list of all the works mentioned which concern his subject, then goes to some library which contains them and spends a few days in carefully examining them—so that he may know what they contain and in what form the information is presented—will in his knowledge of how to set about whatever piece of work he has in mind be months or even years ahead of one who has no such guide"—(ENGLISH STUDIES, May, 1928, 374–375).

GOHDES, CLARENCE.

Bibliographical Guide to the Study of the Literature of the U.S. Durham, North Carolina: Duke University Press, 1970. 133 p.

A list of books designed to assist students and teachers and librarians. Does for those who are interested in the literature of the United States what guides such as those by Spargo and Cross do for students of English literature. Special stress is given to the relationship of national literature to the literature of foreign countries.

MURPHEY, ROBERT W.

How and Where to Look It Up: A Guide to Standard Sources of

Information. New York: McGraw-Hill Book Company, Inc., 1958. 721 p.

A guide to sources of information planned with the needs of the layman in mind, rather than with those of the professional librarian. Thus Part I outlines basic criteria for making an intelligent selection; explains the ways of traditional library organization; expounds some basic mechanics of research. Part II comprises an annotated list of selected sources of information.

"Only a reference librarian can appreciate fully what Robert Murphey has accomplished in this book. He has organized the more important "half of knowledge"—'Knowing where to find it'—so systematically and yet so alluringly, that libraries everywhere are bound to profit from the increased skill and hunger for knowledge that will be engendered in patrons by these pages"—("FORWARD" BY LOUIS SHORES, v).

KENNEDY, ARTHUR G.
Concise Bibliography for Students of English, 4th ed. Stanford: Stanford University Press, 1960. 467 p.

This edition of a well-known manual provides greater emphasis on modern literature and gives more attention to the scholarly techniques of the New Criticism. Lists more than 5000 titles in a classified arrangement, and includes material on literary forms; serials; folklore; language; methods and style of writing; printing and the book trade; bibliographical and reference guides. Virtually no annotations.

ROBERTS, ARTHUR D.
Introduction to Reference Books. 2d ed. London: Library Association, 1951. 214 p.

A revision of the work published in 1948, differing from it, in addition to some textual changes, in virtue of a new chapter on biographical works of reference and three short appendixes.

VITALE, PHILIP H.
An Outline Guide for English Majors. Chicago: Auxiliary University Press, 1959. 246 p.

Originally designed as a guide for graduate students in the

Department of English of DePaul University. Basic contents include: list of primary readings in English and American literatures; an annotated list of selected learned journals; an annotated list of secondary readings in English and American literatures; and one hundred representative questions covering ten areas of graduate study. The "Appendix" comprises a systematic arrangement of some three hundred basic reference works.

Guides to the Use of Libraries

ALDRICH, Ella V.
Using Books and Libraries. Englewood Cliffs, New Jersey: Prentice-Hall, Inc., 1951. 101 p.

In addition to the chapters on basic reference books, the manual contains chapters on "College and University Libraries" (the regulations and routines of the typical college or university library; "The Book" (the important parts of and the ways of intelligently using books); "Classification and Arrangement of Books" (a brief explanation of the Dewey Decimal Classification and the Library of Congress Classification systems).

HUTCHINS, Margaret, A. S. Johnson, M. S. Williams.
Guide to the Use of Libraries. 3rd ed. New York: H. W. Wilson Company, 1920. 251 p.

Originally a manual for students in the University of Illinois; based upon outlines and lectures used in the presentation of actual classes in reference work. Contains nothing particularly new, but the well-known facts and principles are logically integrated and clearly explained.

"The book has a distinct purpose and a definite scope. It carries out its purpose as a class manual consistently and confines itself clearly to its scope"—(LIBRARY QUARTERLY, XLVII, November 1, 1922).

Guides to the Famous Libraries and Their Collections

American Literary Manuscripts. Modern Language Association of America. American Literature Group. Committee on Manu-

script Holdings. Austin: University of Texas Press, 1961. 421 p.
Brief information about the types and quantities of literary manuscripts held in more than 270 academic, historical, and public
libraries in the United States. Entries for about 2,350 authors are
arranged alphabetically. Not intended to be definitive or exhaustive.

BURTON, Margaret.
Famous Libraries of the World. London: Crafton and Company, 1937. 458 p.

A companion volume to Esdaile's THE NATIONAL LIBRARIES OF
THE WORLD. Among the libraries included are those of: the
British Empire, France, Germany, Greece, Italy and the Vati-
can City, Poland, Spain, Portugal, Sweden, U.S.S.R., and the
United States (specifically, Army Medical Library, Boston
Public Library, Harvard University Library, Huntington Library,
New York Public Library, and the Yale University Library).

For each library considered, the author conveys information
relative to: foundation collection, special treasures, current acquisitions, librarians, buildings, catalogues, conditions of admission, facilities for photography, staff, finances, and library
hours.

"The principle has apparently been to select libraries from
as many different countries as possible. There is much to be
said for this, but the result naturally is that many libraries are
excluded to make room for others far less famous. . . . We
have no account of the National Central Library, or of any
Scottish or Welsh university, or of any modern English university, or of any Oxford or Cambridge college. Only one
French, two German, and two American universities are described. No British public library is included nor any special
libraries. The accounts are on the whole accurate, although
there are some strange slips"—(THE LONDON TIMES LITERARY
SUPPLEMENT, Aug., 1937).

"Altogether this book will prove of great value not only to
libraries and members of governing bodies, but also to scholars
in general"—(LIBRARY JOURNAL, November 15, 1937).

CRASTER, Sir Edmund.
History of the Bodleian Library. Oxford: The Clarendon Press,
1952. 372 p.

Originally begun as a revision of W. C. Macrays ANNALS OF THE
BODLEIAN LIBRARY, a work which first appeared in 1868. Craster
however does not confine himself entirely to a chronological
treatment. He divides the history of the famous library into
three periods—1845–1881, 1881–1912, 1912–1945—and re-
counts the development of the library during each period in
terms of: administration, finance, catalogues, accessions, treasures, and physical expansion.

"Though Sir Edmund reminds the reader that he has not
written an official history, his book is likely to serve as a principal source of information about the Bodleian for a long time
to come. Its facts are arranged according to a perspicuous plan;
the difficult task of maintaining the pace of a narrative which
must include hundreds of titles and consolidate a thousand details is fairly faced; and the problems of half-a-dozen librarians
are presented with sympathy and understanding"—(LIBRARY
QUARTERLY, October, 1953).

Directory of Libraries of the Chicago Area. Chicago: Chicago
Library Club, 1945.

The publication is jointly sponsored by the Chicago Library
Club and the Illinois Chapter of the Special Libraries Association. Over eight hundred private and public libraries are
covered. The following is a sample entry:

MUNDELEIN COLLEGE, 1930
6353 Sheridan Road. Bri 3806
SPECIAL COLLECTIONS: Rothensteiner Collection contains
some 622 rare items, including early complete folio editions
of St. Augustine, St. Ambrose, St. Thomas Aquinas, St.
Chrysostom, and St. Robert Bellarmine; the OLD TESTAMENT
published by the Platins, 1565; and two incunabula. Library
also has a third incunabulum presented by His Eminence
George Cardinal Mundelein.
An invaluable directory to anyone doing scholarly research
in the Chicago area.

ESDAILE, ARUNDEL.
The British Museum Library. London: George Allen and
Unwin, 1946. 388 p.

The first part constitutes a historical survey; the second part
constitutes an explanation of the collections and catalogs. As

the author notes in the "Preface": the work is a "summary
account, historical and descriptive . . . full enough to be useful for reference and information, and . . . to bring out the
true significance of the collections and the tales of their gathering."

"While the book is not, and makes no claim to be, an adequate history of the library, still it is a most readable book,
both useful and entertaining"—(THE LIBRARY, VOLUME 11,
1947–1948, 207).

ESDAILE, ARUNDELL.
National Libraries of the World. 2d ed. London: Library Association, 1957. 413 p.

An account of the history, administration, and public services
of over thirty of the principal national libraries of the world.
Each library is treated in terms of: history—foundation, collections, eminent librarians; manuscripts, buildings; catalogues;
departments; staff; place in the national system; finances. A
rather complete bibliography complements each chapter.

"Its only really weak section is its meagre preface of three
pages in which Mr. Esdaile makes no attempt to deal with the
numerous interesting problems which his book raises"—(LON-
DON TIMES LITERARY SUPPLEMENT, November 1, 1934).

". . . a well-timed, well-planned, well-executed and much
needed book. It gives a vast amount of desired information
about the library, government, organization, finances, buildings,
catalogs, classifications, special services, users, librarians, staff,
bibliography, and uniquely 'the place of the library in the
national system' "—(LIBRARY JOURNAL, VOLUME 59, 968).

KRUZAS, ANTHONY T., ed.
Directory of Special Libraries and Information Centers. Detroit:
Gale, 1963. 767 p.

Lists more than 10,000 libraries of all types and sizes, noting
their special collections. Entries are arranged alphabetically by
name of library and provide the following information: name,
address, telephone number, name of director, services available
to outside inquirers, publications, etc.

PREDEEK, ALBERT.
A History of the Libraries in Great Britain and North America.
Chicago: American Library Association, 1947. 158 p.

A concise and balanced outline of the development of libraries in the British Isles and the United States from 1500 to the beginning of World War II. The work is, in fact, the author's contribution to the third volume of the HANDBUCH DER BIBLIOTHEKSWISSENSCHAFT, a monumental history of libraries.

"Leaning heavily upon secondary sources, especially the work of Edwards for the treatment of British libraries, superficially buttressed with an impressive bibliography which the author has obviously read neither wisely nor too well, and filled with errors of fact and interpretation, these chapters contribute nothing to existing knowledge of library history in either Great Britain or the United States. This is especially unfortunate since the reputation of the HANDBUCH will add to the treatment an authenticity, at least with librarians, that it does not deserve"— (LIBRARY QUARTERLY, July, 1948).

Standard Catalog for Public Libraries: An Annotated List of 12,300 Titles with a Full Analytical Index. New York: Wilson, 1950. 2057 p.

The main part of the work comprises a list of books which the average public library or medium-sized library will be able to afford and find most useful. A secondary part comprises an author, title, subject, and analytical index which, in addition to indexing all the titles in the main part contains analytical entries to parts of some 2,000 books. Comment, sometimes fairly extensive, more often brief, are given for virtually all the titles. Kept up by supplements issued annually and cumulating at intervals.

The fourth edition, published in 1958, is a more highly selective catalog, listing 7,610 volumes as compared with 12,300 titles in the preceding edition.

"A classified list, completely indexed, exceedingly useful"— (THE BOOKLIST, XXXI, January, 1935, 175).

"The analytical index that takes up 650 of the nearly 2,000 pages of the work is a masterpiece of modern indexing"—(BOOK REVIEW DIGEST, 1935).

THOMPSON, James.
The Ancient Library. Chicago: College and Research Libraries, 1941. 120 p.

A lucid and organic, but rather sketchy account of the libraries of the East, of Rome and Greece.

"It is too brief for its theme. Fifty pages attempt to summarize our knowledge of Egyptian, Mesopotamian, Greek, and Roman libraries. Forty-eight pages discuss various technical matters, e.i., format of books, library architecture, cataloging and classification, administration, book production and bookselling throughout the whole ancient period. . . . On the one hand it is over-journalistic; on the other hand, over-erudite. . . . The book is not a satisfactory contribution to the historical literature of librarianship. Treatment of Egyptian and Mesopotamian libraries is inadequate and sometimes inaccurate. . . . In spite of imperfections every historical library should have a copy. . . . Professor Thompson makes comparisons, gives suggestions and opens perspectives which will help later compilers of the same subject"—(THOUGHT, VOLUME 16, June, 1941).

THOMPSON, James W.
The Medieval Library. Chicago: University of Chicago Press, 1939. 661 p.

A comprehensive, scholarly, and very readable account of the libraries in the Middle Ages, the four parts being: (1) The Early Middle Ages (2) The High Middle Ages (3) The Close of the Middle Ages and the Italian Renaissance (4) The Making and Care of the Book in the Middle Ages. Contains no bibliography, but copious footnotes—some 2,228 of them—are scattered throughout the work.

"For lovers of books and students of culture, Professor's work is a chest of buried treasure"—(CHRISTIAN CENTURY, August 30, 1939).

". . . if it were later found practical to publish a supplement containing a general index and bibliography, every reader of the book—and over the years in which this volume will remain useful, they will be many—would be grateful"—(SATURDAY REVIEW OF LITERATURE, December 23, 1939).

"The chapter on Jewish and Moslem Libraries might have been extended considerably by consulting G. Sartois' works more thoroughly. What is said on Egyptian monastic libraries is quite inadequate, misleading, and all but useless"—(CATHOLIC WORLD, March, 1940, 112–114).

THOMSON, SARAH KATHARINE.
Interlibrary Loan Procedure Manual. Chicago, Illinois: American Library Association, 1970. 116 p.

Purposes: to interpret the policy stated in the "National Interlibrary Loan Code, 1968"; to present the standardized, efficient methods of transacting interlibrary loan; and to explain the details of the procedure to be followed.—(Pref).

Bibliographies of Bibliographies

BESTERMAN, THEODORE.
A World Bibliography of Bibliographies and of Bibliographical Catalogues, Calendars, Abstracts, Digests, Indexes, and the Like. 4th ed. Totowa, New Jersey: Rowman & Littlefield, 1964–1965. 5 vols.

A classified list of some 117,000 separately published bibliographies under 16,000 headings, including lists of archive materials, calendars, as well as lists of abridgements of patent specifications issued by the patent offices. The specific aim of the work was to bring up to date Petzholdt's BIBLIOTHECA BIBLIOGRAPHICA.

"Bibliography cannot be an art for its own sake; its merits must be judged solely by the standards of its usefulness for a definite purpose. I am afraid that the actual use of the WORLD BIBLIOGRAPHY will by no means be commensurate with the immense labor involved in its compilation"—(PAPERS OF THE BIBLIOGRAPHICAL SOCIETY OF AMERICA, VOLUME 36, 1942, 321–324).

Bibliographical Index: A Cumulative Bibliography of Bibliographies, 1937—. New York: Wilson, 1938—. Volume 1, 1937–1942 (published in 1945), 1780 p.; Volume II, 1943–1946 (published in 1948), 831 p.

An extensive and useful list of separately published bibliographies and bibliographies included in books and periodicals (as many as 1,500 being examined regularly). The arrangement is alphabetical by subject only.

"The librarian expects a bibliography to perform a service similar to that of the library catalog, only on a broader basis, since it is not limited to the contents of one library and·includes "analytical" entries of articles in periodicals, of parts of books, etc., as very few library catalogs do at all extensively. The BIBLIOGRAPHICAL INDEX cuts the scope in two in that it 'locates' material by subject only and not by author. . . . A bibliography arranged under detailed 'specific subject' entries, supplemented by no classified arrangement, and with no author index, thus functions in only one of the three ways of the library catalog"—(LIBRARY QUARTERLY, April, 1940, 272–274).

Volume five, published in 1961, covers the years 1956–1959; volume six, published in 1963, covers the years 1960–1962; volume seven, published in 1967, covers the years 1963–1965.

CONOVER, HELEN F.
Current National Bibliographies. Washington: U.S. Library of Congress, 1955. 132 p.

Supersedes the listings published in preliminary form in the Library of Congress Quarterly Journal of Current Acquisitions, first accumulated in 1950, and the Supplement covering February 1950 through November 1952. In addition to the regular records of the book trade, the annotated lists include periodical indexes, government publications, and directories of periodicals and newspapers.

COURTNEY, WILLIAM P.
Register of National Bibliography: With a Selection of the Chief Bibliographical Books and Articles Printed in Other Countries. London: Constable, 1905–1912. 3 Volumes. 631 p.

Volumes I and II comprise a list of bibliographies published before 1905; volume three comprises a supplement containing about 10,000 additional references principally to bibliographies published 1905–1912. All of the items are listed alphabetically over the span of the three volumes. Each volume is indexed; the third volume contains an appendix which includes materials not included in Volume I and Volume II. Each page is divided into two columns with the first and last captions of the page listed at the top of the column for ready reference.

"This work possesses the exactness and the completeness which was to be expected of the joint-compiler of the BIBLIOTHECA CORNUBIENSIS and contributor to the D.N.B. It includes references not only to separate bibliographical monographs, but also to such lists as are to be found in periodicals and other works—after the manner of Mr. Whitney's most useful catalog of bibliographies. Moreover, it comprises references not simply to those works which are also to be found only in the largest libraries, but also to those popular lists which are to be found in every library"—(LIBRARY JOURNAL, VOLUME 30, 426–427).

"An admirable volume by a master of the subject. Such careful and thorough work will be properly valued by all experts"—(ATHENAEUM, March 23, 1912, 338).

"Useful it certainly is, with its wealth of information, especially on the minutiae of bibliography and on material buried in out-of-the-way places. But one cannot help thinking how much more useful it would have been if more care had been exercised in its preparation, and if Mr. Courtney had confined his efforts, as was originally his intention, to English bibliography"—(THE NATION, 81, 365).

HEYL, LAWRENCE.
Current National Bibliographies. A List of Sources of Information Concerning Current Books of all Countries. Rev. ed. Chicago: American Library Association, 1942. 20 p.

Lists sources of information concerning the books of sixty-two countries. Arranges material alphabetically according to country. Has no index; but the list is so brief that the lack of an index makes for no serious hardship.

HOWARD-HILL, TREVOR HOWARD.
Bibliography of British Literary Bibliographies. Oxford: Clarendon Press, 1969. 570 p.

Constitutes the first volume of the INDEX TO BRITISH/LITERARY/BIBLIOGRAPHY, which is intended to cover books, substantial parts of books, and periodical articles, written in English and published in the English-speaking Commonwealth and the United States after 1890, on the bibliographical and textual examination of English manuscripts, books, printing, publishing, from the establishment of printing in England. The second volume will record the bibliographies of Shakespeare (excluded from volume one); the final volume will list material not included in the prior volumes.

JOSEPHSON, A. G. S.

Bibliographies of Bibliographies: Chronologically Arranged, with Occasional Notes and An Index. Chicago: Bibliographical Society of Chicago, 1901. 45 p.

The first edition is a chronological list of 156 bibliographies of bibliographies. In a second edition, the compiler replaced the chronological arrangement by a classified arrangement, within which he arranges the titles chronologically.

"About two-thirds of the titles cataloged have been personally examined by the author. . . . This little list, with the help of the very full author and subject index supplies an excellent key to sources of information which cannot be readily found elsewhere" — (LIBRARY JOURNAL, April, 1901, 578).

NILON, CHARLES H.

Bibliography of Bibliographies in American Literature. New York: Bowker, 1970. 483 p.

Lists separately published bibliographies and those appearing as periodical articles and parts of books. Index of names and titles.

NORTHUP, CLARK S.

A Register of Bibliographies of the English Language and Literature. New York: Hafner Publishing Company, 1962 (reprinted from 1925 edition). 507 p.

Includes many related bibliographies of other subjects and hence serves to a degree as a general bibliography of bibliography. The main divisions of the work are: I (general, 9–33); II (individual authors and topics, 34–417); additions and corrections (419–449); index (451–507).

"A new bibliography of literary bibliographies, the importance of which in a college or reference library it would be difficult to over-estimate. . . . All entries are given with exact reference, there are some critical and descriptive notes, and reference to reviews is made" — (LIBRARY JOURNAL, January 15, 1926).

"This very substantial dictionary of bibliographies of English authors and of works bearing on English literature contains about 10,000 entries, and is a good example of the laborious thoroughness of the present-day school of American bibliographers"—(LIBRARY ASSOCIATION RECORD, VOLUME 4, NUMBER 28, 143).

VAN PATTEN, NATHAN.
Index to Bibliographies and Bibliographical Contributions Relating to the World of American and British Authors, 1923–1932. California: Stanford University Press, 1934. 507 p.

Aims to make more accessible information regarding the printed and manuscript work of individual authors—binding, paper, pagination, illustration, variants, editions, issues, value, and location. Chronologically, continues the work of Northup's REGISTER.

". . . the compiler has covered a wide field, and assembled a mass of useful information, otherwise difficult to obtain, in a conveniently small compass"—(LONDON TIMES LITERARY SUPPLEMENT, May, 1934).

Universal Bibliographies

PEDDIE, ROBERT A.
Subject Index of Books Published Before 1800. London: Grafton, 1933—.

The first series, 745 p., was published in 1933; the second series, 857 p., was published in 1935; the third series, 945 p., was published in 1939; and the last series, 872 p., appeared in 1948.

Each issue constitutes an alphabetical subject list of some 50,000 books in many languages, published before 1800. The third series includes in its alphabetical arrangement all the headings employed in the three series with cross references to the first and second series. The last series does not continue this record.

WATT, Robert.
Bibliotheca Britannica: Or a General Index to British and Foreign Literature. Edinburgh: Constable, 1824. 4 vols.

Volumes one and two contain authors and their works; volumes three and four contain subjects that have been written about. Includes British authors and authors whose works have been translated into English.

More fully, Volumes I and II comprise an alphabetical list of authors and their works, providing full name and dates, brief biographical data, and, for each book, brief information which generally includes title, date, size, and number of volumes. Volumes III and IV constitute a chronological arrangement of the subject headings, with the references being made, not to the author, but to the page and marginal index letter in the author volumes where the full entry is to be found.

"This is a very useful work; a must for every library" — (BLACKWOOD'S MAGAZINE REVIEW, 553).

"On the whole, it seems to us that all those who prize the honour of British literature, will do well to contribute, as far as in them lies, to the success of this admirable book. . . . for it is quite impossible that the time consumed on the BIBLIOTHECA BRITANNICA should ever be adequately paid for in the usual routine of the trade" — (BLACKWOOD'S EDINBURGH MAGAZINE, August, 1819, 555).

International Bibliographies

BALDENSPERGER, F. and W. Friederich.
Bibliography of Comparative Literature. New York: Russell, 1960 (reprint from 1950 edition). 705 p.

A comprehensive bibliography. The first and third books deal with generalities — themes, motifs, genres, international literary relations; the second and fourth, with specific literatures and their contributions — of one country on another, of one author on another, then the influence of a country on an individual author. The bibliographical citations are brief, the table of contents is quite detailed, but the index is lacking.

"It is the most comprehensive and effective tool ever placed in the hands of comparatists, and should for many years to come do much to center attention on comparative literature. It is excellently printed, clear and readable, firmly bound for every duty, and accurate. It is an almost superhuman task of painstaking scholarship" — (GERMANIC REVIEW, XXVI, 165–166).

The work makes available to students of literature "an invaluable, indispensable tool, an up-to-date, very full, and generally accurate survey of all scholarship which can be called comparative literature. . . . The arrangement, which repeats Betz's scheme with some modifications, seems lucid and logical, once one has grasped the main principle that always the 'emitter' of an influence is the guide for the listing. . . . A weak section is that on the main literary genres. . . . The section on the novel is particularly defective. . . . The list of the general works on literary criticism is also quite small and defective. . . . The part on 'Literature and Politics,' which opens with a chapter on sociology and lists Marxism expressly among its topics, is possibly even more deficient. . . . . A second major deficiency of the work is the step—motherly treatment of Slavic matters. . . . The work could be made nearly perfect by small corrections, if substantially supplemented in the two directions I have indicated—literary theory and Slavic titles" — (COMPARATIVE LITERATURE, VOLUME 3, 90–92).

EDWARDES, MARIAN.
Summary of the Literatures of Modern Europe (England, France, Germany, Italy, Spain) From the Origins to 1400. London: Dent, 1907. 352 p.

An annotated and classified bibliography with references to most authoritative scholarly discussions of the writings included. Major arrangement is by countries; subordinate arrangement is by principal writers. Provides brief biographical data, list of works, notes about works, and bibliographical references to editions, translations, and critical works and articles. Manuscripts in various English libraries are located.

"Such a book . . . is not likely to appeal to any but professional students, and this class of readers will surely prefer to go at once to the sources for the individual literatures which Miss Edwardes herself has used, rather than consult them at second hand in the present work. . . . We have no space to record the innumerable omissions and errors which we have

observed in the English Literature division of this work. . . .
It is no better with the sections on French Literature. . . .
But enough has been said, we believe, to show how defective
this work is, notwithstanding its occasionally useful citations
of recent literature"—(THE NATION, VOLUME 85, November
21, 1907, 424).

"It seems a very careful and painstaking work, and should be
found useful by students"—(THE SPECTATOR, March 16, 1907,
469–470).

In spite of certain defects "the compilation is distinctly
serviceable. With careful revision it might be made indispensable"—(ATHENAEUM, VOLUME 1, June 29, 1907, 789).

FARRAR, C. P., A. P. EVANS.
A Bibliography of English Translations From Medieval Sources.
New York: Columbia University Press, 1946. 643 p.

Compiled in response to a demand for a reasonable, accurate
guide to existing translations from medieval sources. Official
papers are excluded; the aim is to "include English translations
of important literary sources from Constantine the Great to the
year 1500 within an area roughly inclusive of Europe, North
Africa, and West Asia, generally." Most translations from Latin
are excluded. Arrangement is alphabetical, chiefly by author.
Each separate item is numbered. Annotations describe content,
convey translator's comment. Contains an extensive index to
authors, translators, editors, titles, subjects.

"This bibliography fills a critical need at a critical time; it
reflects scholarship of the highest sort, and on every page shows
the industry, patience, and skill of all who aided in its production. . . . Students and scholars can rejoice in the possession
of a work on which they will all lean heavily, and librarians
should consider themselves thrice blest to have such an aid at
hand"—(AMERICAN HISTORICAL REVIEW, LII, 1946, 108).

"Fills a great need and will prove an invaluable tool for all
students of the medieval period. . . . An excellent index, over
seventy pages in length, and adequate cross references will
please the many future users"—(UNITED STATES QUARTERLY
BOOKLIST, 11, 1946, 260).

GOFF, FREDERICK RICHMOND.
Incunabula in American Libraries: a third census of fifteenth

century books recorded in North American collections. New York: Bibliographical Society of America, 1964. 798 p.

Follows the second census compiled by Margaret Stillwell in 1940. A much enlarged edition recording 47,188 copies of 12,599 titles held by 760 owners. The method of listing follows that of the second census; the style is virtually the same.

HOPPER, V. F. and B. N. GREBANIER.
Bibliography of European Literature. New York: Barron's Educational Series, Inc., 1954. 158 p.

Conceived as a companion to the authors' ESSENTIALS OF EUROPEAN LITERATURE, this bibliography is limited to books in English on the subjects covered in the companion volume: the leading writers and their works, the key periods and literary productions, minor figures, national literatures in general.

"It appears that not all English translations, or even the best, are necessarily listed. But in spite of this inadequacy, it does make available in a small, inexpensive volume, a guide for the study of European literature in translation and, with the authors, we may hope that it 'will encourage a vaster work on the subject' " — (WILSON LIBRARY BULLETIN, XXIX, September, 1954, 85).

Modern Language Association of America. MLA international bibliography of books and articles on the modern languages and literatures, 1969–. New York. Modern Language Association of America, 1970. (Pub. as supplement to PLMA. Vol. 85).

Each volume has its own front matter, table of contents, individual paging, and author index.

STILLWELL, MARGARET B.
Incunabula and Americana, 1450–1800. Key to Bibliographical Study. New York: Columbia University Press, 1931. 483 p.

Lists 35,232 copies of 11,132 titles owned by 332 public and 390 private collections. In part one, Incunabula, the contents are: (ch. 1) printed books of the 15th century; (ch. 2) identification and collation; (ch. 3) bibliographical reference material. In part two, Americana, the contents are: (ch. 1) preliminary survey of sources and methods; (ch. 2) century of maritime discovery; (ch. 3) two centuries of colonial growth;

(ch. 4) later Americana and the Revolutionary periods; (ch. 5) early printing in America. The Reference Sections contain: (1) notes and definitions; (2) foreign bibliographical terms; (3) Latin contractions and abbreviations; (4) placenames of 15th century printing towns; (5) Bibliography—some 1,300 items.

"Altogether, the work seems admirably adequate to its purpose and sets a high standard . . ."—(TRANSACTIONS OF THE BIBLIOGRAPHICAL SOCIETY, VOLUME 22, 4).

U.S. Library of Congress: A Catalog of Books Representing Library of Congress Printed Cards, issued to July 31, 1942. Ann Arbor, Michigan: Edward Bros., 1942–1946. 167 v.

An author and main entry catalog of books for which Library of Congress Cards have been printed in the Library of Congress, the many government department libraries, or the various libraries throughout the nation that take part in the cooperative cataloguing program.

U.S. Library of Congress Author Catalog: A Cumulative List of Works Represented by Library of Congress Printed Cards, 1948–1952. Ann Arbor, Michigan: J. W. Edwards, 1953.

Sometimes called the Cumulative Catalog of Library of Congress Printed Cards. Contains not only main entries, but also essential entries and cross references. Volumes 1–23, Authors, A–Z; volume 24, Films. Many cards represented in these volumes were prepared by cooperating libraries, so that for a large number of books not in the Library of Congress at least one location is indicated. Starting with January, 1953, entries are listed separately for Motion Pictures and filmstrips, music and phonorecords.

U.S. Library of Congress Catalog: A Cumulative List of Works Represented by Library of Congress Printed Cards. Books, Subjects, 1950–1954. Ann Arbor, Michigan: J. W. Edwards, 1955. 20 v.

Motion pictures and music scores are included through 1952, but are listed separately since January, 1953. As is the case with the Author section, many of the cards were prepared by cooperating libraries; so that for many books not in the Library of Congress, at least one location is indicated.

National Bibliographies

ALSTON, ROBIN CARFRAE.
A Bibliography of the English Language from the Invention of Printing to the Year 1800. Bradford, England: E. Cummins, 1970. Vol. 3, pt. 1 (In progress).

Contents: Old English, Middle English, early modern English miscellaneous works, vocabulary. 204 p.

American Catalogue of Books, 1876–1910. New York: Publisher's Weekly, 1876–1910. 9 v. in 13.

The 1938 reprint is a continuation of BIBLIOTHECA AMERICANA, compiled by Roorbach, the fourth volume of which brought the work down to 1861. The 1941 reprint under the direction of F. Leypoldt in 1880 was compiled by Lynds E. Jones and published by Peter Smith in 1941.

The aim of the work is to include, with certain exceptions, all the books published in the United States which were in print and for sale to the general public on July 1, 1876. The exceptions to this are: local directories, periodicals, sheet music, books chiefly blank, unbound maps, tracts, and other low-priced pamphlets. Entries number 70,000 and represent the work of over 900 firms.

"On behalf of bibliographers and reference workers, this department wishes to pay tribute to Peter Smith and the National Bibliophile Service. From time to time his concern has rendered librarianship and the world of scholarship signal service, both in the location of rare and out of print items and in the reprinting of needed standard works . . . and now comes a most welcome P.S. from Peter Smith: 'We hope to announce shortly our project for a reprint of the AMERICAN CATALOGUE OF BOOKS, 1876–1910 (the whole blessed business)' "—(WILSON LIBRARY BULLETIN, VOL. XIII, 482).

Annual American Catalogue, 1886–1910. New York: Publisher's Weekly, 1887–1911. 25 v.

Directly based upon Publisher's Weekly's cumulated reference lists as preserved by the linotype system, edited and filled out with additional titles brought to notice during the years of publication. Discontinued for lack of support, and now generally superseded by the cumulated volumes of the AMERICAN CATALOGUE, but useful for occasional omissions in the AMERICAN CATALOGUE.

Books in Print: An Author-Title-Series Index to the Publishers' Trade List Annual, 1948—. New York: Bowker, 1948—.

Provides full information concerning author, title, price, publisher, and thus makes possible easy reference to the appropriate catalogue in the Trade List Annual. One alphabet lists authors, editions, compilers, and translators; the other alphabet lists titles, series, and serial publications. Both indexes give bibliographical information.

"The British book trade has long had a toll similar to this index, namely WHITAKER'S REFERENCE CATALOGUE OF CURRENT LITERATURE. American bookstores and libraries have not had any index of books in print since the 1928 volume of the U.S. CATALOG. The major aim of the volume is to provide in a single volume enough information to enable the vast majority of bookseller's inquiries to be turned into orders"—(LIBRARY JOURNAL, April 1948).

British National Bibliography, No. 1, Jan. 4, 1950. London: Council of the British National Bibliography, British Museum, 1950.

A weekly bibliography of books published in Great Britain, compiled by highly trained cataloguers, working on the books themselves as they pass through the copyright Receipt Office at the British Museum. The descriptions are precise and adequate; the subjects are defined and analyzed with clarity. The classified subject section takes up the first 686 pages; the author, title, and subject index takes up the remaining 268 pages. The cataloguing includes: full name of author, title, publisher, date, pagination, illustration, cm. size, binding, series, occasional annotations.

"A careful sampling has produced only a handful of trivial slips, so few that they merely confirm its substantial accuracy. The index is as nearly perfect an instrument as could be contrived. . . . The British National Bibliography has already established itself as a necessary companion in every bookshop and library where English books are to be found" — (LONDON TIMES LITERARY-SUPPLEMENT, July 4, 1952).

"The publication reflects the greatest credit on everyone concerned with it, to whom our warmest congratulations are due" — (LIBRARY ASSOCIATION RECORD, XVII, April, 1950).

Cumulative Book Index. New York: Wilson, 1898 — . Service Basis.

Aims to catalogue all the books in the English language wherever published, and thus to form a complete bibliography of works in English, exclusive of government documents, tracts, propaganda, and issues of very local or ephemeral nature. Published periodically with cumulation to form supplements to the UNITED STATES CATALOG.

"A comprehensive and reasonably accurate record indispensable in any library."

EVANS, CHARLES.
American Bibliography: A Chronological Dictionary of all Books, Pamphlets, and Periodical Publications Printed in the United States of America from the Genesis of Printing in 1639 down to and Including the Year 1820; with Bibliographical and Biographical Notes. Chicago: Privately printed for the author by the Columbia Press, 1903–1934. Vol. 1–12.

The first volume was published in 1903, the twelfth and last volume, covering the years 1798–1799, was published in 1934, just one year before Evans' death. A reprint was made in 1941–42 by Peter Smith, New York. Volume 14, edited by Roger Pattrell Bristol, is a cumulated author-title index to the whole work, including pseudonyms, attributed authors, other names appearing on the title page, governmental bodies, etc. Volume 13 starts with the letter N for 1799 and continues through 1800 with author and subject indexes.

Each book lists author's full name, with dates of birth and death, full title, publication facts, and, in many instances, location. Each volume contains an author index, a subject index, and a publisher or printer index.

"For ten years the AMERICAN BIBLIOGRAPHY has been in practical use, both in this country and abroad, and is recognized everywhere as the bibliographical authority of early American literature" — (LIBRARY JOURNAL, XXXVIII, 46–47).

"The only serious criticism one can make of his plan, is that he never gives any authorities for borrowed information. It is taken as it is found, good, bad or indifferent, and its source is never credited. The taint of uncertainty or unreliability which belongs to titles of this class thus pervades to a certain extent the whole work, and one is not always able to tell whether Mr. Evans has seen the book or has taken the title for an uncertain source" — (LIBRARY JOURNAL, XXXIV, March, 134).

The American Bibliography of Charles Evans: A Chronological Dictionary of All Books, Pamphlets and Periodical Publications Printed in the United States of America from the genesis of printing in 1639 down to and including the year 1800 with bibliographical and biographical notes. Volume 13, 1799–1800, by Clifford K. Shipton. Worcester, Massachusetts: American Antiquarian Society, 1955. 349 p.

A continuation of Charles Evans' AMERICAN BIBLIOGRAPHY, which ended with the letter M for 1799. Shipton's volume starts with the letter N for 1799 and continues through 1800, with author and subject indexes. Titles are shortened and symbols for location adapted. Cross references are given for anonymous works listed under author.

Volume 14, edited by Roger Pattrell Bristol and published in 1959, is a cumulated author-title index to the entire work, including pseudonyms, attributed authors, other names appearing on the title page, governmental bodies, etc. Newspapers and almanacs are grouped under these respective headings, not under specific title.

KELLEY, JAMES.
American Catalogue of Books Published in the United States from January 1861 to January 1871. New York: Wiley, 1866–1871. 2 v.

A continuation of Roorbach's BIBLIOTHECA AMERICANA and, like the latter, neither complete nor entirely accurate. Yet the BIBLIOTHECA AMERICANA and the AMERICAN CATALOGUE OF

BOOKS are the most general lists available for the period 1820–1870.

National Union Catalog, 1956 Through 1967: A Cumulative author list representing Library of Congress printed cards and titles reported by other American libraries. Totowa, New Jersey: Rowman and Littlefield, 1970–. Vol. 1 (In progress).

"A new and augmented twelve-year catalog being a compilation into one alphabet of the fourth and fifth supplements of the National Union Catalog with a key to additional locations through 1967 and with a unique identifying number allocated to each title. . . ."—Title page.

An important feature is the designation of those items for which further locations are given in the REGISTER OF ADDITIONAL LOCATIONS as cumulated in the 1963–67 supplement. Added locations are cited in a separate section at the end of each volume of the new set.

Paperbound Books in Print. New York: Bowker, 1955–. Monthly.

The monthly issues, called THE MONTH AHEAD, presents previews of forthcoming books under general subject groupings with an author-editor index.

ROORBACH, ORVILLE AUGUSTUS.
Bibliotheca Americana, 1820–1861. New York: Roorbach, 1852–61. 4 v.

An alphabetical list of American publications, including reprints. Arrangement is by author and title; gives publication facts, size and price.

"Roorbach, although his work is most imperfect bibliographically, is entitled to credit for his personal labors and professional enterprise in making the first real American Catalogue"—(LIBRARY JOURNAL, August, 1897, 387).

SABIN, JOSEPH.
Dictionary of Books Relating to America from its Discovery to the Present Time. New York: Bibliographical Society of America, 1928–1936. 29 v.

The actual number of entries probably exceed 107,000. The principal plan of arrangement is by author. The facts given include: full title, publication facts, often contents and bibliographical notes with reference to a review in some other work, and, occasionally, location.

"Joseph Sabin's great Dictionary . . . was left incomplete on his death in 1881, when 82 parts, bringing the work into its fourteenth volume, had been put through the press. . . . A truly monumental work"—(LIBRARY JOURNAL, January, 1924, 84).

Subject Guide to Books in Print: An Index to the Publishers' Trade List Annual 1957—. New York: Bowker, 1957—. Annual.

A companion volume to BOOKS IN PRINT, listing under subject the books to be found there. Follows the subject headings and cross references set up by the Library of Congress; does not index works to which the Library of Congress does not assign subject headings (e.g., fiction, poetry, drama, and Bibles).

United States Catalog: Books in Print, 1899. Minneapolis: The H. W. Wilson Company, 1900. 2 v. in 1.

Each volume alphabetically lists entries under author, title, and subject. Whereas the first edition, however, contained separate author and title indexes, the succeeding editions have grouped author, title, and subject in a single alphabet. And whereas the first three editions excluded books published outside the United States, the fourth edition includes Canadian and British publications, privately printed books, and the publications of universities, societies, scientific institutions, as well as a selected list of the publications of the national and state government.

The UNITED STATES CATALOG, together with its supplements and related publication, the CUMULATIVE INDEX, makes available the most complete record of book publishing in America since 1898.

United States Copyright Office: Catalog of Entries, 1891–1946. Washington, D.C. The Government Printing Office, 1891–1947.

The arrangement and format have varied with different issues. With the third series, published in 1947, the Catalog was subdivided into separate parts following the classification noted in the Copyright Act: pt. 1A, Books and Selected Pamphlets; pt. 1B, Pamphlets, Serials, and Contributions to Periodicals; pt. 3 and 4, Dramas and Works Prepared for Oral Delivery; pt. 5A, Published Music; pt. 5B, Unpublished Music; pt. 6, Maps; pt. 7–11B, Works of Art, Reproduction, Prints; pt. 12 and 13, Motion Pictures; pt. 14A, Renewal Registrations, Literature, Art, Film; pt. 14B, Renewal Registrations, Music.

The book sections includes books published in the United States, books in foreign languages published abroad, and books in the English language first published abroad when they are copyrighted in this country.

U.S. Library of Congress. The National Union Catalog: A Cumulative Author List Representing Library of Congress Printed Cards and Titles Reported by Other American Libraries. Compiled by the Library of Congress with the co-operation of the Committee on Resources of American Libraries of the American Library Association. Ann Arbor, Michigan: Edwards, 1958. 28 vols.

Since January, 1956, it has included titles catalogued and holdings reported by some 500 libraries. From January to June, 1956, monthly and quarterly issues had the title: LIBRARY OF CONGRESS CATALOG-BOOKS: Authors; a National Union Catalog Representing Library of Congress Printed Cards and Titles Reported by Other Libraries. In July, 1956, the title changed to THE NATIONAL UNION CATALOG. Symbols are used to indicate copies held by other libraries.

General Bibliographies

American Library Association Catalog: An annotated Basic List of 10,000 Books. Chicago: American Library Association, 1926–.

The 1926 issue, 1,295 pages, covers approximately 10,000 books. It is a classified list, generally following the Dewey Decimal System, which provides the following information for each entry: author, title, date, paging, publishers, price, Library of Congress card number, and an indication of scope and value.

The second issue of the A.L.A. CATALOGUE covers some 3,000 titles appearing in the years 1926–1931 (1930, 340 p.); the third issue covers about 4,000 titles appearing in the years 1932–1936 (1938, 306 p.); the fourth issue covers about 4,000 titles appearing in the years 1937–1941 (1943, 306 p.); the fifth issue covers about 4,500 titles appearing in the years 1942–1949 (1952, 408 p.).

Lists only works published in the United States; does provide annotations from other comments, but without an indication of the source.

"The biography section is a treasure house of good reading. It is impossible to criticize it"—(LIBRARY JOURNAL, LXI, 1081).

"The policy of using notes without giving credit seems a dubious one; yet withal, the ALA CATALOG . . . is certainly a very useful tool, and everyone connected with its fashioning should have the gratitude of the profession"—(LITERARY QUARTERLY, XII, 1120).

Booklist: A Guide to Current Books, 1905—. Chicago: American Library Association, 1905—.

Issued semimonthly September through July—the single August issue being the volume index. Information given includes: author's full name, title, date, paging, publisher, price, Dewey decimal classification number, and a brief description of the basic contents of the book, its general value, and an indication of the type of library for which it is recommended.

The Booklist and Subscription Books Bulletin. Chicago: American Library Association, 1956—.

A combination of THE BOOKLIST and the SUBSCRIPTION BOOKS BULLETIN. The reviews of the Subscription Books Committee are published in the first pages of THE BOOKLIST, but are not separately paged. Generally reviews fewer books per year than the old SUBSCRIPTION BOOKS BULLETIN.

HOFFMAN, HESTER R.
Bookman's Manual: A Guide to Literature. 8th ed. New York: R. R. Bowker Company, 1958. 987 p.

Covers many fields—the humanities, reference works, science, travel, the book trade, and generally provides brief though useful annotations. This revised and enlarged edition includes two chapters which have been almost completely rewritten. "The new chapter on Greek and Roman Classics in Translation has replaced the old chapter on Classics in Translation. The classics in other foreign languages which formerly had a place here . . . have been transferred to the new and greatly augmented chapter on Other Foreign Literature."

GRACE, Sister M. and G. C. Peterson.
Books for Catholic Colleges: A Supplement to Shaw's LIST OF BOOKS FOR COLLEGE LIBRARIES. Compiled under the auspices of the Catholic Library Association. Chicago: American Library Association, 1948. 134 p.

"This book deserves a far greater appreciation than either its appearance or title warrants . . . but for the seven pages on religion, the book is a universal tool. . . . All the books listed, with very few exceptions, are in print, the LC number is given, where it is available, and as a selective list of the best of books in the fields of the humanities, literature, and elementary science, it cannot fail to be an aid"—(LIBRARY JOURNAL).

REGIS, Sister.
The Catholic Bookman's Guide; A Critical Evaluation of Catholic Literature. New York: Hawthorn, 1962. 638 p.

An annotated, classified bibliography covering: Sources and Evaluation; Religion; Philosophy and psychology; Literature; Social sciences.

SHAW, Charles B.
A List of Books for College Libraries: Approximately 14,000 Titles Selected on the Recommendation of 200 College Teachers, Librarians, and Other Advisers. Chicago: American Library Association, 1931. 810 p.

A basic list, with twenty-four major divisions and an author index. The 1931–1938 edition (1940, 284 p.) omits titles published within the period which were definitely regarded as out-of-print. References to book reviews are often given.

Standard Catalog for Public Libraries. 3d ed. New York: The H. W. Wilson Company, 1950. 2057 p.

The main alphabet covers 12,300 titles of books, pamphlets, periodicals, and other publications particularly suitable for small or medium sized public libraries. In addition there are 3,555 titles listed in the notes, including specialized and out-of-print items. Annotations are given for all titles and many editions; preferred items are starred; the Dewey decimal class numbers, subject headings, and Library of Congress card numbers are included.

Subscription Books Bulletin. Chicago: American Library Association, 1930—.

Devoted exclusively to reviews of reference works—encyclopedias, dictionaries, biographical works, atlases, collections, etc. Published as a quarterly from 1930 to September, 1956, when it was combined with the BOOKLIST and began to appear as THE BOOKLIST-SUBSCRIPTION BOOKS BULLETIN. Lists are classified generally: books suitable for smaller libraries; books suitable for children; lists of government publications, etc. Both the Dewey decimal numbers and the Library of Congress classification numbers are given for each publication.

Subscription Books Bulletin Reviews. Prepared by the American Library Association, Subscription Books Committee. Chicago: American Library Association, 1967–68. Vols. 4-5.

Reprints of reviews published in THE BOOKLIST AND SUBSCRIPTION BOOKS BULLETIN. Each issue is arranged alphabetically by the titles of the works reviewed. Volume four (1964–66) and volume 5 (1966–68) include reprints of reviews published from September 1, 1964 to August, 1968.

United States Quarterly Book List. New Brunswick, New Jersey: Rutgers University Press, 1945–1956.

Provides a bibliographical description, in Library of Congress form, with a description of general contents and, whenever possible, a biographical sketch of the author. Covers mainly such areas as: fine arts, literature, philosophy and religion, biography, the social sciences, the biological sciences, the physical sciences, technology, and reference.

English Literature Bibliographies

GENERAL

Cambridge Bibliography of English Literature. F. W. Bateson, ed. New York: The Macmillan Company, 1941. 4 vols.

An extensive, comprehensive, and scholarly bibliography, the standard in its field. Supersedes the bibliographies listed in the CHEL and is supplemented by the works of the MHRA and the CBEL supplement. Fully records newspapers and magazines, as well as books and learned periodicals. Major arrangement is by periods; subordinate arrangement is by literary forms or general topics and by authors. For each author generally gives: bibliographies of the author; collected editions of his works; separate works; biographical and critical works about the author. The bibliographies appear in the first three volumes; a detailed index constitutes the fourth volume.

"The CBEL is a scholar's bibliography compiled by scholars who understand the uses which other scholars will make of it." — (AMERICAN LITERATURE, XIII, 183–184).

"What is impressive in this new bibliography of English Literature is the scope of the undertaking. It will be useful to students of religion, of philosophy, of education, of political and social conditions, of the history of science. . . . The CBEL is more than a catalogue. It is, in addition, a short-hand history of English Literature" — (JOURNAL OF ENGLISH PHILOLOGY, 40, 1941, 464).

"If a work of reference does not function smoothly in its capacity as a machine for answering questions, then certainly it is of little worth. On this score the new Cambridge bibliography is about as useful as anything that exists. Certainly every college and university library will be incomplete without it" — (COMMONWEAL, 33, 568).

Cambridge Bibliography of English Literature, F. W. Bateson, ed. Vol. 5, Supplement: A.D. 600–1900, George Watson, ed. New York: Cambridge University Press, 1957. 710 p.

The Supplement lists publications of scholarly interest down to 1900 which have appeared since the original bibliography was prepared in 1941. "As nearly as possible sections have been brought down to the beginning of the year 1955."

The New Cambridge Bibliography of English Literature. George Watson, ed. Cambridge, England: Cambridge University Press, 1971. 5 vols. Vol. 2, 1660–1800. 2091 p.

Like volume three, which was published in 1969, given priority in the reworking of the CAMBRIDGE BIBLIOGRAPHY OF ENGLISH LITERATURE because of the progress made in the study of Victorian literature, volume two excludes unpublished dissertations, encyclopedia articles, and reviews of secondary works; otherwise, the basic design remains the same, the task of the contributors being "to revise and integrate the existing lists of 1940 and 1957, to add materials of the past ten years, to correct and refine the bibliographical details already available, and to reshape the whole according to the new conventions which have been designed to give the Bibliography a clearer and more consistent air." (Preface). Vol. 4 (1900–1950) appeared in 1972.

KENNEDY, ARTHUR G.
A Bibliography of the Writings on the English Language from the Beginnings of Printing to the End of 1922. Cambridge: Harvard University Press, 1927. 517 p.

Aims to provide students of English with a simple but complete book of reference, and to assist those students who seek to specialize in the history of linguistics. Covers both language and literature, and is classified with indexes to authors and reviewers and to subjects.

"This is without a doubt the most important contribution of recent years within the field of English Language. It is the result of some fourteen years of research and more than 15,000 volumes of serial publications have been checked. With its 13,402 items, the volume is offered as a complete book of reference on the subject of the scientific study of England; books dealing with the artistic aspect, literary style, art of expression, have been omitted, unless they emphasize questions of grammatical usage . . ." — (FEGP, XXVII, 1928, 437–440).

"One section of the book lends itself to considerable comment, that on slang and colloquialisms. This stops at 1900 and so the period of the Great War is ruled out. . . . French and German works are referred to and quoted. It is indeed quite a complete bibliography" — (LONDON TIMES LITERARY SUPPLEMENT, June 16, 1927, 428).

WATSON, George.
**Concise Cambridge Bibliography of English Literature, 600–
1950.** New York: Cambridge University Press, 1958. 271 p.

A condensed treatment of some 400 "major" authors, selected
from the CBEL and its Supplement, with the addition of a
section covering 1900–1950. The six chronological sections are
preceded by a general introductory section providing bibliographies, literary history and criticism, collections, dictionaries,
etc. The bibliographies include both primary and secondary
works.

CURRENT

**Annual Bibliography of English Language and Literature,
1920 – .** Edited for the Modern Humanities Research Association. London: Cambridge University Press, 1921–. Annual.
(Volume 20, covering the year 1939, was published in 1948;
volume 21, covering the year 1940, was published in 1950; volume 22, covering the year 1941, was published in 1952; and
volume 23, covering the year 1942, was published in 1952.

An excellent annual bibliography of English and American literature; aims to provide as complete a list as possible of all the
books and articles of value which deal with the English language
and literature appearing in the previous year. Includes references to all important reviews in British, American, and foreign
periodicals, and thus enables the student to obtain varied and
authoritative comment on most works of significance. Publication was suspended during the war, but an attempt is now being made to bring the work up to date.
  "A fairly prolonged check has revealed only three minor
misprints—a sufficient testimony to the quality of the work of
both editor and printers. The volume maintains the reputation
of the series as an invaluable aid to scholarship"—(MODERN
LANGUAGE REVIEW, XLIII, 561).

Progress of Medieval and Renaissance Studies in the United

States and Canada: Colorado: University of Colorado Press, 1923—.

The first number was limited to historical studies and contained the names of sixty medievalists. The second number was expanded to include those interested in medieval Latin studies. The third number, appearing in 1925, and representing a distinct departure from earlier issues, sought to embrace all phases of interest in the medieval period. The fifteenth number marked the addition of renaissance studies.

Each issue includes: a section entitled General Matters—papers read at learned societies, for example; lists of works published (including publication facts) and a notation as to their being or not being doctoral dissertations, and a list of doctoral dissertations in progress.

Research in Progress in the Modern Languages and Literatures, 1948—. (In PMLA, Vol. 63, Supplement, pt. 2, pp. 143–405.) Takes up the function of WORK IN PROGRESS, previously published by the MODERN HUMANITIES RESEARCH ASSOCIATION, suspended in 1942. Lists research in progress in twenty-nine countries. Contains a subject and author index. The latter also serves as an index to the addresses of 3,550 scholars in various countries.

Speculum: A Journal of Medieval Studies. Cambridge, Massachusetts: The Medieval Academy of America, 1926—.

Each issue of this quarterly journal contains a bibliography of the periodical literature in the Medieval period that appeared during the preceding quarter. Often publishes articles intended to illuminate neglected areas and to open up new fields of research. Publishes reviews.

"MODERN LANGUAGE NOTES extends greetings to SPECULUM, a new mirror through which students of the modern languages may become more richly conscious of their medieval heritage. . . . Of the significance for research in the humanities which this movement connotes there is no need to speak. The officers of the academy and the editors of the journal are men who have won distinction in the classics, in history, in architecture, and in modern scholarship. . . . Since art, beauty and poetry are portions of our medieval heritage, all will be presented in studies that are scholarly and arranged in pleasing form. The journal will also combine detail with synthesis"—(MODERN LANGUAGE NOTES, XLI).

Work in Progress . . . in the Modern Humanities, 1938–1942. Cambridge: Modern Humanities Research Association, 1938–1942.

The predecessor of RESEARCH IN PROGRESS (see above). No longer published.

Year's Work in English Studies. Edited for the English Association. London: Oxford University Press, 1921—.

The ANNUAL BIBLIOGRAPHY OF ENGLISH LANGUAGE AND LITERATURE includes American literature. The YEAR'S WORK IN ENGLISH STUDIES excludes American literature, but embraces comparable areas of English literature as the former, listing fewer titles, but giving brief comment. Emphasis of treatment varies with the occasion. Thus the 1924 issue gives special attention to philology and, since the year represented the Byron centenary, also to the Romantic Movement; whereas the 1928 issue, the year marking the tercentenary of Bunyan's death, provides particular consideration of the Restoration. The later editions of the YEAR'S WORK follow the same pattern and policy of the earlier volumes; the main difference resides in the matter of items listed.

"Each period of literature is supervised by a specialist, who combines summary and assessment very skillfully without arrogance or leniency"—(LONDON TIMES LITERARY SUPPLEMENT, February 15, 1923, 104).

"This volume [XXXV] maintains a steady standard of fullness and judiciousness. The design of the book has been tightened up, with fuller page and smaller, yet quite legible type, all of which keeps it within manageable size, without reducing scope of survey, which continues to astonish by its completeness"—(MODERN LANGUAGE REVIEW, 1954).

Year's Work in Modern Language Studies. Edited for the MODERN HUMANITIES RESEARCH ASSOCIATION. Cambridge: University Press, 1951. Vols. 1–10, 1931–1940; Vol. XI, 1940–1949; Vol. XII, 1950.

The work is edited by a number of scholars; covers medieval Latin, Italian, French, Hispanic, Roumanian, Germanic, and Celtic studies, and, in later volumes, International languages and Slavonic studies.

DISSERTATIONS

Dissertation Abstracts: A Guide to Dissertations and Monographs Available in Microform. Ann Arbor, Michigan: University Microfilms, 1952—.

Formerly called MICROFILM ABSTRACTS. The change in title and format begins with Volume 12, No. 1, 1952. Six issues are published each year, one containing author and subject indexes for the year. Now only available on a subscription basis.

Dissertation Abstracts International. Retrospective index, Vol. 1-XXIX. Ann Arbor, Michigan: University Microfilms, 1970.

The title change from DISSERTATION ABSTRACTS TO DISSERTATION ABSTRACTS INTERNATIONAL was made with volume 30, number 1 (July, 1969), with a view to including foreign dissertations, and a number of European institutions are now represented among the cooperating institutions. Author and keyword-in-title indexes appear in each monthly issue beginning with volume 30, number 1, both indexes cumulating annually.

Doctoral Dissertations Accepted by American Universities. Compiled for the Association of Research Libraries. New York: Wilson, 1934—. Annual.

Twenty-two volumes appeared between the years 1933–1950. The general division of each volume falls typically into seven categories: philosophy, religion, physical sciences, social sciences, and humanities. The arrangement within the various subdivisions is alphabetical by university and by author. The main contents are: Alphabetical Subject Index; Publication and Preservation of American Doctoral Dissertations; List of Periodic University Publications Abstracting Dissertations; Statistical Tables; Lists of Dissertations arranged by Subject.

The entries include the name of the author, the title of his work, and, if the thesis is published, a bibliographical description of it. Also contains a tabular listing of the distribution of doctorates by school and subject, and an author index.

"This volume provides a very useful and complete list of doctoral dissertations accepted during the past year. . . . Much valuable information is given in the introductory pages. A 'Table of Practice of Publication and Loan of Doctoral Dissertations' gives in convenient form information which has been found heretofore only through the trial-and-error method"— (THE LIBRARY QUARTERLY, April, 1935, 250).

Index to American Doctoral Dissertations, 1955/56—. Comp. for the Assoc. of Research Libraries. Ann Arbor: University of Michigan, 1957—. Annual. (Being DISSERTATION ABSTRACTS, v. 16, no. 13, and cont.)

Consolidates into one list dissertations for which doctoral degrees were granted in the United States and Canada during the academic year covered, as well as those available on microfilm. Preliminary tables give information on the publication and lending of dissertations, and the distribution of doctorates by university and subject field. Arranged by subject classification with author indexes.

Index to Theses Accepted for Higher Degrees in the Universities of Great Britain and Ireland. Edited by P. D. Record. London: ASLIB, 1953—.

An annual classified list, alphabetically arranged by university under various heads. Information includes author's name, title of thesis, and degree granted. Contains both subject and author indexes.

List of American Doctoral Dissertations Printed in 1912–1928. Washington, D.C.: Government Printing Office, 1913–1940. 26 vols.

Each volume has four divisions: (1) an alphabetical list of titles; (2) a subject list, classified by the Library of Congress indexing system; (3) a subject index; (4) a list of authors, arranged according to the institutions granting the degrees. Includes some forty-five colleges and universities. No longer published.

LITTO, FREDRIC M.
American Dissertations on the Drama and the Theatre: A Bib-

liography. Kent, Ohio: Kent State University Press, 1969. 519 p.
Aims to include "references to all doctoral dissertations on subjects related to theatre and drama completed in all academic departments of American (the United States and Canada) universities." Arrangement is by "reference code," with author, keyword-in-context, and subject indexes. Cutoff date is 1965. Plans call for annual lists for the years after 1965, with updated editions of the basic volume at 5-year intervals.

McNAMEE, LAWRENCE F.
Dissertations in English and American Literature: theses accepted by American, British and German universities, 1865–1964. New York: Bowker, 1968. 1124 p.

A computer-produced bibliography. Arrangement is by subject; index is by author. Does not wholly supersede Woodress list for American literature, which covers through 1966; or the Altick and Matthews volume for Victorian literature, which includes Austrian, French, and Swiss dissertations.

The first Supplement, published in 1969 (450 p.), covers the period 1964–68.

Microfilm Abstracts: A Collection of Abstracts of Doctoral Dissertations and Monographs Which Are Available in Complete Form on Microfilm. Ann Arbor, Michigan: University Microfilms, 1938– .

This collection of abstracts is distributed to leading libraries and journals accompanied by printed library cards for each abstract. The dissertations themselves are microfilmed in full and copies of the microfilm are available for sale through University Microfilm. Now called DISSERTATION ABSTRACTS.

PALFREY, T. H., H. E. COLEMAN, JR.
Guide to Bibliographies of Theses, United States and Canada.
2d ed. Chicago: American Library Association, 1940. 54 p.

Nothing appears to be known about the first edition. The second edition comprises general lists, lists in special fields, and institutional lists. The third edition was printed in 1950. The arrangement is alphabetical throughout—in the third grouping, according to the schools listed.

"This is a helpful tool for college and university libraries. It contains a reasonably complete listing of theses [although] a few omissions are noted"—(WILSON LIBRARY BULLETIN, 15:683).

"This guide furnishes a convenient aid for the student wishing to know what research work has been completed in his field. For the library itself it is most useful in locating reference materials"—(LIBRARY QUARTERLY, 7:287).

Progress of Medieval and Renaissance Studies in the United States and Canada. (See annotation on pages 161–162.)

ROSENBERG, RALPH P.
Bibliographies of Theses in America. (In the BULLETIN OF BIBLIOGRAPHY for September–December, 1945, and January–April, 1946.)

Constitutes a supplement to GUIDE TO BIBLIOGRAPHIES (Palfrey and Coleman), with corrections and additions.

OLD AND MIDDLE ENGLISH

GENERAL

FARRAR, CLARISSA P., A. PATERSON.
Bibliography of English Translations from Medieval Sources. New York: Columbia University Press, 1946, 534 p.
For annotation, see page 146.

HEUSINKVELD, A. H. AND E. J. BASHE.
A Bibliographical Guide to Old English: A Selective Bibliography of the Language, Literature, and History of the Anglo-Saxons. Iowa City: University of Iowa Press, 1931. 153 p.

Aims to assist student by (1) providing him with "a guide to the bibliographical tools most likely to prove necessary and useful" in a more than superficial study of old English; (2) reminding him that "language and literature are but two of many phenomena in the Anglo-Saxon period"; and (3) providing him with "a list of the most important literary and linguistic monuments" of the period.

". . . fills up far more completely than the authors' modesty will admit a serious gap which has long existed in the equipment of tools at the disposal of students and readers. It is about as complete as the first edition of a work of this sort could reasonably expect to be; it is intelligently and conveniently arranged; it is well-indexed; it is selective yet almost certainly fulfills the authors' hopes 'that the material actually will lead the student to all other works that have been deliberately or inadvertently omitted' " — (SPECULUM, VII, 287).

LOOMIS, ROGER S.
Introduction to Medieval Literature Chiefly in England: A Reading List and Bibliography. 2d ed. New York: Columbia University Press, 1948. 32 p.

"The ten years which have elapsed since the first appearance of Professor Loomis' unassuming but worthwhile syllabus have brought forth no rivals. Revision has allowed the author to keep abreast of the thriving course of medieval scholarship during the decade" — (MODERN LANGUAGE QUARTERLY, March, 1950, 498).

MUMMENDEY, RICHARD.
Language and Literature of the Anglo-Saxon Nations as Presented in German Doctoral Dissertations, 1885–1950: A Bibliography. Charlottesville: Bibliographical Society of the University of Virginia, 1954. 200 p.

Prefatory material and captions are in English and German. Contains 2,989 items arranged by subject field; provides a name and subject index.

ROBINSON, FRED C.
Old English Literature: A Select Bibliography. Toronto: University of Toronto Press, 1970. 68 p.

Undertakes to list the most important and useful writings on each literary work of the period and on the literature in general. Short descriptive notes on references to critical reviews follow most citations.

SEVERS, JONATHAN BURKE, gen. ed.
A Manual of the Writings in Middle English, 1050–1500, by members of the Middle English Group of the Modern Language Association. New Haven, Connecticut: Academy of Arts and Sciences, 1970. Vol. 2.

Volume one was published in 1967. A rewriting and an expansion of A MANUAL OF THE WRITINGS IN MIDDLE ENGLISH 1050–1400 by John Edwin Wells. Bibliographies are updated, the scope is broadened to include the 16th century, and the commentary is a fresh evaluation of the literature and of the scholarship of its critics. Cutoff date for the first volume is 1955; cutoff date for volume two appears to be 1965. A bibliography complements each survey.

STILLWELL, MARGARET B.
Incunabula in American Libraries: A Second Census of Fifteenth Century Books owned in the United States, Mexico, and Canada. New York: Bibliographical Society of America, 1940. 619 p.

In the Census of Fifteenth Century Books Owned in America published in 1919, the Preface notes that "an estimate of 13,200 copies is recorded under 6,292 titles, owned by 173 public and 255 private collections." The second census lists "35,232 copies of 11,132 titles, owned by 232 public and 390 private collections. And of these 35,232 copies, 28,491 copies are owned by institutions, and 6,741 copies are in private hands."

Each entry includes author's name, Hain numbers, short title, place, printer, date, catalogs, and location.

STRATMAN, CARL J.
Bibliography of Medieval Drama. 2d. ed. rev. and enl. 2 vols. Berkeley: University of California Press, 1972. 1035 p.

This new edition of a work which is already a standard reference source adds more than 5000 entries to the 1954 original, carrying the listings, textual and critical, down to about 1968.

TUCKER, LENA AND ALLEN BENHAM.
A Bibliography of Fifteenth Century Literature: With Special Reference to the History of English Culture. Seattle, Washington: University of Washington Press, 1928. 274 p.

Aims to bring together in usable form the material which would be available in a university or research library. Makes no attempt to list manuscripts, first or rare editions. References to these are found in the general bibliography section, as well as in the individual author bibliographies. The main divisions are: Bibliography; Political Background; Social and Economic Background; Cultural Background; Linguistic Background; Literature; Appendix.

The work, "in spite of its title is a bibliography, not of the original texts, but of modern works concerning the 15th century literature. A large number of titles are listed, among them many articles in periodicals which were well worth recording.

WELLS, JOHN E.
Manual of the Writings in Middle English 1050–1400. Published under the Auspices of the Connecticut Academy of Arts and Sciences. 1941. 941 p.

Attempts to treat all the extant writings in print, "from single lines to the most extensive pieces, composed in English between 1050 and 1400." For each piece included, provides probable date, MS or MSS, form and extent, dialect in which first composed, source or sources, bibliography, comment, and, in some cases, abstracts.

The index covers every reference to each work; cross references are numerous. The main work covers bibliography to September, 1915. The first eight supplements include additions and modifications to December, 1941. The ninth supplement, July, 1951, includes additions and modifications to December, 1945.

"A long step towards the writing of the history of medieval literature in England will have been accomplished when the work of such manuals as this of Professor Wells, which engages our notice shall have been fully understood by the critical world. . . . The wideness and fulness of the author's own reading, the evidence on every page that no work has escaped an individual and independent judgment by the compiler, render the work peculiarly valuable to those who have no time for the original. For such the book is more than a bibliographic manual; it is distinctly informative in an encyclopedia way" — (YALE REVIEW, VOL. VI, 659–660).

"The work is well-done and serves at least two purposes, in that it affords a complete view for the first time of a large body of literature, and provides the fullest possible information short of a critical edition, of any given piece to which reference may be sought. It is particularly useful for indicating where the text of such and such a piece may be found" — (LONDON TIMES LITERARY SUPPLEMENT, September 14, 443).

WELLS, John Edwin.
Ninth Supplement to A Manual of the Writings in Middle English, 1050–1400. New Haven, Conn.: Yale University Press, 1951. pp. 1779–1938.

Additions to and modifications of the basic volume and supplements to December, 1945, by Beatrice Daw Brown, Eleanor K. Heningham, and Francis Lee Utley.

RENAISSANCE AND RESTORATION

GENERAL

HAZLITT, William Carew.
Handbook to the Popular, Poetical, and Dramatic Literature of Great Britain, From the Invention of Printing to the Restoration. London: J. R. Smith, 1867. 701 p.

A two-column format, alphabetically arranged according to author. Bibliographical Collections and Notes on Early English Literature, 1474–1700 (London: Quaritch, 1876–1903) in six volumes, a useful supplement, is alphabetically arranged according to title. Also serviceable is G. J. Gray's GENERAL INDEX TO HAZLITT'S HANDBOOK AND HIS BIBLIOGRAPHICAL COLLECTIONS (London: Quaritch, 1893, 866 p.), which indexes the HANDBOOK and all the volumes of the Bibliographical Collections except the fourth series and the second supplement to the third series.

LOGAN, Terence P.
The Predecessors of Shakespeare: A Survey and Bibliography of Recent Studies in English Renaissance Drama. Edited by Terence P. Logan and D.S. Smith. Lincoln, Nebraska: University of Nebraska Press, 1973. 348 p.

This volume, the first of a "project which will survey recent scholarship on English Renaissance drama exclusive of Shakespeare," is devoted to: Christopher Marlowe, Robert Greene, Thomas Kyd, Thomas Nashe, John Lyly, George Peele, and Thomas Lodge. The starting point of the surveys is 1923, the publication date of E.K. Chamber's THE ELIZABETH STAGE; the cut-off date is 1968. Bibliography; Index of Persons; Index of Plays.

POLLARD, Alfred W. and G. R. Redgrave.
Short-Title Catalogue of Books Printed in England, Scotland, and Ireland, and of English Books Printed Abroad, 1475–1640.
London: Bibliographical Society, 1926. 609 p.

A comprehensive record of English books (some 26,000) arranged according to author. Contains abridged entries of all the English books, copies of which exist at the British Museum, the Bodleian, the Cambridge University Library, and the Henry E. Huntington Library, California. For each entry gives: author, brief title, size, printer, date, reference to entry of the book in the Stationers' registers, and location. Of the libraries referred to, 133 are British, 15 are American. It is supplemented by the Huntington Library Supplement compiled by C. K. Edmonds and published by the Harvard University Press in 1933.

STRATMAN, Carl J.
Restoration and Eighteenth Century Theatre Research: a bibliographical guide, 1900–1968. Carbondale: Southern Illinois University Press, 1972. 811 p.

Divided into subject headings, arranged alphabetically. More than 400 categories are devoted to specific actors, actresses, architects, composers, musicians, playwrights, scene designers, stage managers, etc. Other categories include topics such as ballet, burlesque, pantomime, and type characters. The large majority of the items are annotated.

TANNENBAUM, S. and D. R. Tannenbaum.
Elizabethan Bibliographies. New York: The Author, 1937–1947. No. 1–39.

Brief bibliographies of primary and secondary works, including bibliographies of the sonnets and five plays of Shakespeare (MACBETH, KING LEAR, MERCHANT OF VENICE, OTHELLO, TROILUS AND CRESSIDA). Some of the bibliographies are quite short (Cyril Tourner, 14 p.). Others are relatively long (MACBETH, 165 p., BEN JONSON, 151 p., THE MERCHANT OF VENICE, 140 p.).

The **Elizabethan Bibliographies Supplements**, published by the Nether Press (London) in 1967, contains numbers one through 10; the **Elizabethan Bibliographies Supplements**, published by the same press in 1968–1970, contains numbers 11, 12, 15, 18. Plans include preparation of bibliographies of some Elizabethan authors not covered by Tannenbaum.

WING, DONALD GODDARD.
Short-Title Catalogue of Books Printed in England, Scotland, Ireland, Wales, and British America and of English Books Printed in Other Countries, 1641–1700. New York: Columbia University Press, 1948–1951. 3 v.

A continuation of Pollard and Redgrave, SHORT-TITLE CATA-LOGUE. Locates items in more than 200 libraries, many items being given five locations in Great Britain and five locations in America. Location symbols, however, are in accordance with a system devised by the author, not in accordance with the system followed by the S.T.C. or the UNION CATALOG.

"It was a daring, hazardous and some would say foolhardy undertaking for one man, and if the achievement falls a long way short of perfection, this is not to say that Mr. Wing has not made a most important and serviceable contribution to enumerative bibliography"—(LONDON TIMES LITERARY SUPPLE-MENT, November 14, 1952).

CURRENT

Annual Bibliography of English Language and Literature, 1920–. Edited for the MODERN HUMANITIES RESEARCH ASSOCIATION. London: Cambridge University Press, 1921–. (For annotation, see page 161.)

Philological Quarterly: A Journal Devoted to Scholarly Investigation in the Classical and Modern Languages and Literatures. Iowa City: State University of Iowa Press, 1922–. (For annotation see page 118.)

Progress of Medieval and Renaissance Studies in the United States and Canada. Colorado: University of Colorado Press, 1923–. (For annotation see pages 161–162.)

Research in Progress in the Modern Languages and Literatures,

1948—. (In PMLA, Vol. 63, Supplement, pt. 2, pp. 143–405.) (For annotation, see page 162.)

Shakespeare Quarterly. 1950—. New York: Shakespeare Association of America.

Successor to the Shakespeare Association of America BULLETIN. Contains critical and research articles by scholars from here and abroad on all phases of Shakespeare's life, works, and characters; also, lengthy, detailed book reviews, notes, and comments. The spring issue provides a comprehensive annotated annual bibliography of Shakespeare studies.

Studies in Philology. Chapel Hill, North Carolina: University of North Carolina Press, 1906—. (For annotation see page 121).

Work in Progress . . . in the Modern Humanities, 1938–1942. Cambridge: MODERN HUMANITIES RESEARCH ASSOCIATION, 1938–1942.

The predecessor of RESEARCH IN PROGRESS. No longer published.

Year's Work in English Studies. Edited for the English Association. London: Oxford University Press, 1921—. (For annotation see page 163.)

DISSERTATIONS

For an annotated list of dissertations which are useful to the student of the Renaissance and Restoration periods, see pages 164–167.

EIGHTEENTH CENTURY

GENERAL

ARNOTT, JAMES FULLARTON AND JOHN WILLIAM ROBINSON. **English Theatrical Literature, 1559–1900: A Bibliography.** London: Society for Theatre Research, 1970. 486 p.

A revised and expanded edition of Robert W. Lowe's A BIBLI-OGRAPHICAL ACCOUNT OF ENGLISH THEATRICAL LITERATURE published in 1888. Period coverage is extended and American and other overseas editions are noted. Indexes by author, title, and place of publication.

CORDASCO, FRANCESCO.

Eighteenth Century Bibliographies: handlists of critical studies relating to Smollett, Richardson, Sterne, Fielding, Dibdin, 18th century medicine, the 18th century novel, Godwin, Gibbon, Young, and Burke. To which is added John P. Anderson's bibliography of Smollett. Metuchen, New Jersey: Scarecrow Press, 1970. 230 p.

Reprints, without updating, the bibliographies as they appeared in the series 18TH CENTURY BIBLIOGRAPHICAL PAMPHLETS, no. 1-12 (Brooklyn: Long Island University Press, 1947-50).

CRANE, RONALD S., LOUIS I. BREDVOLD.

English Literature, 1660–1800: A Bibliography of Modern Studies. Compiled for PHILOLOGICAL QUARTERLY. Princeton: Princeton University Press, 1950–1952. Vol. I, 575 p., Vol. II, 579–1292.

Volume I includes reprints of the annual bibliographies published in the PHILOLOGICAL QUARTERLY 1926–1938, covering studies published 1925–1937; Volume II includes reprints of the annual bibliographies published in the PHILOLOGICAL QUARTERLY 1939–1950, covering studies published 1938–1949, and an index to both volumes. In a single alphabet, the index lists: (1) the names of modern scholars whose books and articles have been listed; (2) the names of those who have been the subjects of the studies; (3) topical entries—names of periodicals, place names, themes; (4) selected miscellaneous entries—e.g., Gothic voyages. The basic classifications, within which works are arranged in a chronological order according to authors' surnames, are: (1) Bibliography and Bibliographical Studies; (2) Language; (3) Historical and Social Background; (4) Philosophy, Science, and Religion; (5) Arts and Crafts; (6) Literary History and Criticism; (7) Individual Authors; (8) Continental Background. The reviews of books listed are often very full, scholarly, and readable.

The third and fourth volumes were published in 1962: the third volume, 573 pages, covering the years 1951–1956; the fourth volume, pages 575–1133, covering the years 1957–1960.

"The annotations are generally impressive. The lists of abbreviations show that the search of the periodicals has been thorough. In particular attention has been paid to NOTES AND QUERIES, a journal which is far too often overlooked. . . . A full study of the present volume shows that the book is indispensable to members of English faculties, and can be usefully consulted by readers of literature generally"—(LONDON TIMES LITERARY SUPPLEMENT, September 28, 1952).

TOBIN, JAMES E.
Eighteenth Century English Literature and Its Cultural Background. New York: Fordham University Press, 1939. 190 p.

Contains over 7,000 titles, exclusive of diaries, autobiographies, and journals, representing primary and secondary works. Part I includes: (1) Historical Background; (2) Social Thought; (3) Memoirs, Diaries, Anecdotes; (4) Criticism; (5) Poetry; (6) Prose; (7) Journalism; (8) Drama; (9) Extra National Relations. Part II contains the bibliographies of 169 individual authors (pp. 67–180). Does not provide annotations.

"Professor Tobin has performed a meritorious service by collecting within the covers of one volume a selection of this voluminous material and making it available in convenient form. . . . Brief critical notes appended to some of the titles would have increased the bulk of the volume, but would have immeasurably heightened its value. . . . American journals have been combed more thoroughly than foreign; the files of the Athenaeum, particularly, would have yielded a number of important items"—(LIBRARY QUARTERLY, July, 1940, 446–448).

CURRENT

Annual Bibliography of English Language and Literature, 1920 —. Edited for the MODERN HUMANITIES RESEARCH ASSOCIATION. London: Cambridge University Press, 1921 —. Annual. (For annotation see page 161.)

Philological Quarterly: A Journal Devoted to Scholarly Investigation in the Classical and Modern Languages and Literatures. Iowa City: State University of Iowa Press, 1922—. (For annotation see page 118.)

Research in Progress in the Modern Languages and Literature, 1948—. (In PMLA, Vol. 63, Supplement, pt. 2, pp. 143–405). (For annotation see page 162.)

Work in Progress . . . in the Modern Humanities, 1938–1942. Cambridge: MODERN HUMANITIES RESEARCH ASSOCIATION, 1938–1942. (For annotation see page 163.)

Year's Work in English Studies. Edited for the English Association. London: Oxford University Press, 1921—. (For annotation see page 163.)

DISSERTATIONS

For an annotated list of dissertations which are useful to the student of the Eighteenth Century, see pages 164–167.

NINETEENTH CENTURY

GENERAL

DeLAURA, DAVID J. ed.
Victorian Prose: a Guide to Research. Baltimore: Modern Language Association of America, 1973. 560 p.
Serves as a companion volume to Lionel Stevenson's VICTORIAN FICTION and Frederic E. Faverty's THE VICTORIAN POETS. Mainly devoted to Macaulay, Carlyle, Newman, Mill, Ruskin, Arnold, and Pater. Well organized; skillfully written.

EHRSAM, THEODORE G., ROBERT DEILY.
Bibliographies of Twelve Victorian Authors. New York: H. W. Wilson, 1936. 362 p.

The authors treated are: Elizabeth Barrett Browning, Matthew Arnold, Arthur Clough, Edward Fitzgerald, Thomas Hardy, Rudyard Kipling, William Morris, Christina Rossetti, Robert Louis Stevenson, Charles Swinburne, and Alfred Lord Tennyson. The matter is compiled from over two hundred sources and is divided into biographies, pamphlets, bibliographies, essays, critical analysis, foreign material, unpublished articles, doctoral dissertations, and unpublished master's theses.

"The compilers have done a valuable and lasting piece of work which will inevitably place students of Victorian poetry heavily in their debt"—(MODERN PHILOLOGY, 1936–1937).

"An immense amount of work has gone into the preparation of the bibliographies in this volume. . . . it is distinctly a scholarly book"—(LIBRARY QUARTERLY, 1937, 161–162).

ELKINS, A.C. AND L.J. FORSTNER, eds.
The Romantic Movement Bibliography 1936–1970. Ann Arbor: Pierian Press, 1973. 7 vols.

A revised and expanded edition of Robert W. Lowe's A BIBLI- peared annually in ELH, PHILOLOGICAL QUARTERLY, or ENGLISH LANGUAGE NOTES. The seventh volume contains detailed indexes to the bibliographies.

FAVERTY, FREDERIC EVERETT.
The Victorian Poets: A Guide to Research. Cambridge, Mass.: Harvard University Press, 1968. 433 p.

A handbook of bibliography, scholarship, and criticism. Chapters by specialists are devoted to major authors separately, to minor authors and movements collectively.

A revision and updating of the first edition, published in 1956, with generally the same pattern of organization. The closing date for publications is 1966.

HOUTCHENS, CAROLYN WASHBURN AND LAWRENCE HUSTON HOUTCHENS.
The English Romantic Poets and Essayists: a review of research and criticism. New York: Modern Language Association of America, 1957. 363 p.

A companion volume to Raysor, THE ENGLISH ROMANTIC POETS. Evaluates critical material about ten romantic poets and essayists, giving bibliographies, editions, biographies, and criticism.

RAYSOR, Thomas M.
English Romantic Poets: A Review of Research. New York:
Modern Language Association of America, 1950. 395 p.

Aims to assist the graduate student as he begins his specialized
study of the field of English Romanticism. Includes Wordsworth, Coleridge, Byron, Shelley, and Keats. Lists studies of
ideas, general and miscellaneous criticism, and additional
references on individual poems. Major works are discussed at
relative length; minor works are characterized in a sentence or
two. Has no index.

". . . a godsend to graduate students and almost equally, to
practising specialists in the fields of English Romantic poetry.
. . . The absence of an index is by all means the most serious
defect of the book. It is inexplicable and deplorable that a book
produced under the auspices of an association dedicated to
preserving and propagating the highest standards of scholarly
publication should lack a feature no scholarly volume—least of
all, a collection of bibliographical essays—should be without"—
(PHILOLOGICAL QUARTERLY, XXX, April, 1951, 100–101).

"In ENGLISH ROMANTIC Poets, six of the best American
Scholars have united to produce a book whose modest title is
misleading . . . have, in fact, provided not only the graduate
beginning research, but more advanced students with a suc-
cession of bibliographies, and, in addition, wise and balanced
and sometimes witty comments"—(MODERN LANGUAGE RE-
VIEW, XLVI, 547).

RAYSOR, Thomas Middleton.
The English Romantic Poets: A Review of Research. Rev. ed.
New York: Modern Language Association of America, 1956.
307 p.
This, a revised edition of the work published in 1950, con-
stitutes a companion volume to the Faverty title.

SLACK, Robert C.
**Bibliographies of Studies in Victorian Literature for the Ten
Years 1955–1964.** 461 p.

A reproduction of the annual Victorian Bibliographies for the
ten years 1955–1964 published in the journals MODERN PHILOL-
OGY (1956–1957) and VICTORIAN STUDIES (1958–1965). Includes more than 7,900 entries, excluding book reviews.

STEVENSON, LIONEL (AND OTHERS).
Victorian Fiction: A Guide to Research. Cambridge: Harvard University Press, 1967. 440 p.

A companion to Faverty's VICTORIAN POETS. Separate papers on each of the principal novelists; a survey of research, and a critical evaluation of selected writings in the field.

TEMPLEMAN, WILLIAM D.
Bibliographies of Studies in Victorian Literature for the Thirteen Years 1932–1944. Urbana: University of Illinois Press, 1945. 450 p.

A photoprint of bibliographies published originally in the May issues of MODERN PHILOLOGY, 1933–1945. The main divisions are: (1) Individual Authors; (2) Material Contributed from the Continent; (3) Bibliographical Material; (4) Movements of Ideas and Literary Forms; (5) Anthologies. The additions to the original issues of MODERN PHILOLOGY are simply: a preface, a foreword by Howard Mumford Jones, and a helpful index.

"But his attempt is insufficient; mere aggregation is not cumulation, and a scholar who pays five dollars for the volume might fairly expect it to be something more than the thirteen parts he already had in his file of MODERN PHILOLOGY. The brief index of names that has been added tells us only that items are listed each year under major authors, and somewhat intermittently for those who attract less interest; the skeleton given is not a living index. . . . Because of the photographic reproduction all the page references to earlier numbers of the annual bibliography are wrong—a considerable nuisance. The volume is on the whole a convenience, but it contributes little to the solution of the scholar's problem"—(LIBRARY QUARTERLY, 1945–1946, 362–364).

TOWNSEND, FRANCIS G., ed.
Victorian Bibliography, 1957—. In VICTORIAN STUDIES, Vol. 1, June 1958—.

Continues the list previously published in MODERN PHILOLOGY.

WRIGHT, AUSTIN.
Bibliographies of Studies in Victorian Literature, 1945–1954. Urbana: University of Illinois Press, 1956.

Supplements Templeman's BIBLIOGRAPHIES OF STUDIES IN VICTORIAN LITERATURE FOR THE THIRTEEN YEARS 1932–1944. Each chapter (an annual) contains a brief introduction, general information, and a key of abbreviations. The major divisions of each annual are arranged alphabetically under four headings: (I) Bibliographical Material; (II) Economic, Political, Religious, and Social Environment; (III) Movements of Ideas and Literary Forms; (IV) Individual Authors. The Index comprises a single alphabetical arrangement of the names of authors listed, of Victorian figures written about or mentioned, of selected place names, and of headings relating to background.

"A valuable guide to the work done in the study of Victorian literature, both here and in America, during the ten years, and with editorial notes to indicate the content and importance of the items listed"—(LONDON TIMES LITERARY SUPPLEMENT, Oct. 5, 1956, 591).

"The Index is greatly superior to that of 1945. Cross references are useful. A comprehensive "Key to Abbreviations" among the preliminary matter would be an asset. Wright and his ten compilers should be congratulated for their industry and ability. This text will be of great value to students of the period and to all reference librarians"—(LIBRARY JOURNAL, VOL. 82, 2342)

CURRENT

Annual Bibliography of English Language and Literature, 1920
—. For the publication facts and description of contents, see page 161.)

English Literary History; A Journal of English Literary History. For the publication facts and a description of the basic contents see page 111.

Modern Philology. For the publication facts and a description of contents, see page 117.

Philological Quarterly. For the publication facts and a description of contents, see page 118.

Research in Progress in the Modern Languages and Literature, 1948 —. For the publication facts and a description of contents, see page 162.

Work in Progress. For the publication facts and a description of contents, see page 163.

Year's Work in English Studies. For the publication facts and a description of contents, see page 163.

DISSERTATIONS

For an annotated list of dissertations useful to the student of the nineteenth century, consult pages 164–167.

TWENTIETH CENTURY

GENERAL

MILLETT, FRED B.
Contemporary British Literature: A Critical Survey and 232 Author Bibliographies. Third revised and enlarged edition, based upon the second revised and enlarged edition by J. M. Manly and Edith Rickert. New York: Harcourt, 1935. 556 p.

Something more than a revision and expansion. Contains a 110 page "Critical Survey," discussing general background, the bibliographies of some forty authors not included in the earlier edition, and excludes some thirty authors treated in the earlier edition. The arrangement is alphabetical by writer. Provides a short biography for each author, a fairly complete bibliography of his works (with date of publication only), and biographical and critical studies or reviews arranged alphabetically by author or magazine.

"In general . . . this book has been thoroughly edited and presents a great mass of material in a very convenient form. Librarians, scholars, and students can all make use of this handy reference work"—(LIBRARY JOURNAL, LXI, 108).

"The bibliographies themselves are remarkably full for a work of this kind, and endeavor to list the first appearance, in the British Empire or elsewhere, of every book and pamphlet by the author in question published before January 1, 1935, including translations, but excluding "edited works," such as anthologies. This limitation is rather regrettable, and rules out important books such as Mrs. Meynell's FLOWER OF THE MIND, and Mr. de la Mare's COME HITHER. Pseudonyms are unveiled, and sometimes with surprising results"—(LONDON TIMES LITERARY SUPPLEMENT, January 4, 1936, 17).

CURRENT

Annual Bibliography of English Language and Literature, 1920—. For the publication facts and description of contents, see page 161.

Contemporary Authors. Vol. 1—Quarterly. Detroit: Gale, 1962. Bio-bibliographical guide to new and relatively unknown as well as established authors. Includes American (and a few foreign) writers of juvenile books, fiction, poetry, and nonfiction of general interest. Authors of professional level technological, physical, and biological sciences are not included. Works in progress are indicated.

Research in Progress in the Modern Languages and Literature, 1948—. For the publication facts and a description of contents, see page 162.

Twentieth-Century Literature: A Scholarly and Critical Journal, 1955–56—. Quarterly.
Each quarterly issue contains abstracts of current articles on twentieth-century authors from about a hundred and fifty other journals. No cumulations.

Work in Progress. For the publication facts and a description of contents, see page 163.

DISSERTATIONS

ALTICK, RICHARD DANIEL AND WILLIAM R. MATTHEWS.
Guide to Doctoral Dissertations in Victorian Literature, 1886–1958. Urbana: University of Illinois Press, 1960. 119 p.
A list of 2,105 dissertations from universities in the United States,

United Kingdom, Germany, France, Austria, and Switzerland.
Divisions include generalities, literary forms, literary criticism,
individual authors. Author index.

POWNALL, David E.
Articles on Twentieth Century Literature: An Annotated Bibliography, 1954 to 1970. Los Angeles: IHC Press, 1973.

The first three volumes of a projected seven volume series "includes all of 'Current Bibliography' in twentieth century literature, plus 10,000 articles from other sources." Generally excluded are book reviews, review articles, popular journalism, and elementary level articles on teaching literature. Each entry is numbered and will be cross indexed in the last of the projected seven volumes.

For an annotated list of dissertations useful to the student of the twentieth century, consult pages 164–167.

AMERICAN LITERATURE

GENERAL

BLANCK, Joseph
Bibliography of American Literature. New Haven: Yale University Press, 1955–1963. Vol. 1–4 (In progress).

A selective bibliography of American authors which, when completed, will include the book publications of approximately 300 authors from the beginning of the Federal period up to and including persons who died before the end of 1930.

Material for each author is arranged chronologically and includes: first editions of books and pamphlets; reprints containing textual or other changes; selected lists of biographical, bibliographical, and critical works. Location is indicated for copies examined.

"The study is so thorough that this seems to be the definitive work on its subject. . . . Here is a great encyclopedia of bibliography with which every student of American literature will be delighted and by which he will be aided"—(american literature, volume 28).

"This BIBLIOGRAPHY OF AMERICAN LITERATURE is "skeletal, monumental, and authoritative. It replaces Merle Johnson as he replaced Foley. It holds its place with Allibone, the CAMBRIDGE HISTORY OF AMERICAN LITERATURE, and the post World War II bibliography of Spiller. Collectors will consider it essential and textual students will discover it to be 'exasperatingly helpful'" —(THE BOOK COLLECTOR, SUMMER, 1956, 185–186).

Volume 5, published in 1969, covers Washington Irving to Henry Wadsworth Longfellow.

BRYER, JACKSON R., ed.
Fifteen Modern American Authors: a Survey of Research and Criticism. Durham, North Carolina: Duke University Press, 1969. 493 p.

Patterned after Stovall's EIGHT AMERICAN AUTHORS, this work has similar survey chapters by different scholars, each covering editions, manuscripts and letters, biography, bibliography, critical studies of the individual author. Treated are: Sherwood Anderson, Will Cather, Hart Crane, Theodore Dreiser, T. S. Eliot, William Faulkner, F. Scott Fitzgerald, Robert Frost, Ernest Hemingway, Eugene O'Neil, Ezra Pound, Edwin Arlington Robinson, John Steinbeck, Wallace Stevens, and Thomas Wolfe.

CANTRELL, CLYDE H. AND WALTON R. PATRICK.
Southern Literary Culture: A Bibliography of Masters' and Doctors' Theses. Tuscaloosa: University of Alabama, 1955. 124 p.

A list of masters' and doctors' theses completed through the summer of 1948 in the graduate schools of the United States, dealing with southern culture and literature.

EVANS, CHARLES.
American Bibliography: A Chronological Dictionary of all Books, Pamphlets, and Periodical Publications Printed in the United States of America from the Genesis of Printing in 1639 Down to and Including the Year 1820; with Bibliographical and Biographical Notes. Chicago: Columbia Press, 1903–1934. Vols. 1–12.

For further comment see page 151.

FOLEY, PATRICK K.
American Authors, 1795–1895. A Bibliography of First and Notable Editions Chronologically Arranged with Notes. With an Introduction by W. L. Sawyer. Boston: Publishers' Printing Company, 1897. 350 p.

When published in 1897, it was the most useful work of its kind; although now out-of-date, it still retains some value: It provides: (1) an indication of authors and works that were considered notable at the time; (2) it may serve as a supplement to the CHAL and, when completed, to Blanck's BIBLIOGRAPHY OF AMERICAN LITERATURE for the period 1795–1895.

"Of the 300 authors given, over thirty are unknown even by name to the reviewer, who has been acquainted with the writings of his own countrymen for many years. The omissions are most glaring, among them being Charles A. Dana, Emily Dickinson, Horace Greely, Judge O. W. Holmes, Henry James, and Herbert D. Ward. . . . It is a fairly accurate checklist of the American authors it includes. It contains, also, much information generally unknown before, and is a step in advance of 'Leon's' and 'Stone's' but it falls far short of its opportunities" — (THE CRITIC, September 4, 1897, 123–124).

FULLERTON, BRADFORD M.
A Selective Bibliography of American Literature, 1775–1900. New York: William Payson, 1932.

The aim of the book is to briefly estimate the more important American authors, and to describe their more representative works. The authors are listed alphabetically. Has no index.

"Bradford M. Fullerton manifests fine selective judgement, not merely in the authors presented, but in the details related of them; included are all the writers whom we would expect to find, and many of the less prominent whom we are surprised and also pleased to see. Accuracy and brevity are combined with an interest that only first-hand familiarity with his matter could give" — (AMERICA, XLVIII, 487).

"Mr. Fullerton's SELECTIVE BIBLIOGRAPHY is a handbook that both dispenser and absorber of American first editions must whole-heartedly welcome. If it did nothing but chart new or little trod paths it would fulfill an eminently praiseworthy purpose, but it does more than that. For Mr. Fullerton has made of what might easily have been as arid a performance as a

telephone directory a readable as well as a serviceable manual"
— (THE SATURDAY REVIEW OF LITERATURE, x, 321).

GERSTENBERGER, Donna Lorine and George Herrick.
The American Novel, 1789–1968; A Checklist of Twentieth-
Century Criticism. Denver: A. Swallow, 1970. Vol. 1, 333 p.;
Vol. 2, 459 p.
Three parts: (1) criticism of individual authors (specific novels,
general studies, bibliographies); (2) studies of the American
novel generally (classified as far as possible by century); (3)
bibliographies of sources consulted.

The first volume, published in 1962, covers criticism written
to 1960; the second volume, published in 1970, covers criticism
written 1960 to 1968.

GHODES, Clarence.
Literature and Theater of the States and Regions of the U.S.A.:
an Historical Bibliography. Durham, North Carolina: Duke University Press, 1967. 276 p.

A preliminary checklist of books, chapters from books, pamphlets, periodical articles, anthologies, and monographs from the
earliest times to 1964. Excludes listings of unpublished theses
or dissertations and works dealing with individual authors.

GROSS, Theodore L.
Hawthorne, Melville, Stephen Crane: A Critical Bibliography.
New York: The Free Press, 1972. 301 p.

The selections are generally well chosen, and the annotations
are competent; the emphasis is at times questionable. For Hawthorne there are 196 entries; for Melville there are 186; and
for Crane there are 105. Each section contains a brief survey of
the subject's critical reputation, a biographical chronology, and
bibliographical entries.

JONES, Howard Mumford and Richard M. Ludwig.
Guide to American Literature and its Backgrounds Since 1890.
3rd edition, revised and enlarged. Cambridge, Mass.: Harvard
University Press, 1964.

A guide listing works presenting the intellectual, sociological, and
political backgrounds of American literary history, followed by
reading lists on various aspects and schools in American litera-

ture. Updated by the addition of new lists on biography and drama, new information on periodicals, recent material to the table of events. Indexed by author only.

LEARY, Lewis Gaston.
Articles on American Literature, 1900–1950. Durham, North Carolina: Duke University Press, 1954. 437 p.

A revision and extension of ARTICLES ON AMERICAN LITERATURE, APPEARING IN CURRENT PERIODICALS, 1920–1945. The main part of the work comprises an alphabetical list of articles about the American authors (the American authors being the basis of the arrangement), followed by subject and form groupings.

LEARY, Lewis Gaston.
Articles on American Literature, 1950–1967. Compiled with the Assistance of Carolyn Bartholet and Catherine Roth. Durham, North Carolina: Duke University Press, 1970. 751 p.

A continuation of Leary's bibliography for the 1900–1950 period, compiled on the same principles and employing the same arrangement; but more inclusive (relative to foreign periodical matter) and more selective.

MARSHALL, T. F.
American Literature: An Analytical Index to American Literature, Volumes 1–30 (March, 1929–January, 1959). Durham: Duke University Press, 1963.

Divided into two sections: Author-Subject Index and Book Review Index. The latter has entries for subject as well as for author of book reviewed.

MILLETT, Fred B.
Contemporary American Authors: A Critical Survey and 219 Bio-bibliographies. New York: Harcourt, 1940. 716 p.

A revised and expanded edition of the work of Manly and Rickert. Contains a lengthy critical survey of American literature since 1900 (pp. 1–204). The main part of the text comprises biographical and bibliographical information and a list of studies and articles about the author. The foreword notes: "107 authors have been dropped from the second edition; six authors who were dropped in the second edition have been restored; 30 authors who appeared for the first time in the second edition have been retained and 101 new authors have been added."

"For it is certainly the finest large scale bibliography of contemporary American literature to be issued within the covers of one volume. . . . The book unquestionably belongs in every library and on the desk of every student of contemporary literature" — (THE CHRISTIAN CENTURY, March 6, 1940, 321).

". . . a variety of checkings have led me to a respectful confidence in the accuracy of the book. And I have not only examined it: I am referring to it all the time" (a review of the original edition by P. H. Boynton, NEW REPUBLIC, January 3, 1923).

PALMER, HELEN H. AND ANNE JANE DYSON.
American Drama Criticism: Interpretations, 1890–1965 Inclusive, of American Drama Since the First Play Produced in America. Hamden, Connecticut: Shoe String Press, 1967. 239 p.
Book and periodical materials, arranged by playwright, with index of titles and playwrights.

RUBIN, LOUIS DECIMUS, ed.
A Bibliographical Guide to the Study of Southern Literature. With an appendix containing sixty-eight additional writers of the colonial South. Baton Rouge, Louisiana: Louisiana University Press, 1969. 351 p.
Selected checklists, compiled by one hundred scholars, of literature on twenty-three general topics and more than two hundred individual writers. Following bibliographical surveys of general topics (literary periods, genres, etc.) are checklists of biographical and critical writings on about 135 individual authors. An impressive work.

RUSK, RALPH L.
The Literature of the Middle Western Frontier. New York: Columbia University Press, 1925. 2 vols.

A comprehensive survey and bibliography of the literature of the West before 1840. Volume one contains a history of the pioneer period and a discussion of such interests as cultural beginnings, newspapers and magazines, controversial writings, and fiction. Volume two is a bibliographical volume, following the arrangement of the companion volume, and covering:

cultural beginnings, travel, newspapers, and magazines, controversial writings, scholarly writings, and schoolbooks, fiction, poetry, and drama. Locates copies.

"With the utmost thoroughness and impartiality, Dr. Rusk has traversed every department of literature within his period. . . . His painstaking bibliography will be of permanent value to students of early American literature" — (NORTH AMERICAN REVIEW, CCXII, 1925, 354–357).

"This is a laborious, learned, and useful contribution to the history of the West. It represents a relatively clean sweep of the material on the literary aspect of Western culture, classifying with intelligence and appraising with fairness. . . . We need more books like this, dealing with the bed-rock of Western fact" — (AMERICAN HISTORICAL REVIEW, VOLUME 31, 366).

SABIN, JOSEPH.
Dictionary of Books Relating to America from Its Discovery to the Present Time. New York: Bibliographical Society of America, 1928–1936. 29 v.

For an annotation consult pages 153–154.

SHAW, RALPH R. AND RICHARD H. SHOEMAKER.
American Bibliography. New York: Scarecrow Press, 1963. 3 volumes.
With the publication of these three volumes, two additional volumes in 1964, and a volume of addenda in 1965, Shaw and Shoemaker have continued with their twenty volumes covering the period 1801–1819. These volumes are meant to be a continuation of the work by Evans, also called AMERICAN BIBLIOGRAPHY.

SPILLER, ROBERT E. (AND OTHERS).
Literary History of the United States. New York: Macmillan, 1948. 3 vols.

Volume I constitutes a history of American literature from Colonial beginnings to the Civil War; Volume II constitutes a history of American literature from the end of the Civil War to the present; Volume III constitutes the Bibliography, the main divisions of which are: Guide to resources; Literature and culture; Movements and Influences; and Individual authors. In addition to the 207 individual author bibliographies there is information on separate and collected works, edited texts and reprints, biography and criticism, primary sources, and bibliographies. Volumes one and two have no footnotes; volume three contains an author and subject index.

In the third edition, published in 1963, the main text remains the same, except for minor corrections, but two chapters have been added: one covering the period between the two World wars, the other covering the period since 1945. In addition, the two bibliographical volumes have been combined into one with a general index integrating the entries of the two earlier volumes.

"Editors and contributors seem to have no clear conception of their function as either literary historians or literary critics. They are little concerned with theories as to how a literary history should be written. They have a great concern with social backgrounds and implications of our literature. The soundest discussions are those which sum up what is known and thought about the major writers in New England. The weakest chapters are those about writers and topics which have attracted little attention from scholars. The least satisfactory chapters are on twentieth century authors and on writers of the South and West in all periods"—(SOUTH ATLANTIC QUARTERLY, 48:452–467).

STOVALL, FLOYD.
Eight American Authors: a Review of Research and Criticism. New York: Modern Language Association of America, 1956. 418 p.

Eight essays, each by a different scholar, commenting on the published bibliographies, editions, biographies, and critical studies of the authors treated. The eight American authors treated are: Poe, Emerson, Hawthorne, Thoreau, Melville, Whitman, Mark Twain, and Henry James. "A Bibliographical Supplement," compiled by J. Chesley Mathews (New York, 1963), lists a selection of later studies, to the early part of 1962.

TRENT, WILLIAM P. (AND OTHERS).
Cambridge History of American Literature. New York: Putnam, 1917–1921. 4 vols.

The 1954 reissue by Macmillan in three volumes is textually complete, but lacks the bibliographies (indexed in Northup's REGISTER) which are an important feature of the original edition.

Volume one covers colonial and revolutionary literature; volume two, early and later national literature; volumes three and four, later national literature. In its time, and perhaps at present, the most important history of American literature.

"A valuable, comprehensive, and from beginning to end, a more interesting book. Emphasis must be laid upon the care and detail which the authors and editors have devoted to the early literature of our land . . . is of the utmost importance" — (THE NEW YORK TIMES, November 25, 1917).

"This history brings to our notice writers whom we should otherwise have overlooked; fills up gaps in our knowledge of the literary history of the country, and supplies accurate data as to the various activities of the press and the biographies of writers" — (SATURDAY REVIEW OF LITERATURE, May 31, 1919).

"This lack of balance, together with the lack of contagious enthusiasm in the writing, and the dearth of comparative estimates, constitute in our view faults which prevent us from extending such a cordial reception to the second volume as we did to the first" — (THE TIMES LITERARY SUPPLEMENT, July 17, 1919).

WRIGHT, LYLE HENRY.
American Fiction, 1774–1850: A Contribution Toward a Bibliography. 2d rev. ed. San Marino, California: Huntington Library, 1969. 411 p.

This edition has one hundred and forty-three titles not found in the revised edition of 1948. The appendix, however, has been eliminated since virtually all the titles listed have been located, and those which qualified incorporated into the main work.

CURRENT

American Literature, 1929 — . North Carolina: Duke University Press, 1929—. For an annotation see page 109–110

American Literature Abstracts: A Review of Current Scholarship in the Field of American Literature. Vol. 1, no. 1—, Dec. 1967—.

San Jose, California: Department of English, San Jose State College, 1967.

Publication is semiannual, December and June. Includes abstracts of periodical articles and a "Book Review Consensus" which reports the tenor of reviews of recent books in the field. Author and subject index in each issue.

Annual Bibliography of English Language and Literature, 1920—. Edited for the MODERN HUMANITIES RESEARCH ASSOCIATION. See page 161.

Publications of the Modern Language Association of America. Baltimore, 1884—.

For an annotation see pages 118–119.

DISSERTATIONS

Dissertation Abstracts: A Guide to Dissertations and Monographs Available in Microform. Ann Arbor, Michigan: University Microfilms, 1952—. (For an annotation see page 164.)

Doctoral Dissertations Accepted by American Universities. Compiled for the Association of Research Libraries. New York: Wilson, 1934—. Annual. (For an annotation, consult page 164.)

LEARY, LEWIS G.
Doctoral Dissertations in American Literature, 1933–1948. Durham, North Carolina: Duke University Press, 1950. 230 p.

Basically a reprint from the May, 1948 issue of AMERICAN LITERATURE, with corrections and additional titles. Dissertations in progress are printed in roman type; those completed are printed in italics. Titles are listed alphabetically in two groups: (1) "Dissertations on Individual Authors"; (2) "Dissertations on General Topics."

LEISY, ERNEST E. AND JAY B. HUBBELL.
Doctoral Dissertations in American Literature. Durham, North Carolina: Duke University Press, 1933.

Basically a reprint from the May, 1933 issue of AMERICAN LITERATURE, with corrections and some additional titles.

List of American Doctoral Dissertations Printed in 1912–1928. Washington, D.C.: Government Printing Office, 1913–1940. 26 vols. (For an annotation see page 165.)

Microfilm Abstracts: A Collection of Abstracts of Doctoral Dissertations and Monographs Which are Available in Complete Form on Microfilm. Ann Arbor, Michigan: University Microfilms, 1938–. (For an annotation see page 166.)

PALFREY, T. H., H. E. COLEMAN.
Guide to Bibliographies of Theses, United States and Canada. 2d ed. Chicago: American Library Association, 1940. 54 p. (For an annotation see page 166–167

ROSENBERG, RALPH P.
Bibliographies of Theses in America. (In the BULLETIN OF BIBLIOGRAPHY for September–December, 1945, and January–April, 1946.)

Constitutes a supplement to GUIDE TO BIBLIOGRAPHIES (Palfrey and Coleman), with corrections and additions.

WOODRESS, JAMES L.
Doctoral Dissertations in American Literature 1891–1966. Newly rev. and enl. ed., with the assistance of Marian Koritz. Durham, North Carolina: Duke University Press, 1968. 185 p.

Comprises theses written at approximately one hundred universities in the United States and Western Europe. Includes completed theses and those in progress. The arrangement is alphabetical according to author and according to topic.

The 1962 edition, published in 1962, includes the years 1956–1961 and adds to the entries in the 1957 publication the following: 809 new titles and 150 titles previously reported as in progress. This edition represents a complete resetting, incorporating into the main body of the work materials from the supplement of the 1962 edition and new materials through 1966.

". . . the whole is carefully prepared and, of course, offers a most valuable tool to all advanced students and researchers in the field of American literature"—(AMERICAN LITERATURE, XXIX, November, 1957, 343).

AUTHOR BIBLIOGRAPHIES

English

Beowulf, and The Fight at Finnsburh: A Bibliography. Edited by Donald K. Fry. Charlottesville (published for the Bibliographical Society of the University of Virginia): The University Press of Virginia, 1969. 222 p.

Listed by author; subject index; 2,280 entries.

MATTHEW ARNOLD

SMART, THOMAS BURNETT.
The Bibliography of Matthew Arnold. London: J. Davy & Sons, 1892.

Provides a list of poems in each Arnold volume, a record of exclusions and republications, a "synoptical index," and a chronological arrangement of critical material regarding Arnold. In volume fifteen of THE WORKS OF MATTHEW ARNOLD, published in 1904, the Smart bibliography, although expanded, lacks the list of criticisms and reviews of Arnold's writings. (A more recent bibliography of Arnold is found in TWELVE VICTORIAN AUTHORS by Ehrsam, Deily, and Smith.)

JANE AUSTEN

CHAPMAN, ROBERT WILLIAM.
Jane Austen: A Critical Bibliography. Oxford: The Clarendon Press, 1953.

In a sense, an exceptionally selective bibliography since, as Chapman himself notes in the "Preface," it does not include editions of Austen's works beyond 1890; nor does it aim to be as complete, up to 1938, as is the CAMBRIDGE BIBLIOGRAPHY OF ENGLISH LITERATURE. Well annotated references to books, magazines, and journals; includes "numerous references to Austen in letters, diaries, and books . . . usually hard to find." (The G. L. Keynes bibliography of Jane Austen, published in 1929, provides more details of publication, but is less fully annotated.)

FRANCIS BACON

GIBSON, R. W.
Francis Bacon: A Bibliography of His Works and His Baconiana to the Year 1750. Oxford: The Scrivener Press, 1950. 369 p.

The introductory pages (xiii–xvii) list chronologically, according to the date of their first separate appearance in print, the editions of the works of Bacon and, through the use of the asterisk, the reproduction (or not) of the title page in the bibliography. Under the heading of Baconiana are included all the works of Francis Bacon which have been issued as supplements to or as parts of works by other authors: minor pieces; works ascribed to him; excerpts or quotations from his works; dedications and allusions to him, etc. (pp. 223–227). Also notes the works and editions which are erroneously cited by "authorities," those which have not been traced to a definite source, and items wrongly attributed to Bacon (pp. 325–327).

WILLIAM BLAKE

BENTLEY, G. E. AND MARTIN K. NURMI.
A Blake Bibliography: Annotated List of Works, Studies, and Blakeana. Minneapolis, Minn.: University of Minnesota Press, 1964. 393 p.

Aims to list every reference to William Blake published between 1757 and 1863 and every criticism and edition of his works from the beginning to the present. An introductory essay defines the best work that has been done and the areas that have been neglected. Specimen copies of all works published before 1831 are traced to specific libraries, and each of Blake's manuscripts is traced to its present owner. Includes hundreds of articles (in many languages) not found in earlier bibliographies of Blake. The contents of the work are: Blake's Chronology; I, Editions of Blake's Writing; II, Reproductions of Drawings and Paintings; III, Engravings; IV, Catalogues and Bibliographies; V, Books Owned by Blake; Index.

ROBERT BROWNING

BROUGHTON, L. NATHAN, CLARK SUTHERLAND NORTHUP, ROBERT PEARSALL.
Robert Browning: A Bibliography, 1830–1950. Ithaca, New York: Cornell University Press, 1953. 446 p.

The most complete record of the works of Robert Browning, of his correspondence, and of writings about him. The poet's separate works are elaborately described in chronological order, with the later editions following the original issue; fugitive pieces, those published in periodicals, and posthumous poems are given a separate arrangement, as are the collections and selections of his poetry beginning with the POEMS OF 1849; critical notices, other than those formally listed, are conveyed through the practice of citing reviews and articles "referring to or inspired by major biographical or critical items under those items;" the letters are arranged chronologically, noting the place of composition, the name of addressee, the place of first or most convenient later publication, and, where possible, the location of the holograph. Also contains: "a list of translations of Browning into European languages, a list of 419 musical settings of his works, and a most interesting bibliography of criticism, appreciation, and parody in verse."

DeVANE, W. C.
A Browning Handbook. New York: Crofts & Company, 1955.

Attempts to deal with each of Browning's poems in chronological order, giving, as far as possible, the genesis, sources, history, and appropriate critical and scholarly works on it.

ROBERT BURNS

EGERER, J. W.
A Bibliography of Robert Burns. Edinburgh. London: Oliver & Boyd, 1964. 396 p.

A chronological arrangement of the editions and translations of Burns's works, with full descriptions for editions 1786–1802, and briefer listings for later editions.

CHAUCER

GRIFFITH, DUDLEY DAVID.
Bibliography of Chaucer, 1908–1953. Seattle, Washington: University of Washington Press, 1955. 398 p.

Continues Caroline E. Spurgeon's FIVE HUNDRED YEARS OF CHAUCER CRITICISM AND ALLUSION: 1357–1900 and Eleanor Prescott Hammond's CHAUCER, A BIBLIOGRAPHICAL Manual. It is not only more current than the Spurgeon and Hammond works; it supplies some significant omissions in the earlier bibliographies. It contains a fuller index than Griffith's 1926 edition and is the result of a study of a larger number of periodicals. It is provided with a supplement designed to enable scholars to limit the references they need to consult to three: the Hammond, the Spurgeon, and the 1955 Griffith volumes. Among the background sections having unquestionable usefulness is: "General Backgrounds."

CRAWFORD, WILLIAM R.
Bibliography of Chaucer, 1954–63. Seattle: University of Washington Press, 1967. 144 p.

A supplement to Griffith's BIBLIOGRAPHY OF CHAUCER, 1908–1953.

SAMUEL TAYLOR COLERIDGE

HANEY, JOHN LOUIS.
A Bibliography of Samuel Taylor Coleridge. Philadelphia, 1903. 144 p.

Enumerates all the editions of the poet's works—English, American, Continental, and arranges them in chronological order. Although dated it is still useful especially for the list of books containing Coleridge's marginalia.

KENNEDY, V. W. AND M. N. BARTON.
Samuel Taylor Coleridge: A Selected Bibliography. Baltimore: Enoch Pratt Free Library, 1935. 151 p.

A list of all the available editions of his writings, of biographies and criticisms of him, and of references showing his relations with contemporaries. Selected for its usefulness to students and teachers. Favors recent editions to older ones; most of the critical works listed appeared between 1914–1934.

WISE, THOMAS J.
A Bibliography of the Writings in Prose and Verse of Samuel Taylor Coleridge. London, 1913.

Lists memoirs, periodical publications, and collected editions of the works of Coleridge. Three principal parts are: I, "Editiones Principes," which includes some 107 items written by the subject; II, "Contributions to Periodical Literature," which consists of poems and minor verses that appeared for the first time in the pages of annuals, magazines, and newspapers, or in books by other authors; III, "Collected Editions of the Poetical and Dramatic Works."

JOSEPH CONRAD

EHRSAM, THEODORE GEORGE.
A Bibliography of Joseph Conrad. Metuchen, New Jersey: Scarecrow, 1969. 448 p.

Includes editions and studies to early 1968. Thoroughness most apparent in the largest section "Bibliographical and Critical Material," which lists books and articles about Conrad in English, French, German, Polish, Dutch, Italian, and Spanish.

TEETS, BRUCE E.
Joseph Conrad: An Annotated Bibliography of Writings about Him. Comp. and ed. by Bruce E. Teets and Helmut E. Gerber. Illinois: Northern Illinois University Press, 1971. 671 p.

The 1977 entries, dated between 1895 and 1966, include abstracts of writings in about fourteen languages and publications of all kinds: reviews, general appreciations, bibliographies, biographies, critical studies, articles, dissertations.

DANIEL DEFOE

MOORE, JOHN ROBERT.
A Checklist of the Writings of Daniel Defoe. Bloomington: Indiana University Press, 1960, 254 p.

A chronological arrangement of Defoe's works in three sections: Part I, Books, Pamphlets, Poems, and Manuscripts; Part II, Undated Works Published Posthumously; Part III, Periodicals (those edited by Defoe and those to which he contributed). For each book and pamphlet, Moore provides a transcript of the title page, including mottoes, contents, imprints, and prices (where possible). He records format and pagination and, for most entries, gives explanatory notes. Problems of issue and edition are raised and, at times, resolved. Reissues under variant titles are identified. Each entry concludes with a listing of libraries where copies, particularly first editions, can be acquired. Two indexes are included, an alphabetical list of Defoe's known printers and booksellers, and an alphabetical list of Defoe's works.

CHARLES DICKENS

GOLD, JOSEPH.
The Stature of Dickens: a Centenary Bibliography. Toronto,
Canada: University of Toronto Press, 1971. 236 p.

The introduction provides a list of sources and aids to the bibliographer and scholar. The four main sections contain: I, lists of
books, essays, and articles primarily on Dickens and includes
selected reviews of some . . . recent works of criticism; II, list
of books, essays, selected early reviews and articles on single
novels and on A CHRISTMAS CAROL, and a section on Dickens'
Letters; III, list of Doctoral Dissertations; IV, books either making significant mention of Dickens or which seem important to
the background study of some aspect of Dickens' work. Listing
is chronological.

KITTON, F. G.
**Dickensiana: A Bibliography of the Literature Relating to
Charles Dickens and His Writings.** London: George Redway,
1886.

A comprehensive catalogue of all the writings of Dickens and
of many works about him, with copious extracts from reviews
of his works and comments on his character.

MILLER, WILLIAM.
The Dickens Student and Collector: A List of Writings Relating
to Charles Dickens and His Works, 1836–1945. Cambridge:
Harvard University Press, 1946. 351 p.

An extensive list of writings about Dickens and his work arranged
by subject and, under subject, chronologically. Chapter headings include the biographical, critical, dramatic, musical, antho-
logical, topographical, plagiaristic, and bibliographical. The index
is detailed. However, as more than one reviewer has indicated,
the work of Miller has serious omissions. Compared to the bibliography of Templeman, covering the years 1932–1944, the
former work misses "ten out of seventy-nine books and pamphlets, five out of forty-four portions of books, thirty-five out of
119 major articles of three pages or more, and forty-four out of
fifty articles of less than three pages." In addition, over the same
period, it fails to include thirty-five articles contained in THE

TIMES LITERARY SUPPLEMENT, forty-six which are present in NOTES AND QUERIES, and over four hundred which are contained in Frederic G. Kitton's DICKENSIANA.

JOHN DONNE

KEYNES, GEOFFREY.
A Bibliography of Dr. John Donne. 3rd ed. Cambridge: Cambridge University Press, 1958. 195 p.

A revised and enlarged edition of the Keynes bibliography first printed in 1914. The major divisions are: Prose Works, Poetical Works, Walton's LIFE OF DONNE, Biography and Criticism, Appendixes, Libraries Consulted, List of Printers and Publishers from 1607 to 1719, and a General Index. The prose pieces are arranged as follows: Pseudo-martyr, Conclave Ignati, Sermons, Devotions, Juvenalia, Biathanatos, Essays in Divinity, and Letters. The poetical works are divided into: Occasional Pieces, Anniversaries, and Collected Poems. The section on Biography and Criticism contains a short introduction and the list of books and articles about Donne and his work. A comprehensive, scholarly, and well annotated bibliography.

ROBERTS, JOHN R.
John Donne: An Annotated Bibliography of Modern Criticism, 1912–1967. Columbia, Missouri: University of Missouri Press, 1973. 323 p.

Extends significantly, but does not replace, the bibliography by Geoffrey Keynes. The 1280 annotated entries (articles, books, parts of books) are arranged alphabetically by author for each year covered. There are three indexes: authors and editors of works cited, subjects mentioned in the entries, and title of Donne's works mentioned in entries.

JOHN DRYDEN

MACDONALD, HUGH.
John Dryden: A Bibliography of Early Editions and of Drydeniana. New York: Oxford University Press, 1939, 358 p.

A thorough, scholarly, and virtually definitive primary bibliography "interspersed with valuable disquisitions on biographical and literary background." Among the twelve sections of the work are those covering: poems, plays, prologues and epilogues, prose, letters, and Drydeniana. With slight exceptions, the year 1700 is the terminal date for entries. A thiry-two page author-subject index.

MACDONALD, HUGH AND JAMES MARSHALL OSBORN.
Macdonald's Bibliography of Dryden: An Annotated Check List of Selected American Libraries. Chicago: University of Chicago Press, 1941. (Extract from *Modern Philology* 39: 69–98, 197–212. Aug. and Nov. 1941.)

Locates copies in ten American libraries and includes "notes and additions and corrections to more than a third of Macdonald's descriptions."

MONK, S. H.
Dryden: A List of Critical Studies, 1895–1948. Minneapolis, 1950.

Contains 768 entries, arranged alphabetically in eleven divisions. Many cross references. Asterisks indicate those titles which are considered to present new material or interesting and new points of view. The year 1948 is the terminal date for the entries.

T. S. ELIOT

GALLUP, DONALD CLIFFORD.
T. S. Eliot: A Bibliography. Rev. and extended ed. New York: Harcourt, Brace & World, 1969. 414 p.

Extends through 1967 (a few 1968 items) the material contained in the 1952 edition.

MARTIN, MILDRED.
A Half-Century of Eliot Criticism: An Annotated Bibliography of Books and Articles in English, 1916–1965. Lewisburg, Pa.: Bucknell University Press, 1972. 361 p.

An exhaustive, annotated bibliography containing almost 2700 entries arranged chronologically. Works of special value are starred. Author, subject, and periodical indices quite useful.

HENRY FIELDING

CORDASCO, F.
"Henry Fielding." A List of Critical Studies Published from 1875–1946. **18th Century Bibliographical Pamphlets, No. 5.** Brooklyn: Long Island University Press, 1948.

A handlist of general histories and articles. Cites reviews only for important works. Little annotation. The general section titles are: Bibliography, Biography, General Criticism. Some works are listed by name of author; others by name of magazine. Many important studies appear to be omitted, particularly relative to JOSEPH ANDREWS and AMELIA.

OLIVER GOLDSMITH

SCOTT, TEMPLE.
Oliver Goldsmith, Biographically and Bibliographically Considered, Based on the Collection of Materials in the Library of W. M. Elkins, Esq. New York: Bowling Green Press, 1928.

A weaving of bibliographical details and the facts of publication into the story of Goldsmith's life. Even the letters of the subject are included in the text. The general result is twofold: the reader or student not only understands the exact chronological order of the works, but appreciates the circumstances under which they were composed; on the other hand, he is hampered by the omission of proper documentation. The bibliography is very full and painstaking; the indexes are inadequate.

THOMAS GRAY

NORTHUP, CLARK SUTHERLAND.
A Bibliography of Thomas Gray. New Haven: Yale University Press. 1917. 296 p.

Aims to record all the editions of Gray's work and of the reviews, critical notices, and studies relating to him from the beginning to the year of publication. For the ELEGY alone, there are over 650 entries; comprising some 250 editions, and including more than 130 translations into fifteen different languages, among them Hebrew, Russian, and Japanese; and upwards of 150 parodies and imitations. Admirably planned and arranged, with a useful (if not exhaustive) index.

STARR, HERBERT W.
A Bibliography of Thomas Gray, 1917–1951. Philadelphia: University of Pennsylvania Press for Temple University Publications, 1953.

An excellent supplement to C. S. Northup's A BIBLIOGRAPHY OF THOMAS GRAY (1917); for as Professor Starr notes in his Preface: "Most of the material represented is that published since 1916, the last year covered in Professor Clark S. Northup's" work. Some of the entries in Starr's work, as he also observes, are from an earlier period; namely, publications omitted by Northup or supplementary to those which he has included. Finally, to expedite the location of the new entries in his bibliography, Professor Starr prints after the number of each item the number which does or should accompany the entry in Professor Northup's compilation. The more important treatments of Gray are in most instances indicated by an asterisk; and, when the title fails to define the contents of a volume of material, a brief descriptive note accompanies the entry. The index is unusually useful and frequently must be consulted to note additional information, since, among other things, it refers the reader "to critical articles which mention or discuss one of Gray's works that it has not seemed necessary to list in the description of the article given in the text of the bibliography."

THOMAS HARDY

GERBER, HELMUT E. AND W. EUGENE DAVIS.
Thomas Hardy: An Annotated Bibliography of Writings about Him. Illinois: Northern Illinois University Press, 1973. 841 p.

A year-by-year annotated listing of over 3000 items (1871–1969), most of which were written in English and published in England or America. Annotation consists of abstracts of the authors' arguments, as often as possible in his own words. American dissertations are listed, with Dissertation abstracts references. Index of authors; titles of secondary works; periodicals and newspapers; foreign languages; primary titles. Annotations are almost entirely descriptive, rather than critical or evaluative.

PURDY, RICHARD LITTLE.
Thomas Hardy: A Bibliographical Study. London: Oxford University Press, 1954.

An attempt to record every printing of Hardy's works, to give full and detailed descriptions of the appearance of all first editions as far as possible, and to locate and describe manuscripts.

Does not attempt to record translations of Hardy's works. The divisions and organization of the work are as follows; I. "Editiones Principes," II. "Collected Editiones," III. "Uncollected Contributions to Books, Periodicals, and Newspapers." The Appendixes include: I. "A Calendar of Hardy-Tinsley Letters 1860–75," II. "Six Letters of Leslie Stephen as Editor of the CORNHILL relating to FAR FROM THE MADDING CROWD," III. "A Note on Tillotson and Son and their Newspaper Fiction Bureau," IV. "A Note on the Honorable Mrs. Arthur Henniker," V. "A Note on the Privately Printed Pamphlets of Clement Shorter and Mrs. Hardy," VI. "A Note on the Hardy Players, with a List of their Productions." An Excellent work. According to Professor Weber: "Every serious student of Hardy, every library where his works are studied, will want a copy of this bibliography. It is a definitive piece of work—thorough, authoritative, clear, methodical, precise, and in all but a few instances accurate."

WEBER, C. J.

The First Hundred Years of Hardy, 1840–1940: A Centenary Bibliography of Hardiana. New York: Russell and Russell, 1965. 276 p.

An attempt to list everything written about Hardy anywhere during the period 1840–1940, including works about him in foreign languages, such as Swedish, Russian, Italian, Polish, Chinese, Japanese. Weber does not include writings by Hardy himself because, as he explains in the Preface, Professor Purdy was, at that time, preparing his bibliography of all of Hardy's works. Authors are listed alphabetically and, under each author, works are listed alphabetically. Where articles are unsigned, they are given chronologically under the name of the publication in which they appeared. According to one reviewer (MP XL, 1942–43), the Weber work is "remarkable for its variety, pervasiveness, and persistence." A glaring shortcoming is the lack of an index.

GERARD MANLEY HOPKINS

COHEN, EDWARD H.

Works and Criticism of Gerard Manley Hopkins: A Comprehensive Bibliography. Washington: Catholic University of America Press, 1969. 217 p.

A chronological listing with an index of critics.

SEELHAMMER, Ruth.
Hopkins at Gonzaga. Chicago: Loyola University Press, 1970. 272 p.

A bibliography based on the collection in the Crosby Library at Gonzaga University, Spokane, Washington. Includes works by and about Hopkins.

ALFRED E. HOUSMAN

EHRSAM, T. G.
A Bibliography of Alfred E. Housman. Boston: F. W. Faxon Company, 1941.

The main sections are: (1) material written by Housman, with reviews thereof; (2) volumes edited by Housman, with reviews thereof; (3) translations by Housman; (4) prefaces by Housman; (5) material written about Housman; and (6) bibliographical material about Housman. Section five comprises about half of the volume; in this the books and articles are arranged alphabetically by author or, in the case of anonymous materials, by title. The closing date for the books and articles is 1940. A thorough and conscientious work. Does not have an index. Additions to the Ehrsam bibliography are supplied by Stallman (PMLA, 1960), in whose supplement there is full information for all entries.

SAMUEL JOHNSON

ADAM, R. B.
The R. B. Adam Library Relating to Dr. Samuel Johnson and his Era. 3 volumes. New York: Oxford University Press, 1930.

Records and reproductions of the greatest Johnsonian collection in the world. Includes: portraits of members of the Johnson Club; Letters of Johnson and his friends; corrected proof pages and fragments of memoirs and notes; drafts of Johnson for his DICTIONARY, autographs of the period.

CLIFFORD, James L.
Johnsonian Studies, 1887–1950: A Survey and a Bibliography.

Minneapolis, Minnesota University of Minnesota Press, 1951. 140 p.

This bibliography is divided into twenty-four parts, among which are: the catalogues and bibliographies proper, Boswell, Johnson's personal relationships, miscellaneous, Johnson's prose style, and sections on Johnson's individual works. The most important items are indicated by an asterisk; cross references, where called for, are given. An attempt is made to list every separately printed book and pamphlet and to track down private printings and scrappiana in remote and widespread collections. The index is limited. Only proper names 1887–1950 are given; titles of articles and books are omitted, as well as general classification by subject.

CLIFFORD, JAMES LOWRY AND DONALD J. GREENE.
Samuel Johnson: A Survey and Bibliography of Critical Studies. Minneapolis: University of Minnesota Press, 1970. 333 p.

Combines the listings in Clifford's JOHNSONIAN STUDIES 1887–1950 and the supplementary listing for 1950–60 which appeared in Magdi Wahba's collection of Johnsonian studies, with new listings for the 1960–68 period. Chronological arrangement within topical divisions; author and subject index.

COURTNEY, WILLIAM PRIDEAUX AND DAVID NICHOL SMITH.
Bibliography of Johnson. Oxford: Clarendon Press, 1915 (reissue, 1925). 186 p.

The aim, as stated in the Preface, is to record the publication of Johnson's writings, but it does more than merely list the editions, "the bibliography being so treated as to present the main facts of Johnson's literary career in the form of a series of interesting CAUSERIES, in which is incorporated not only matter that has hitherto been more or less inaccessible, but also much that is new." Thus fourteen pages are devoted to RASSELAS and some thirty pages to the DICTIONARY and the LIVES OF POETS. There are many quotations from Johnson himself and many from friends and acquaintances about him; and the work is so thorough that it provides the source of every quotation, comment, and criticism made in it. Lists over thirty editions of THE LIVES OF THE MOST EMINENT ENGLISH POETS, tells when and where they were published, and includes notes of particular interest concerning them. As enjoyable and readable a work as it is useful.

JAMES JOYCE

DEMING, ROBERT H.
A Bibliography of James Joyce Studies. Lawrence, Kansas: University of Kansas Publications, 1964.

Complements Slocum and Cahoon's bibliography, providing material about Joyce up to 1961. Annotated. Contains an index of authors, reviewers, and editors.

PARKER, ALDEN.
James Joyce: A Bibliography of His Writings, Critical Materials and Miscellany. Boston, 1948.

The critical material is comprised of two divisions: books, and periodicals and reviews. The articles are briefly annotated, unless the title is sufficiently explanatory. The inclusion dates are 1914–1947.

SLOCUM, JOHN J. AND HERBERT CAHOON.
A Bibliography of James Joyce, 1882–1941. London: Hart-Davis, 1953. 195 p.

Does not include critical works about Joyce. A listing of the Slocum collection of Joyce materials now in the Yale University Library.

SLOCUM, J. J. AND HERBERT CAHOON.
Bibliography of James Joyce, 1882–1941. New Haven: Yale University Press, 1953. 195 p.

Extensive compilation, including much data previously unrecorded. Surviving manuscripts of James Joyce are described at length. Does not include critical works about Joyce. Based on the Slocum collection of Joyce material now in the Yale University Library. The collations include data on the author's books and their editions, periodical and newspaper contributions, translations into foreign languages and unlisted printings of books and pamphlets.

JOHN KEATS

MACGILLIVRAY, J. R.
Keats, A Bibliography and Reference Guide. Toronto: University of Toronto Press, 1949. 210 p.

A comprehensive survey of Keats' scholarship to 1949. Contains about 1250 entries, many of them annotated. The starting date is 1816. Omits certain classes of material, including Keats' manuscripts.

RUDYARD KIPLING

MARTINDELL, E. W.
A Bibliography of the Works of Rudyard Kipling 1881–1921. London, 1922.

The two principal divisions are: "Early and Collected Editions" (by far the larger section) and "Uncollected Contributions to Periodical Literature, Books, Etc." The compilation is, for the period covered, thorough. When reviewed in 1922 (TIMES LITERARY SUPPLEMENT, July 13), the author of the article stated that the "Martindell bibliography is not likely to be superseded for some time." A serious omission in the work, however, is the exclusion of manuscript data.

STEWART, JAMES McG.
Rudyard Kipling: A Bibliographical Catalogue. Toronto: Dalhousie University Press and University of Toronto Press, 1959. 673 p.

A descriptive bibliography of Kipling's published works appearing in book form, based largely on the author's collection bequeathed to Dalhousie University. Appendices include: Items in sales catalogues; Uncollected prose and verse; Works in anthologies and readers; Collected sets; Musical settings; Unauthorized editions.

D.H. LAWRENCE

ROBERTS, WARREN.
A Bibliography of D.H. Lawrence. London: Hart Davis, 1963. 399 p.

The main contents are: Books and Pamphlets; Contributions to Books; Contributions to Periodicals; Translations; Manuscripts; Books and Pamphlets about D. H. Lawrence. Appendices list parodies, piracies, and forgeries of *Lady Chatterley's Lover* and other Spurious Works. Index. Manuscripts are not cross-referenced with published versions, but the work is generally thorough and scholarly.

CHRISTOPHER MARLOWE

TANNENBAUM, Samuel Aaron.
Christopher Marlowe: A Concise Bibliography. New York: Scholars' Facsimiles and Reprints, 1937.

A list of poems, plays, and reference sources gathered almost wholly from the books and periodicals in the New York Public Library and in the Library of Columbia University and from unpublished theses and dissertations. In 1947 Samuel and Dorothy Tannenbaum published a Supplement. The basic bibliography has two principal divisions; (1) plays and poems by Marlowe; (2) biography and commentary. Entries in part one are alphabetically arranged by title; entries in part two are alphabetically arranged by author. In the Supplement there are nine divisions: (1) plays; (2) poems; (3) apocrypha; (4) collected works; (5) selection; (6) commentary; (7) Marlowe in fiction; (8) bibliography; (9) addenda. All entries in each division are alphabetically arranged by author. Both the original bibliography and the supplement have an "Index of Names and Subjects."

JOHN MILTON

FLETCHER, Harris Francis.
Contributions to a Milton Bibliography, 1800–1930. Urbana: University of Illinois Press, 1931.

A list of addenda to Stevens' Reference GUIDE TO MILTON.

HUCKABY, Calvin.
John Milton: A Bibliographical Supplement, 1929–1957. Pittsburgh: Duquesne University Press, 1960. 211 p.

Designed to supplement the bibliographies by David Harrison Stevens and Harriet F. Fletcher. Lists significant books and articles of the period covered and includes some doctoral dissertations and master's theses.

STEVENS, David Harrison.
Reference Guide to Milton: From 1800 to the Present Day. Chicago: University of Chicago Press, 1930. 302 p.

Editions, translations, biography, criticism, etc., from 1800 to about 1928. Includes even the simpler school editions and brief articles of slight originality for the value they may have for students, rather than for the bibliographer as such.

SIR THOMAS MORE

GIBSON, R. W.
St. Thomas More: A Preliminary Bibliography of His Works and of Moreana to the Year 1750. With a bibliography of Utopiana compiled by R. W. Gibson and J. Max Patrick. New Haven: Yale University Press, 1961. 499 p.

Published in connection with the projected edition of More's works now in preparation at Yale. A revised edition, which will include all new materials discovered by the editors of the projected edition will be issued upon the completion of the work. Includes works by and about More published up to 1750.

JOHN HENRY NEWMAN

SLOAN, C. E.
Newman: An Illustrated Brochure of his First Editions. Worcester, Mass.: Holy Cross College Press, 1953.

Describes the many first editions exhibited in the Museum of the Dinand Library of Holy Cross College in 1952. Follows Newman's life chronologically by periods and lists the works published in each along with the dates. Illustrations of the first editions, frequently with a short description, but no critical analysis.

ALEXANDER POPE

GRIFFITH, H.
Alexander Pope: A Bibliography. 2 vols. London: Holland Press, 1962.

A careful examination and description of the editions of Pope's works. Volume one contains twenty-four pages of introduction, 264 pages of text, and thirty-three pages of index; volume two contains eighteen pages of introduction, 271 pages of text, fifty-four pages of additions and corrections to volume one, and twenty-two pages of index. A total of 752 books are classified which are entirely or partly by, or have been attributed to, Pope from complete books to a newspaper or magazine contribution.

Chronologically arranged, each entry details the time and circumstances attending the publication, the format and contents of the published work, and the collection to which each item belongs. The additions and corrections compiled in volume two constitute the supplements to volume one which were published by George Sherburn (MP, XXII, 327–336) and Arthur Case (MP, XXIV, 297–313).

LOPEZ, Cecilia L.
Alexander Pope: an Annotated Bibliography, 1945–1967. Gainesville, Florida: University of Florida Press, 1970. 154 p.

Lists 682 editions, books, and articles, in addition to reviews, alphabetically arranged under 23 headings, such as editions, bibliography, manuscripts, biography, style, etc. Annotations are descriptive, rather than critical.

WISE, Thomas James.
A Pope Library: A Catalogue of Plays, Poems and Prose Writings by Alexander Pope. London, 1931. 112 p.

Two parts: the first part comprises a chronological listing of Pope's writings, with reproductions of the original folio pages; the second part, entitled "Popeiana," lists works about him and provides a brief résumé of the contents.

SAMUEL RICHARDSON

CORDASCO, Francis.
Samuel Richardson: A List of Critical Studies Published from 1896 to 1946. Brooklyn, 1948.

Intended to serve "as a guide to the criticism of Richardson in the last half century."

SALE, W. M.
Samuel Richardson: A Bibliographical Record of His Literary Career with Historical Notes. New Haven: Yale University Press, 1936.

The three main divisions of the work are: the novels, edited works, pamphlets, and books written in collaboration; contributions to periodicals; works inspired in part or completely by the publication of Richardson's novels. Includes almost a hundred small but legible reproductions of title pages. Regarded by one reviewer (SATURDAY REVIEW, January 10, 1937) as "the first definitive bibliography of Richardson."

JOHN RUSKIN

COOK, E. T. AND ALEXANDER WEDDERBURN.
The Works of John Ruskin. Library Edition. Vol. XXXVIII. Bibliography. 1912.

Regarded by many as the most comprehensive and reliable bibliography of Ruskin. Includes: (1) all Ruskin volumes current at time of publication; (2) reissue of all publications by him and "now out of print or only privately collected;" (3) all letters, articles and other scattered writings not heretofore collected; and (4) a collection of all the different editions. Also contains all the illustrations inserted by Ruskin in his books, and all drawings by him which have appeared in publication; unpublished MSS. by Ruskin; collations of Ruskin's MSS. of published works; letters and diaries.

WISE, THOMAS J. AND JAMES P. SMART.
A Complete Bibliography of the Writings in Prose and Verse of John Ruskin. London, 1893. Reprinted for Dawsons of Pall Mall, London, 1964.

In nineteen parts, a minute account of the various early editions of Ruskin and so-called "major" and "minor" Ruskiniana. Part III, Division A, for example, deals with the complete volumes of biography and criticism; Division B lists "Minor Ruskiniana" or, as the compilers put it: "reviews and criticisms of Professor Ruskin and his writings contained in books and magazines, with a selection from the literary weekly periodicals." Excludes American editions.

SIR WALTER SCOTT

CORSON, JAMES CLARKSON.
A Bibliography of Sir Walter Scott. London: Oliver and Boyd, 1943.

A classified and annotated List of Books and Articles Relating to his life and works, 1797–1940. Excludes those which do not deal exclusively with Scott, as well as supposititious works, poetical tributes, dramatized versions of his poems and novels, engravings, parodies, accounts of the centenary celebrations of 1871 and 1932 and clubs formed in his honor. The four principal sections are: I Bibliographical Material, II Biographical Material, III Literary Criticism, IV Literary-Biographical Material and Special Topics. An excellent bibliography with an author and subject index.

WILLIAM SHAKESPEARE

EBISCH, WALTER AND LEVIN LUDWIG SCHUCKING.
A Shakespeare Bibliography. Oxford: Clarendon Press, 1931. 294 p.

A selective bibliography covering Shakespeare's life, times, personality, texts, sources, literary influence, language art, production, influence, individual plays, etc. Although many of the titles are from the nineteenth century and in languages other than English, it provides an adequate sampling of recent criticism that is readily accessible to the student who knows only English. The two principal divisions are: A) General and B) The Works of Shakespeare Individually Examined. As an illustration of the manner of division, the arrangement of section B is as follows: (1) Shakespeare Bibliography (2) Elizabethan Literature (3) Shakespeare's Life (4) Shakespeare's Personality (5) Text: Transmission and Emendation (6) Shakespeare's Sources, Literary Influence and Cultural Relations (7) The Art of Shakespeare (language and style) (8) The Art of Shakespeare (dramatic art) (9) Shakespeare's Stage and the Production of His Plays (10) Literary Taste in Shakespeare's Time (11) Aesthetic Criticism of Shakespeare (12) Shakespeare's Influence through the Centuries (13) Civilization in Shakespeare's England (14) The Shakespeare-Bacon Controversy and Similar Theories. A Supplement to the Ebisch and Schucking Bibliography, covering the years 1930–1935 (104 p.) was published in 1937.

SMITH, ROSS GORDON.
A Classified Shakespeare Bibliography 1936–1958. University Park, Pennsylvania: The Pennsylvania State University Press, 1963. 784 p.

A continuation of the Ebisch and Schucking bibliographies, compiled from the annual bibliographies from SHAKESPEARE QUARTERLY, SHAKESPEARE ASSOCIATION BULLETIN, PMLA, STUDIES IN PHILOLOGY, LITERATURE AND PSYCHOLOGY, MODERN HUMANITIES RESEARCH, YEAR'S WORK IN ENGLISH STUDIES, and dissertation lists and bibliographies. Follows the arrangement in Ebisch and Schucking; contains 344 sources on psychology.

SIR PHILIP SIDNEY

TANNENBAUM, SAMUEL.
Sir Philip Sidney: A Concise Bibliography. New York: Samuel A. Tannenbaum, 1941.

Material under the following headings: Works, Correspondence, Translations, Selections, Music and Songs, Poems in Praise of Sidney, Biography and Commentary, Sidney in Fiction. Provides publication dates, but is not annotated. Contains an index of names and subjects.

WASHINGTON, MARY A.
Sir Philip Sidney: an Annotated Bibliography of Modern Criticism, 1941–1970. Columbia, Missouri: University of Missouri Press, 1972. 199 p.

A continuation of Tannebaum's SIR PHILIP SIDNEY: A CONCISE BIBLIOGRAPHY. Lacks material from the 1970 MLA international bibliography, since it was not published early enough to be used.

TOBIAS GEORGE SMOLLET

CORDASCO, F.
Smollet Criticism, 1925–45. New York: Long Island University Press, 1947. **Smollet Criticism, 1770–1924.** New York: Long Island University Press, 1948.

Published as an enumerative and annotative bibliography. Regarded generally as a useful listing of materials, if not exhaustive; but the annotations are quite inadequate, at times less illuminating than the titles themselves.

KORTE, DONALD M.
An Annotated Bibliography of Smollet Scholarship, 1946–1968. Toronto: University of Toronto Press, 1969. 54 p.

Intended as a supplement to Francesco Cordasco's SMOLLET CRITICISM, 1925–1945.

EDMUND SPENSER

ATKINSON, DOROTHY F.
Edmund Spenser; A Bibliographical Supplement. Baltimore; Johns Hopkins Press, 1937, 242 p.

Designed as a supplement to Carpenter's A REFERENCE GUIDE TO EDMUND SPENSER.

CARPENTER, FREDERICK IVES.
A Reference Guide to Edmund Spenser. Chicago: University of Chicago Press, 1923.

A reliable work. Arrangement is chronological. Many useful summaries.

MCNEIR, WALDO F. AND GEORGE FOSTER PROVOST.
Annotated Bibliography of Edmund Spenser. Pittsburgh: Duquesne University Press, 1962.

Covers the period following that embraced in Atkinson's SUPPLEMENT to Carpenter.

PARROT, ALICE.
A Critical Bibliography of Spenser from 1923 to 1928. Studies in Philology XXV, 1928.

Supplements the Carpenter bibliography.

LAWRENCE STERNE

CORDASCO, FRANCESCO.
Lawrence Sterne. New York: Long Island University Press, 1948.

Critical studies from 1896 to 1946. Virtually no annotations. Includes only important reviews. The fullest section is "Biography and General Criticism."

ROBERT LOUIS STEVENSON

PRIDEAUX, W. F.
**A Bibliography of Robert Louis Stevenson. New York: Charles
Scribner's Sons, 1903.**

A well documented bibliography of 548 writings of Stevenson,
illustrated with original title pages, a description of the form
of the book, pamphlet or paper. Also indicated are the publishing procedure involved, the publishing dates, advertisements
that introduced the work in its original form, and the names
of the periodicals that they first appeared in. The seven main
sections are: I. "First Editions and Separate Works," II. "Ju-
venilia, Toy-Books, and Nugae," III. Contributions to Books,"
IV. "Contributions to Periodicals in Prose," V. Contributions
to Periodicals in Verse," VI. "The Edinburgh Edition," VII.
"Selections from the Works." The Appendix contains: "Complete Volumes of Biography and Criticism," "Critical and Biographical Notices in Books," "Critical and Biographical Articles
in Magazines, Newspapers, etc." Edited and enlarged by F. V.
Livingston, 1917.

JONATHAN SWIFT

STATHIS, James J.
**A Bibliography of Swift Studies, 1945–1965. Nashville, Ten-
nessee: Vanderbilt University Press, 1967. 110 p.**

A comprehensive and succinctly annotated bibliography of critical studies.

TEERINK, Herman.
**A Bibliography of the Writings of Jonathan Swift. 2nd ed. re-
vised and corrected H. Teerink and edited by Arthur Scouten.
Philadelphia: University of Pennsylvania Press, 1963. 453 p.**

A considerable improvement over the first edition, retaining the
original Teerink numbers and providing meticulous bibliographical description for each work. Divided into seven sections: (1)
Collected Works; (2) Smaller Collections; (3) A TALE OF A
TUB, etc.; (4) GULLIVER'S TRAVELS (5) Separate Works; (6)
Doubtful Works; (7) Biography and Criticism, 1709–1895. In
the first edition, the listing of criticisms of Swift's writings covers the period 1790 to 1935; in the second edition the reader is

referred to JONATHAN SWIFT, A LIST OF CRITICAL STUDIES PUB-
LISHED from 1895 to 1945. Most of the entries are well annotated; locations are given. Includes a Table of Symbols and
Abbreviations, a Table of Location of Teerink Numbers, and
an Index of Titles.

ALFRED TENNYSON

TENNYSON, SIR CHARLES AND CHRISTINE FALL.
Alfred Tennyson: An Annotated Bibliography. Athens: University of Georgia Press, 1967. 126 p.

About Tennyson and his works.

WILLIAM MAKEPEACE THACKERAY

FLAM, DUDLEY.
Thackeray's Critics: An Annotated Bibliography of British and
American Criticism 1836–1901. Chapel Hill: University of North
Carolina Press, 1967. 184 p.

Lists critical and biographical books and articles on Thackeray.

VAN DUZER, HENRY SAYRE.
Thackeray Library. New York, 1919, 198 p.

A list of first editions, first publications, portraits, water colors,
etchings, drawings, and manuscripts; also miscellaneous items.
A fairly complete bibliography.

OSCAR WILDE

MILLARD, CHRISTOPHER SCLATER.
Bibliography of Oscar Wilde. New ed. London: Rota, 1967.
605 p.

A reprint of the earlier edition, with a new introduction which
makes note of a few omissions from the original work.

WILLIAM WORDSWORTH

BALD, R. C.
The Cornell Wordsworth Collection. Ithaca, New York: Cornell
University Press, 1957. 458 p.

A catalogue of books and manuscripts given to the University by

Mr. Victor Emmanuel. Not simply a revision of the 1931 list based on the same collection, but a new work. Contains a section entitled "Wordsworthiana," in which there are entries of books, magazines, and reviews about Wordsworth and his works year by year. An excellent source.

HENLEY, ELTON F. AND DAVID H. STAM.
Wordsworthian Criticism 1945–1959. New York: New York Public Library, 1960. 61 p.

An annotated bibliography, conceived as a supplement to the Logan bibliography.

LOGAN, JAMES VENABLE.
Wordsworthian Criticism: A Guide and Bibliography. Columbus, Ohio: Ohio State University Press, 1947. 304 p.

Two principal parts. Part I presents a body of Wordsworthian criticism, extending from his own day to the present. In the section dealing with Wordsworth's contemporaries, the author's aim is to include primarily formal criticism.

WILLIAM BUTLER YEATS

CROSS, K. G. W.
A Bibliography of Yeats Criticism, 1887–1965; with a Foreword by A. Norman Jeffares. New York: Macmillan Company, 1972. 341 p.

An eight page chronology of Yeats' work, reviews of his writings, and books, pamphlets, and articles wholly or partly about him. Also included are bibliographies, concordances, and descriptions of Yeatsiana. A monument of Yeats scholarship.

WADE, ALLAN.
A Bibliography of the Writings of W. B. Yeats. 2nd. ed. rev. London: Hart-Davis, 1958. 449 p.

The first edition of Allan Wade's bibliography was published in 1951. Soon thereafter he began the work of revision, but his sudden death in 1955 intervened, and Mr. Hart-Davis took Allan Wade's papers and, with the assistance of a number of Yeats scholars, completed the work. The "First Preface" in the

1958 edition is that of Allan Wade from the first edition; the "Second Preface," that of Hart-Davis, defines the corrections and the new publications of the intervening years. The 1958 edition, some fifty-nine pages longer, retains the same format, cross-references, and numbers, but has a very superior index of titles, subjects, authors, and persons. A comprehensive work, it includes: a catalogue of Yeats's books; books and periodicals edited by him, and books containing contributions by him, including letters; a catalogue of contributions to periodicals; translations into other languages; translations into Japanese.

EDWARD YOUNG

CORDASCO, F.
Young: A Handlist of Critical Notices and Studies. New York, 1950.

A list of thirty-nine titles covering the period 1892 to the present.

American

JAMES FENIMORE COOPER

SPILLER, Robert E. and Philip C. Blackburn.
A Descriptive Bibliography of the Writings of James Fenimore Cooper. New York: R. R. Bowker Co., 1934.

Only those volumes which are all or primarily by Cooper are listed in the numerical sequence of his works; others are grouped with the contributions to periodicals and collections. Books or periodicals first published in America, England, or Europe are described in full—title, author, publisher, copyright date, descriptions of illustrations, replicas of title pages, number of volumes, number of pages, description of binding, and a brief summary of the story. Brief entries are employed for collected editions, translations, and periodical contributions; mere mentions are made of second and third editions with changes in prefatory material only. The bibliography of books and periodicals covers the years 1820–1855; that of the collected works cover the years 1820–1934. In the section entitled "Attributions, Adaptations, Etc.," are listed Cooper's unpublished writings, writings attributed to him by publishers or foreign translators, writings associated with Cooper but not written by him, and dramatizations of his stories by others. The index includes all bibliographical entries, important proper names, titles of periodicals, and cross references for foreign titles of Cooper's works.

STEPHEN CRANE

STALLMAN, R.W.
Stephen Crane: a Critical Bibliography. Ames, Iowa: Iowa University Press, 1972. 642 p.

Parts A and B are "facsimile sections" of the Williams and Starrett STEPHEN CRANE: A BIBLIOGRAPHY (1948). The main portion of the work is a 463 page bibliography of criticism from contemporary reviews and subsequent expressions down to 1972. In a sense, an anthology of criticism on Crane compiled by a scholar who has devoted more than twenty years of study to his subject.

WILLIAMS, AMES W. AND VINCENT STARRETT.
Stephen Crane: A Bibliography. Glendale, California: John Valentine, 1948. 165 p.

Contains: a chronological list of Crane's writings alphabetically arranged by title; a list of works, biographical and bibliographical about Crane; a chronological listing of contemporary reviews of all Crane's books. A careful work of sifting and collating. Today, it should be supplemented with the annual bibliographies edited by Robert N. Hudspeth appearing each spring in *Thoth* (Syracuse University). Also still useful is the bibliography published in the Stephen Crane number of *Modern Fiction Studies*, V (Autumn 1959), 282–291.

THEODORE DREISER

MCDONALD, EDWARD D.
A Bibliography of the Writings of Theodore Dreiser. New York: Putnam, 1928. 130 p.

A complete, annotated listing; includes earliest writings and contributions to periodicals.

RALPH WALDO EMERSON

BRYER, JACKSON R. AND ROBERT A. REES.
A Checklist of Emerson Criticism 1951–1961. Hartford: Transcendental Books, 1963. 50 p.

Covers the decade immediately following the period indexed in

Leary's ARTICLES ON AMERICAN LITERATURE 1900–1950. Divided into five sections: (1) Books, (2) Articles, (3) Doctoral Dissertations, (4) Index of Topics, (5) The Old Manse and Emerson. The entries are arranged alphabetically in each section; most entries are annotated. Detailed index. Also cites reviews of books devoted entirely to Emerson.

COOKE, GEORGE WILLIS.
A Bibliography of Ralph Waldo Emerson. Boston, 1908.

Aims to provide a complete list of Emerson's writings, translation, and critical material. Includes: Emerson's single works—book publications, reviews, pamphlets, periodical articles, with prose works listed in roman type, poetry in italic type, and books in capital letters; biographical works, listed alphabetically under the author's name; critical books and articles, listed alphabetically. Each entry is briefly annotated. An orderly arrangement, covering an impressive amount of information.

WILLIAM FAULKNER

MERIWETHER, JAMES B.
The Literary Career of William Faulkner: A Bibliographical Study. Princeton, New Jersey: Princeton University Library, 1961. 192 p.

An extensive catalog of a Faulkner exhibit held at Princeton in 1957; a classified bibliography of his work. Has a title index.

SLEETH, IRENE.
William Faulkner: A Bibliography of Criticism. Denver: Alan Swallor, 1962.

Aims to provide an accurate, complete, and useful arrangement of materials—books, essays in collections, and periodical articles, for the years 1920–1961. No annotations or comments.

F. SCOTT FITZGERALD

BRYER, JACKSON R.
The Critical Reputation of F. Scott Fitzgerald: A Bibliographical Study. New York: The Shoe String Press, 1968. 434 p.

An annotated listing of reviews and literary criticism, suggesting the problems involved in any assessment of Fitzgerald's works and literary career. Some of the annotations are rather long; others are quite short; all are precise and scholarly. Excellent index.

ROBERT FROST

CLYMER, W. B. AND CHARLES R. GREEN.
Robert Frost: A Bibliography. Amherst, Mass.: The Jones Library, 1937. 158 p.

Provides collations, first appearance of poems in periodicals, first appearance in books, translations and appreciations in foreign languages, essays and reviews in periodicals, essays and reviews in books, books dedicated to Robert Frost, a brief but very useful secondary bibliography, and a chronology of his life.

MERTINS, LOUIS AND ESTHER.
The Intervals of Robert Frost: A Critical Bibliography. Los Angeles: University of California Press, 1947. 91 p.

An annotated listing of primary and secondary sources. In compiling the listing, Mertins and Frost worked together. It is divided into the seven intervals of Robert Frost's life and gives a brief account of the publication of each poem through 1947.

NATHANIEL HAWTHORNE

BROWNE, NINA E.
A Bibliography of Nathaniel Hawthorne. Boston and New York: Houghton, Mifflin & Company, 1905.

A scholarly listing of Hawthorne's published work, whether in book form, magazines, or newspapers, and of everything that Miss Browne was able to discover in print about him. Contains a double-entry author and magazine index, a list of pseudonyms used by Hawthorne, and a list of previous bibliographies of Hawthorne. Dated, but excellent for the years covered.

GROSS, THEODORE L. AND STANLEY WERTHEIM.
Hawthorne, Melville, Stephen Crane: A Critical Bibliography. New York: The Free Press, 1972. 301 p.

Each section contains a brief survey of the subject's critical reputation, a biographical chronology, and bibliographical entries with summaries and evaluations. 196 entries for Hawthorne; 186 entries for Melville; and 105 entries for Crane. Bibliographical indexes.

OLIVER WENDELL HOLMES

CURRIER, Thomas Franklin.
A Bibliography of Oliver Wendell Holmes. New York: New York University Press, 1953.

Lists editions of Holmes' books, leaflets, and broadsides, and gives for each a full transcription of the title, size, collation by pages, by gatherings, and by printings. Locates manuscripts. Ten appendixes list special kinds of publications, such as sheet music, printed letters, biographies and critical studies of Holmes. Contains a vast amount of hitherto unknown or unpublished information by and about Holmes.

WILLIAM DEAN HOWELLS

BRENNI, Vito J. comp.
William Dean Howells: A Bibliography. New Jersey: Scarecrow Press, 1973. 212 p.
The arrangement is by form (short stories, poems, novels, plays, etc.), not by chronology. Broader in scope than any earlier bibliography on Howell.

WASHINGTON IRVING

WILLIAMS, Stanley T. and Mary Allen Edge.
A Bibliography of the Writings of Washington Irving. 1937.

A thorough listing of all of Irving's writings from the year of first publication to 1936. The eleven divisions are: I. Complete Works, II. Selected Works, III. Poems, IV. Individual Works, V. Journals, VI. Individual Works, VII. Works Ascribed to Irving, VIII. Life and Letters, IX. Periodicals and Collections, X. Miscellanea, XI. Criticism of Irving. The arrangement of material for which dates are available is chronological; that for titles for which dates are not certain is alphabetical.

HENRY JAMES

EDEL, Leon and Dan. H. Lawrence.
A Bibliography of Henry James. 2nd. ed. rev. London: Hart-Davis, 1961. 427 p.

A comprehensive list of publications—books, periodical materials, letters, translations, and miscellaneous. Provides precise dates of publication, details relative to English and American issues, original pieces, additional information. Useful index. Supersedes LeRoy Philips' bibliography. Regarded by Edel and Lawrence as the "fullest account yet set down, descriptive and historical, of the physical form in which the novelist's works and ephemeral writings were made public." Lists the exact number of copies delivered by the printer; fully describes works according to size, binding, color, binder's fly, signatures, and revisions made by novelist. In addition to the novels, the BIBLIOGRAPHY supplies a check list of books containing Henry James's letters and fragment writings.

SIDNEY LANIER

ANDERSON, CHARLES.
Sidney Lanier: Centennial Edition. Baltimore: The Johns Hopkins Press, 1945. 10 vols.

Volume six contains a thirty-three page bibliography, probably the most comprehensive listing of the works of Lanier. Compiled by Philip Graham and Frieda Theis, the bibliography is divided into three parts: a chronological listing of the works of Sidney Lanier, together with a statement regarding content, and a chronological listing of the first printing of poems by Lanier, together with a listing of his musical compositions; the second part contains an alphabetical listing of selected biography and criticism of Lanier, without annotation; the third part lists selected reviews of Lanier's published volumes, arranged chronologically according to the volume treated.

HENRY WADSWORTH LONGFELLOW

LIVINGSTON, LUTHER S.
A Bibliography of the First Editions in Book Form of the Writings of Henry Wadsworth Longfellow. New York: Privately Printed, 1908. 127 p.

Aims to describe each work "which contained for the first time *in a book* anything of Longfellow's writings." The arrangement is chronological, according to the actual date of publication as far as it can be determined. Each entry is carefully annotated, giving title page information, notations as to the size of the paper and the type of binding, the material contained in each work, and remarks Longfellow is known to have made about the work.

HERMAN MELVILLE

SHERMAN, Stuart, John Birss, Gordon Roper.
Melville Bibliography, 1952–1957. Providence Public Library, 1959. 35 p.

Includes published works and research completed or in progress during the years 1952–1957. Based on the following sources: AMERICAN DOCTORAL DISSERTATIONS ACCEPTED BY AMERICAN UNIVERSITIES, DISSERTATION ABSTRACTS, AMERICAN LITERATURE, BOOKS IN PRINT, MELVILLE SOCIETY NEWSLETTER, PMLA, NATIONAL UNION CATALOGUE, and others. An excellent arrangement for the years covered.

EDGAR ALLAN POE

ROBERTSON, John W.
Bibliography of the Writings of Edgar A. Poe. San Francisco: Grabhorn, 1934. 2 vols.

Volume one lists work by Poe; volume two constitutes a commentary on the works listed in volume one.

HEARTMAN, Charles Frederick and James R. Canny.
A Bibliography of the First Printings of the Writings of Edgar Allan Poe. Hattiesburg, Miss.: The Book Farm, 1943. 294 p.

A revised edition of A CENSUS OF FIRST EDITIONS AND SOURCE MATERIALS BY EDGAR ALLAN POE IN AMERICAN COLLECTIONS, compiled by Charles F. Heartman and Kenneth Rede and published in 1932. Records first and later printings of his contributions to annuals, anthologies, periodicals and newspapers issued during his lifetime. Includes some spurious Poeana and fakes.

KATHERINE ANNE PORTER

WALDRIP, Louise.

A Bibliography of the Works of Katherine Anne Porter; and A Bibliography of the Criticism of the Works of Katherine Anne Porter. New York: Scarecrow Press, 1970. 219 p.

Among the works of Katherine Anne Porter are included translations and contributions to books and periodicals; in the section on criticism are magazine and newspaper materials, dissertations and theses, book reviews, and foreign language criticism. The index is devoted to the authors of the critical works. A thorough work.

EZRA POUND

GALLUP, DONALD CLIFFORD.
A Bibliography of Ezra Pound. London: Hart-Davis, 1963. 454 p.

Divided into five sections: books and pamphlets by or translated by Pound; books and pamphlets edited or with contributions by Pound; periodical contributions; translations; an appendix of miscellaneous items, such as syllabi, leaflets, broadsides, music, musical settings, recordings. Entries on books and pamphlets are particularly well annotated.

HENRY DAVID THOREAU

ALLEN, FRANCIS H.
A Bibliography of Henry David Thoreau. Boston: Houghton Mifflin Co., 1909. 201 p.

Contains the following: (1) Thoreau's books, single and collected publications; (2) Selections from Thoreau's writings, articles and poems by Thoreau; (3) biography and books relating exclusively to Thoreau; (4) critical and biographical materials; (5) newspaper and periodical articles; (6) auction prices; (7) addenda; (8) erratum; (9) index. Each source is concisely annotated. The closing date is 1908. A thorough guide for the period covered.

HARDING, WALTER.
A Bibliography of the Thoreau Society Bulletin Bibliographies, 1941–1969; a Cumulation and Index. Whitson, 323 p.

More than 4,000 items alphabetically arranged by author; includes books and articles about Thoreau as well as new editions

of Thoreau's own works in all languages. Serves as a supplement
to the standard bibliographies of F. H. Allen and William White.

WHITE, WILLIAM.
A Henry David Thoreau Bibliography, 1908–1937. Boston: F. S.
Faxon Company, 1939. 51 p. Reprinted from BULLETIN OF BIB-
LIOGRAPHY, No. 35.

Based on a study of fifty bibliographical sources. The main divisions are: (1) Bibliography (2) Bibliography and Criticism (3)
Periodical Articles (4) Dissertations (5) Books entirely Devoted
to Thoreau (6) Biographical and Critical Material in Books (7)
Selections from Thoreau's Writings (8) Addenda. Some annotations are given. Reviews of books and articles are indicated.

MARK TWAIN

ASSELINEAU, ROGER.
The Literary Reputation of Mark Twain from 1910 to 1950.
Paris: Librari Marcel Didier, 1954. 240 p.

Two principal divisions. Part one is a critical essay which concentrates on the major critical attitudes, by American authors,
from 1910 to 1950. The critical works, mainly biographies, are
described and evaluated. The arrangement is chronological,
evidencing the development of critical thought during the forty
years surveyed. Part two is the bibliography proper, a comprehensive listing covering 160 pages and listing chronologically 1,333
entries. Each year is given separate treatment and has the following recurring subdivisions: 1. Bibliography and Criticism; 2. Introductions and Prefaces; 3. Other books; 4. Periodicals; 5. Unpublished theses. Each entry includes a note definitive of contents; more important works are fully annotated.

JOHNSON, MERLE.
A Bibliography of the Works of Mark Twain. Rev. and enl. New
York: Harper, 1935. 274 p.

A list of first editions in book form; of first printings in periodicals; occasional publications of his varied literary activities.

WALT WHITMAN

FREY, ELLEN FRANCIS.
Catalogue of the Whitman Collection in the Duke University

Library. Durham, North Carolina: Duke University Library, 1945. 148 p.

A part of the Trent collection given by Dr. and Mrs. Josiah C. Trent. Includes material by and about Whitman.

TANNER, JAMES T. F.
Walt Whitman: A Supplementary Bibliography, 1961–1967. Kent, Ohio: Kent State University Press, 1968. 59 p.

Intended as an extension of the bibliography of 1945–1960 by E. A. Allen, appended to Gay Wilson Allen's WALT WHITMAN AS MAN, POET, AND LEGEND (Carbondale: Southern Illinois University Press, 1961).

WELLS, CAROLYN AND ALFRED F. GOLDSMITH.
A Concise Bibliography of the Works of Walt Whitman with a Supplement of Fifty Books about Him. Boston: Houghton, 1922. 106 p.

A concise and extensive bibliography.

JOHN GREENLEAF WHITTIER

CURRIER, THOMAS FRANKLIN.
A Bibliography of John Greenleaf Whittier. Cambridge, Massachusetts: Harvard University Press, 1937. 650 p.

An extremely valuable work. Includes 400 poems by Whittier not in the so-called complete Whittier edited by Pechiod and fifty pieces of literary criticism which are omitted in the complete Whittier. Divided into five parts: editions and leaflets arranged chronologically; poems arranged alphabetically; prose essays and tales arranged alphabetically; letters to the press arranged chronologically; and criticism by Pauline S. Pulsifer arranged chronologically. Bibliographical information is brief, but all available information essential to identify the items is furnished. Eleven appendices cover such subjects as pseudonyms, sheet music editions, editions for the use of the blind, and incorrect attributions. A work of immense scholarship. So thorough, it seems to be a definitive work.

Recent, separately published author bibliographies include: HART CRANE: AN ANNOTATED BIBLIOGRAPHY, by Joseph Schwartz (N.Y., David Lewis, 1970); EMILY DICKINSON: AN ANNOTATED

BIBLIOGRAPHY, by Willis J. Buckingham (Bloomington, Indiana University Press, 1970); AUTHUR MILLER CRITICISM, by Tetsumaro Hayashi (Metuchen, N.J., Scarecrow, 1969); ALLEN TATE: A BIBLIOGRAPHY, by Marshall Fallwell (N.Y., David Lewis, 1969); A BIBLIOGRAPHY OF SCHOLARSHIP ABOUT HENRY DAVID THOREAU 1940–1967, by Christopher A. Hilldenbrand (Hays, Fort Hays Kansas State College, 1967); W. SOMERSET MAUGHAM: AN ANNOTATED BIBLIOGRAPHY OF WRITINGS ABOUT HIM, by Charles Sanders (De Kalb, Illinois, Northern Illinois University Press, 1970); A BIBLIOGRAPHY OF ELIZABETH BARRET BROWNING, by Warner Barnes (Austin, University of Texas Press, 1968); GODWIN CRITICISM: A SYNOPTIC BIBLIOGRAPHY, by Burton R. Pollin (Toronto, University of Toronto Press, 1967); EMILY DICKINSON: A BIBLIOGRAPHY, by Sheila T. Clendenning (Kent, Ohio, Kent State University Press, 1968); ERNEST HEMINGWAY: A COMPREHENSIVE BIBLIOGRAPHY, by Audre Hanneman (Princeton, N.Y., Princeton University Press, 1967); JOHN STEINBECK: A CONCISE BIBLIOGRAPHY, by Tetsumaro Hayashi (Metuchen, N.J., Scarecrow, 1967); JAMES TURBER: A BIBLIOGRAPHY, by Edwin T. Bowden (Columbus, Ohio State University Press, 1968); ROBERT PENN WARREN: A BIBLIOGRAPHY, by Mary Nance Huff (N.Y., David Lewis Publ., 1968).

CONCORDANCES

English

MATTHEW ARNOLD

PARRISH, S. M.
A Concordance to the Poems of Matthew Arnold. Ithaca: Cornell University Press, 1960. xxiii + 965 p.

The first concordance produced by an electronic computer, an IBM 704 Data Processing Machine which, according to the preface, made 42,000 logical decisions per second. Based upon: Tinker and Lowry's POETICAL WORKS (1950) which is indexed to its entirety even to the variant readings, their COMMENTARY (1940), G. W. E. Russell's edition of Arnold's LETTERS (1895), and the Lowry edition of the LETTERS TO CLOUGH. The format, described by one reviewer (A. Dwight Culler) is as follows: "The text of each line of poetry is printed entire under its index word and is followed by a page reference to the POETICAL WORKS (if that is where the line appears), by the title of the poem, by the line number, and by an indication of whether the line is a variant or part of the established text. The entire volume is printed in Roman capitals and without punctuation, these limitations being imposed by the capacity of the IBM Printer. A special feature of the concordance is that it lists at the end of the volume all the index words in the order of the frequency of their use. These range from I, which was used 1,045 times, to a group of 4,358 words which were used only once. Omitted from the indexing, both in the frequency list and the main concordance, were 151 nonsignificant words which would simply have cluttered up the concordance had they been included. They are listed in the preface . . . The total number of words indexed is 9,946, which, with the 151 words not included, makes a total poetic vocabulary for Arnold of 10,097. This number, as Professor Parrish points out, is somewhat inflated by the peculiarities of computer indexing."

BEOWULF

BESSINGER, J. B.
A Concordance to Beowulf. Ithaca, New York: Cornell University Press. 1969. 378 p.

A concordance of every word in the poem in the context of its verse-pair, followed by a key-word-in-context concordance, "which groups together any sections containing 12 consecutive common characters." Also included are a word frequency list, as well as a checklist of homographs.

COOK, ALBERT S.
A Concordance to Beowulf. Halle, Max Niemeyer, 1911. 436 p.

Based on the text of Wyatt's second edition (Cambridge, 1898). Except for common words such as numerals, prepositions, many pronouns, conjunctions, and adverbs (which are omitted), lists the occurrence of every word and quotes passages sufficiently to evidence context. Exceptionally free of error.

WILLIAM BLAKE

ERDMAN, DAVID V., ed.
A Concordance to the Writings of William Blake. Ithaca, New York: Cornell University Press, 1967. 2 Vols.

Based on the text THE COMPLETE WRITINGS OF WILLIAM BLAKE: with all the variant readings, ed. by Geoffrey Keynes (London and New York, Random, 1957). Aims to include everything that Blake wrote, in poetry and prose. All entries are in upper-case lettering.

ROBERT BROWNING

BROUGHTON, LESLIE N. AND BENJAMIN F. STELTER.
A Concordance to the Poems of Robert Browning. New York: G. E. Stechert and Company, 1924–1925. 2 vols. 2,658 p.

Two huge quartos containing about 500,000 entries, with each entry giving one complete line of poetry. The basic text for the concordance is the Globe Edition of Browning's work, the errors of which are corrected, especially in reference to the line numbers of the poems. A list of the "Catch Titles," with the corresponding titles and page numbers in the Globe Edition precede each entry; and to facilitate use the line number and the title of the poem are given after each entry. Quotations which are not contained in the Globe Edition are listed in the Addenda at the end of Volume II. Listed immediately after the preface are certain pronouns, conjunctions, prepositions, auxiliaries, and articles which are omitted within the quotations. An immensely useful work.

GORDON LORD BYRON

HAGELMAN, CHARLES W., JR. AND ROBERT J. BARNES. **Concordance to Byron's Don Juan.** Ithaca, New York: Cornell University Press, 1967.

Based on the monumental variorum edition of *Don Juan*, edited by Truman Guy Steffan and Willis W. Pratt and published by the University of Texas Press in 1956. Indexes not only the complete poem but, also, the sixteen so-called "rejected stanzas" and 634 complete-line variant readings. It is easily usable with any edition of *Don Juan*, it is claimed, "since each line is identified by canto, stanza, and line number as well as by the volume and page number in the variorum edition." Because the variorum edition of *Don Juan* does not regularize Byron's spellings, several changes were made to integrate and align individual entries. For example, whereas Byron uses both *Saint* and *St.*, the concordance lists all these entries under *Saint*. And because it was considered virtually impossible to list all the variant readings, the editors decided to include: (1) only relatively complete alternate lines; and (2) only those complete lines which reflect a significant change of diction—"two or more words." The total number of variant lines included is 634. Added to the 16,064 published lines and the 127 lines in rejected stanzas, the grand total of lines in the concordance is 16,825.

GEOFFREY CHAUCER

TATLOCK, JOHN STRONG PERRY AND ARTHUR G. KENNEDY. **A Concordance to the Complete Works of Geoffrey Chaucer and to the Romaunt of the Rose.** Washington: The Carnegie Institute of Washington, 1927. 1110 p.

A virtually exhaustive compilation, based on the text of the Globe Edition. Approximately 2500 variant readings are included, with modern spelling dominating the head-words, except those that have become obsolete. For the word CAN there are over 600 references; for words like GOOD, GREAT, and HEART, there are about 1000; for the word GOD, there are some 1400 references;

and for the word DO (including DOTH, DID, DONE), there are nearly 2000 references. The 300 emendations of the Globe text are indicated. Employs a dictionary arrangement. Beneath the head-words are the words in part of the line in which they occur. To the right is both the work from which the line was taken and the number of that line in the word.

SAMUEL TAYLOR COLERIDGE

LOGAN, Sister Eugenia.

A Concordance to the Poetry of Samuel Taylor Coleridge. St. Mary of the Woods, Indiana: Private Printing, 1940. 901 p.

Based on the two-volume edition of Coleridge's POEMS by E. H. Coleridge. Deals not only with the standard Oxford text, but with the variant readings included therein. Indexes every line of poetry; makes note of all the changes in spelling, punctuation, and use of capital letters, all the erasures and emendations. One of the major divisions "List of Titles" is broken down into: 1. Index to Poems, 2. Index to First Drafts and Early Versions. A second major division "Index to Sources of Variant Lines" is broken down into: 1. MSS and Notebooks; 2. Various Editions of the Works of Samuel Taylor Coleridge; 3. Newspapers and Periodicals; 4. Letters of Samuel Taylor Coleridge; 5. Miscellaneous Works of the Authors.

WILLIAM CONGREVE

MANN, David.
A Concordance to the Plays of William Congreve. Ithaca, New York: Cornell University Press, 1973. 888 p.

Another of the computer-assisted concordances, providing an alphabetical index, with cross references, to the dramatic vocabulary of the playwright, and including page, title, act, scene and line citations, and the name of the character speaking. Appendixes list stage directions, common words, and words arranged by frequency of usage.

CHARLES DICKENS

WILLIAMS, Mary.
The Dickens Concordance, 1950.

A compendium of names, characters, and major places referred to in all the works of the novelist.

JOHN DONNE

COMBS, HOMER CARROL AND ZAY RUSK SULLENS.
Concordance to the English Poems of John Donne. Chicago: Packard, 1940. 418 p.

Based on the revised, one-volume edition of THE POETICAL WORKS OF JOHN DONNE, edited by Professor H. J. C. Grierson, and Published by the Oxford University Press in 1929. Does not include quotations from the Latin poems and translations in Appendix A or from the "doubtful poems," listed in the Appendix B of the 1929 edition. But it does cover all the English poems which the 1929 edition attributes definitely to Donne. The guide words appear in modern spelling, while the poet's spelling is retained in the quoted lines. Following each line is the number of the page from which it is taken, an abbreviation of the title of the poem, and the number of the line in the poem. Homographs are not differentiated when the citations are few or the danger of confusion is slight. Contractions are spelled out in most of the guide words.

JOHN DRYDEN

MONTGOMERY, GUY.
Concordance to the Poetical Works of John Dryden . . . Assisted by Mary Jackman and Helen S. Agoa. Berkeley: University of California Press, 1957. 722 p.

"Based on the Cambridge edition of the POETICAL WORKS OF JOHN DRYDEN, edited by George Rapall Noyes (revised and enlarged) in 1950. The list of titles taken from the Table of Contents of this edition are alphabetically arranged, and the page numbers indicate pages in this edition on which the poems begin. Some 208,000 word occurrences are listed in the concordance, about one-sixth of which consist in the repetition of a few adjectives, nouns, and verbs ranging in use from 400 to 1100 times; but the word occurrences are merely listed, outside of context. Some 200 key symbols are used to identify the poems; homonyms and parts of speech are not distinguished."

EDWARD FITZGERALD

TUTIN, JOHN RAMSDEN.
Concordance to Fitzgerald's Translation of the Rubaiyat of Omar Khayyam. London, New York: Macmillan, 1900. 169 p.

Indexes every word in the last edition issued during Fitzgerald's lifetime; every word in the first edition, 1859; and all variations in the second, third, and other editions. References are to edition, quatrain, and line.

OLIVER GOLDSMITH

PADEN, WILLIAM DOREMUS AND CLYDE KENNETH HYDER.
A Concordance to the Poems of Oliver Goldsmith. Lawrence, Kansas: University of Kansas Press, 1940.

Based on THE POETICAL WORKS OF OLIVER GOLDSMITH, edited by Austin Dobson and published by the Oxford University Press, 1906. Fairly adequate listing of the occurrences of the more commonly used words and terms in Goldsmith's poetry.

THOMAS GRAY

COOK, ALBERT STANBURROUGH.
Concordance to the English Poems of Thomas Gray. Boston: Houghton, 1908. 160 p.

Based on Gosse's edition of Gray (4 vols., London and New York, 1884); follows the order of poems in the edition by Gosse, except that variants are placed under the poems to which they belong. Where orthography presents a problem, the preference is for full forms (ROUSED rather than ROUS'D) and for forms generally preferred by scholars, "for etymological or other reasons." Words hyphenated by Gray are retained and the second element of such words is entered in its alphabetical place, with a cross-reference to the complete word. Punctuation by Gray, even where erratic, is kept. Homonyms, when different parts of speech, are occasionally differentiated.

GERARD MANLEY HOPKINS

BORRELLO, ALFRED, ed.
A Concordance of the Poetry in English of Gerard Manley Hopkins; programmed by James Anderson and Angelo Triandafilou. Metuchen, New Jersey: Scarecrow Press, 1969. 780 p.

Based on the text of the 4th edition of the collected poems published by Oxford University Press. An alphabetized list of Hopkins' vocabulary and the number of times each word appears; and a list of words used in the order of their frequency of appearance are included in the appendices.

DILLIGAN, ROBERT J. AND TODD K. BENDER.
A Concordance to the English Poetry of Gerard Manley Hopkins. Madison: University of Wisconsin Press, 1970. 321 p.

Based on the text edited by W. H. Gardner and N. H. MacKenzie (Oxford University Press, 1967). A computer print-out. To facilitate cross reference and to aid users who do not have the fourth edition at hand, the table of contents to that edition is included.

SAMUEL JOHNSON

NAUGLE, HELEN HAROLD AND PETER B. SHERRY.
A Concordance to the Poems of Samuel Johnson. New York: Cornell University Press, 1973. 578 p.

An alphabetical index to Johnson's poetic vocabulary, based on the Oxford University Press edition of THE POEMS OF SAMUEL JOHNSON edited by David Nichol Smith and Edward L. McAdam. The text is divided into English poems, Latin poems, and poems of doubtful attribution. A list of words arranged by use of frequency follows each section.

JAMES JOYCE

HANCOCK, LESLIE.
Word Index to James Joyce's Portrait of the Artist. Carbondale: Southern Illinois University Press, 1967.

Based on the edition published in 1964 (New York, Viking Press).

HART, CLIVE.
A Concordance to Finnegans Wake. Minneapolis: University of Minnesota Press, 1963. 516 p.

JOHN KEATS

BALDWIN, DANE LEWIS, L. N. BROUGHTON (AND OTHERS).

Concordance to the Poems of John Keats. Washington: Carnegie Institute, 1917. 437 p.

Based on the Buston Forman editions of 1910 and 1914. Provides a complete record of all words used by Keats, save for fifty-nine common words, which are omitted, and ten others which are recorded partially.

CHRISTOPHER MARLOWE

CRAWFORD, Charles.
The Marlowe Concordance. Louvain: Uystpruyst, 1911–1932. 1453 p.

"Very few words have been omitted from the concordance, and only those which are of little aid to study, such as auxiliary verbs, pronouns, and insignificant prepositions and conjunctions."—Pref.

JOHN MILTON

BRADSHAW, John.
Concordance to the Poetical Works of John Milton. London: Sonnenchein, 1894. 412 p.

Based upon the Aldine Edition (Bell, 1894). Includes all the works except the "Psalms" and the prose translations; and all words with the exception of certain pronouns, conjunctions, adverbs, and prepositions. Orthography seems inconsistent.

INGRAM, William, and Kathleen Swaim, eds.
A Concordance to Milton's English Poetry. New York: Oxford University Press, 1972. 683 p.

A computer-produced concordance, based not on any single edition, but chiefly on texts published during the poet's lifetime and authenticated by manuscripts. Milton's original orthography is preserved in citations, and alternative text readings and manuscript variants are noted.

ALEXANDER POPE

ABBOTT, Edwin.
Concordance to the Works of Alexander Pope. New York: Appleton, 1875. 365 p.

Lists every word contained in the first authorized edition of Pope's complete works, edited by Warburton in 1751, except the translations from Greek and Latin, the adaptations of Chaucer, and the imitations of English poets; also lacks the minor poems found in subsequent editions. Both the modern spelling and Pope's spelling of a given word are indicated, and the line of verse in which the word is found is reprinted in its entirety. Contains about 40,000 references. The introduction prefixed to the CONCORDANCE contains specimens from Johnson's LIVES OF POETS, providing a brief study of the revisions to which Pope subjected his couplets; a letter by Pope to Cromwell, expressing the rules according to which he constructed his verse; and a list of irregular rhymes, noting their frequency of occurrence.

WILLIAM SHAKESPEARE

BARTLETT, JOHN.
New and Complete Concordance or Verbal Index to Words, Phrases, and Passages in the Dramatic Works of Shakespeare with a Supplementary Concordance to the Poems. London: MacMillan, 1894. 1910 p.

Based on the text of the Globe Edition. Lists each word in full context, providing exact reference to act, scene, and line as numbered in the 1891 Globe Edition. A comprehensive work. Does not list the word Bible, but contains hundreds of references to GOD and to phrases such as GOD IN HEAVEN. There are at least fifteen references of JESUS, and many more names generally found in the Bible, and several hundred references to the word BLESSING.

DONOW, HERBERT S.
A Concordance to the Sonnet Sequence of Daniel, Drayton, Shakespeare, Sidney, and Spenser. Carbondale: Southern Illinois University Press, 1970. 772 p.

A computer programmed concordance of 525 sonnets by key words. Each entry consists of an index word, under which are grouped those lines from each sonnet in which the word appears. Number code identifies author, sonnet, and line location.

SPEVACK, Marvin.

The Harvard Concordance to Shakespeare. Cambridge, Mass.: The Harvard University Press, 1974. 1612 p.

Based on the six volume A COMPLETE AND SYSTEMATIC CONCORDANCE TO THE WORKS OF SHAKESPEARE (1968–70) —specifically on volumes IV, V, and VI, the one volume edition provides entries for every one of the more than 29,000 words used by Shakespeare, as well as contexts for all but 43 of the most frequently used words. A worthy successor to Bartlett's one-volume concordance.

PERCY BYSSHE SHELLEY

ELLIS, Frederick S.
Lexical Concordance to the Poetical Works of Percy Bysshe Shelley. London: Quaritch, 1892. 818 p.

Based upon the text of the Forman Edition, 1880, 2 Vols. "Reveals, as no mere concordance can, the Shelleyan characteristics of the vocabulary, in all their diversity of significance, to the nicest shades of sensitive discrimination." Thus, six significations are given to the word "dream"; twenty-two meanings are noted of the word "fresh." Locates many of the vague geographical places mentioned by Shelley.

EDMUND SPENSER

OSGOOD, Charles Grosvenor.
Concordance to the Poems of Edmund Spenser. Washington: Carnegie Institute, 1915. 997 p. (Reprinted: Gloucester, Mass.: Peter Smith, 1963).

Based upon the R. E. Neil Dodge's edition (Cambridge, 1908), with record of all variants in the Oxford edition, 1909–1910. Provides complete listing of all words, except for one hundred and seventy-four common terms for which only selected references are provided.

JONATHAN SWIFT

SHINAGEL, Michael, ed.
A Concordance to the Poems of Jonathan Swift. Ithaca, New York: Cornell University Press, 1972. 977 p.

A carefully produced book of reference, covering in addition poems which have been attributed doubtfully to the subject. The appendix gives Swift's poetic vocabulary in order of frequency.

ALFRED LORD TENNYSON

BAKER, ARTHUR ERNEST.

A Concordance to the Poetical and Dramatic Works of Alfred, Lord Tennyson. New York: Barnes & Noble, 1966 (reprinted from the 1914 ed.). 1212 p.

Includes reference to, not only the Macmillan edition (6 vols.), but to poems from the LIFE OF LORD TENNYSON by his son and to SUPPRESSED POEMS edited by J. C. Thomson. The key words are arranged alphabetically; the line references are given for each word; cross-references are supplied in the case of compounds and dialect forms; duplicate titles and poems without titles are differentiated. In all, contains 150,000 quotations and references. The last section of the work has a "Corrigenda, with a table of contents and two pages which list short titles and abbreviations. The main divisions are: (1) short titles and abbreviations; (2) poetical works; (3) dramatic works; (4) poems contained in LIFE OF ALFRED, LORD TENNYSON by his son; (5) SUPPRESSED POEMS 1830–1868; (6) addenda, composed of words using the Old English spelling. Supplemented by Baker's CONCORDANCE to the DEVIL AND THE LADY (London: Golden Vista Press, 1931).

DYLAN THOMAS

WILLIAMS, ROBERT COLEMAN, ed.
A Concordance to the Collected Poems of Dylan Thomas. Lincoln, Nebraska: University of Nebraska Press, 1967. 579 p.

Based on the 1954 reprinting of the COLLECTED POEMS (London, Dent, 1952) and the 18th printing of the American edition (New York, New Directions, 1953).

WILLIAM WORDSWORTH

COOPER, LANE.
Concordance to the Poems of William Wordsworth. London: Smith, Elder (New York, Dutton), 1911. 1136 p.

Based upon the text of the Oxford WORDSWORTH edited by Hutchinson, 1907. A complete list of references for all words, except for fifty-two of the most common words, for which only a selection is given.

WILLIAM BUTLER YEATS

PARRISH, STEPHEN MAXFIELD.
A Concordance to the Poems of W. B. Yeats . . . Programmed by James Allan Painter. Ithaca, New York: Cornell University Press, 1963. 967 p.

Like the Matthew Arnold Concordance, produced by means of an IBM 704 electronic data-processing machine. Based on the VARIORUM EDITION OF THE POEMS OF W. B. YEATS (New York: MacMillan Company, 1957). An alphabetical list of every word, excepting common words such as A and AND, giving the page and line number for every occurrence in the VARIORUM EDITION. According to the frequency list, the most frequent nouns used by Yeats were: man (456), love (353), heart (272), eyes (244), night (197), thought (196), day (194), moon (176), world (174), and time (162). Contains 17,000 lines and 65,000 words.

American

HART CRANE

LANDRY, HILTON.
A Concordance to the Poems of Hart Crane. New Jersey: Scarecrow Press, 1973. 379 p.

Based on the COMPLETE POEMS AND SELECTED LETTERS AND PROSE OF HART CRANE (Liverright, 1966). Each entry contains a page number, the line using the key word (without end punctuation), an abbreviation of the poem's title, and the number of the line in the poem. (Pref.)

EMILY DICKINSON

ROSENBAUM, S. P.
A Concordance to the Poems of Emily Dickinson. Ithaca, New York: Cornell University Press, 1964. 912 p.

The third volume in the distinguished series "Cornell Concordances"; and like the first two, programmed on an IBM 704 electronic computer. It is based on Thomas H. Johnson's three-volume edition of all the known texts of Emily Dickinson's poems and provides an alphabetical list of all significant words (and variants) in context. Also included are an analytical preface by the editor and an index of words in the order of frequency. Thus, as listed in the appendix, 'I' appears, as the first word, 1,682 times, as the second word, 908 times; 'my' appears 755 times; 'be' 616 times; "and so on, through a long list of words which are used only once, ending with 'Zodiac'."

RALPH WALDO EMERSON

CAMERON, KENNETH WALTER.
Index-Concordance to Emerson's Sermons. Hartford: Transcendental Books, 1963. 2 Vols.

These two volumes, totalling seven hundred and nine pages and arranged alphabetically, attempt to cover everything in every version of Emerson's sermons as well as many unclassified manuscript fragments; to "unlock the resources of imagery, quotation, and verbal expression" in Emerson's approximately 150 unpublished sermons, composed immediately preceding the publication of "Nature" (1836).

HUBBELL, GEORGE SHELTON.
Concordance to the Poems of Ralph Waldo Emerson. New York: Wilson, 1932. 478 p.

Based on the text of volume nine of the Centenary Edition of Emerson (Houghton); hence does not include the uncollected poems scattered through the other volumes of the edition. Gives only selected references to 172 common words, but full references for all occurrences of words used in the ninth volume of the Centenary Edition. The arrangement is alphabetical. Inflected forms which have an apostrophe precede other forms which are identical save for the apostrophe; the sequences of quotations under one word are in the alphabetical sequence of the catchword titles of the poems from which the quotations are taken. If a poem does not have a title, the first line is listed in quotation marks. Variant spellings are listed with cross-references.

WILLIAM FAULKNER

SMART, George K.
Religious Elements in Faulkner's Novels: A Selective Concordance. Coral Gables: University of Miami Press, 1965. 144 p.

In the Introduction Smart gives a brief account of the many differences of opinion concerning the meanings attached to Faulkner's spiritualisms, and asserts that his study is "designed to provide textual evidence which may contribute a moderate speculative approach to the problem." Included in the CONCORDANCE are references to Biblical accounts, the Church, motifs which parallel the religious themes, and rhetorical devices which come from or reflect the language of religion. Also arranged alphabetically are the names of characters which have religious connotations. Mentions are only given to the first published edition of the novels. The three appendices provide: (a) expletives and religious uses; (b) characters related to selective religious allusions found in SOLDIERS' PAY, MOSQUITOES, and SARTORIS; (c) sketches of the small pieces of Faulkner.

ROBERT FROST

LATHEM, Edward Connery.
A Concordance to the Poetry of Robert Frost. New York: Holt, 1971. 640 p.

Omits about 153 high-frequency words (not including *like* and *as*) and word contractions; yet lists over 100,000 words. Based on the standard THE POETRY OF ROBERT FROST (Holt, 1969) by Lathem himself. A "model concordance."

EUGENE O'NEILL

REAVER, Joseph Russel.
An O'Neill Concordance. Detroit: Gale Research, 1969. 3 vols.

Based on the latest standard Random House edition of O'Neill in three volumes, the Random House edition of "A Moon for the Misbegotten," and the individual plays published by the Yale University Press. Omits certain early plays.

EDGAR ALLAN POE

BOOTH, Bradford A. and Claude E. Jones.

A Concordance of the Poetical Works of Edgar Allan Poe.
Baltimore: The Johns Hopkins Press, 1941. 211 p.

An exhaustive and meticulous work. Basel upon Killis Campbell's edition. A useful Introduction explains the difficulties encountered in interpolating the rest of Poe's work in the concordance (in the absence of a standard text for all of Poe's poetry). Among the interesting facts revealed by a perusal are the following frequencies: "all," 168 times; "love," 95 times; "heart," 77 times; "heaven" and "night," each 69 times; "soul," 66 times.

WALLACE STEVENS

WALSH, Thomas F.
Concordance to the Poems of Wallace Stevens. University Park: Pennsylvania State University Press, 1963. 341 p.

A strict alphabetical arrangement of every word in the poetry of Stevens and, under each word, arrangement in text order, with title and line number, of the lines in which they appear. Thus the reader is enabled, not only to note the words which the poet has used, but to note the range of uses: "to note the chronologies of usage and emphasis, to identify passages from a phrase or two, to note the interplay of homonyms and synonyms, to note large and small frequencies of word use . . ."

WALT WHITMAN

EBY, Edwin Harold.
A Concordance of Walt Whitman's "Leaves of Grass" and Selected Writings. Seattle, Washington: The University of Washington Press, 1949–54. 964 p.

The Subtitle is: Including DEMOCRATIC VISTAS; "A Backward Glance O'er Travelled Roads"; Preface to the 1855 Edition; Preface, 1872; Preface, 1876; and Preface Note to 2d Appendix. Issued in five fascicules. For each entry two references are given: one to THE COMPLETE WRITINGS OF WALT WHITMAN (New York: Putnam, 1902; 10 Vols.), volume, page, and line; the other to individual poems, indicated by group, providing title of poem, section, and line. The concordance is thus keyed to all complete editions of LEAVES OF GRASS.

GUIDE TO BOOK REVIEWS
AND BOOK SELECTION

Indexes

Book Review Digest, 1905—New York: Wilson, 1905—.

A digest and index of selected book reviews appearing in more than seventy-five English and American periodicals and newspapers. Books are alphabetically listed by author, and each entry gives bibliographical information, Dewey classification number, LC card number, subject headings, a descriptive annotation, and quoted passages from reviews with full reference to sources. Indicates length of review in number of words. Most of the books listed are of general interest, but many are of scholarly nature. Monthly (except February and July), with a semi-annual cumulation in August, and an annual cumulation of the main list in February.

Book Review Index. Vol. I—January 1965—. Detroit: Gale, 1966.

Monthly publication, with quarterly cumulations, indexing reviews appearing in more than two hundred periodicals, primarily in the fields of general fiction and non-fiction, humanities, social sciences, librarianship, bibliography, juvenile and adult books. Entries, arranged by author's names, are brief, but quite adequate to locate reviews.

Contemporary Literature. Madison, Wisconsin: University of Wisconsin Press, 1960–. (For annotation see page 110.)

Criticism: A Quarterly for Literature and the Arts. Detroit, Michigan: Wayne State University Press, 1959–. (For annotation see page 111.)

Critique: Studies in Modern Fiction. Atlanta, Georgia: Georgia Institute of Technology, 1956–. (For annotation see page 111.)

GRAY, Richard A.
A Guide to Book Review Citations: A Bibliography of Sources.
Columbus, Ohio: Ohio State University Press, 1968. 221 p.

An annotated list of sources of book review citations—both continuing series and separately published works which include such references. Arrangement by class; author, title, and subject index.

EICHELBERGER, Clayton L.
A Guide to Critical Reviews of United States Fiction, 1870–1910.
Metuchen, New Jersey: Scarecrow Press, 1971. 576 p.

A good source of book reviews from thirty American and English periodicals, including the NEW ORLEANS DAILY PICAYUNE and other regional and seldom indexed sources.

Index to Book Reviews in the Humanities. Vol. 1, no. 1, March 31, 1960—Annual.

The term "Humanities" is broadly interpreted to include social sciences. Indexes almost 700 periodicals (all in English), both popular and scholarly. Each issue includes several thousand book titles and contains a list of periodicals indexed, specifying actual issue numbers. While it does not indicate whether the reviews are favorable or not, and does not provide quotations from the reviews, it attains extensive coverage. Only slightly duplicates entries in BOOK REVIEW DIGEST.

SALEM, James M.
A Guide to Critical Reviews: 4 pts. pt. 1, 181 p.; pt. 2, 353 p.; pt. 3, 209 p.; pt. 4, 2 vols., 1420 p. Metuchen, New Jersey: Scarecrow Press, 1971.

The first part (American drama O'Neil to Albee) cites reviews of the works of fifty-two playwrights from 1920 to 1965. The second part (The Musical from Rodgers-and-Hart to Lerner-and-Loewe) cites critical reviews from 1920 to 1965. The third part (British and Continental Drama from Ibsen to Pinter) constitutes a bibliography of reviews of modern British and Continental plays produced on the New York stage from 1909 to 1966. The fourth part (The Screenplay from the Jazz Singer to Dr. Strangelove, volumes 1 and 2) comprises a bibliography of critical reviews of feature-length movies from October, 1927, through 1963.

Periodicals, Journals, and Newspapers

American Journal of Philology, 1800—.

The extensive book review sections contain long and detailed signed reviews. List of books received. (For more detailed annotation, see the section on Serials.)

American Literature, 1929—. North Carolina: Duke University Press, 1929—.

Contains long critical reviews and an annotated listing of other recent books. (For more detailed annotation, see section on Serials.)

American Quarterly, 1949—. Philadelphia, Pa.: American Studies Association, 1949—.

Aims to "aid in giving a sense of direction to studies in the culture of the United States" and to contribute "to the entire American scene and to world society." Contains scholarly articles on American politics, society, history, art, belles-lettres, etc. Since 1955 it has published an annual annotated bibliography (covering approximately 200 periodicals) of "articles that manifest relationships of various aspects of American civilization." Occasional review articles; many critical, signed book reviews.

American Scholar, 1932—. Quarterly. Richmond, Va.

Non-technical articles, essays, and discussions devoted to all fields of learning. Brief, signed book reviews.

American Speech, 1925—. Quarterly. New York.

Articles deal with current usages, pronunciation, lore of place names, local dialects, non-English languages in North America. Regular features: "Of matters lexicographical," "Among the new words," and a bibliography of present-day English and phonetics. Includes book reviews.

Antioch Review. Yellow Springs, Ohio: The Antioch Press, 1941—.

A quarterly publication, devoted largely to progressive articles on current social and political problems and theory, "and all areas important for contemporary understanding." Includes scholarly articles in the humanities, short stories, and poetry; also book reviews, mainly of poetry, literature and criticism. "Style is important, but content more so."

Atlantic Monthly. Concord, New Hampshire: The Rumford Press, 1941—.

Covers literature, economics, politics and social affairs, and includes essays, poetry, and stories. Regular features are: the "Atlantic Report on the world today," which provides background material on some of the places and issues of current interest; the "Atlantic Serial," which gives chapters from a forthcoming novel or biography; and short stories by established writers, published as "Atlantic Firsts." Brief, informative book reviews and commentary.

Booklist and Subscription Books Bulletin. Chicago: American Library Association, 1956—.

The SUBSCRIPTION BOOKS BULLETIN section describes and evaluates sets of books or single works which are generally sold by agents or by institutions on the extended payment plan; but it is principally useful to librarians and the student for reviews of important reference works. Each review gives a critical evaluation of the work and author and indicates the type of library for which the work is suitable or necessary. (For fuller annotation, consult the BOOKLIST entry in the "Bibliography" section.)

Books Abroad. Norman, Oklahoma: University of Oklahoma Press, 1927—.

An international literary quarterly featuring articles on a wide range of subjects of international interest in the fields of drama, prose, poetry, and, even more pointedly, reviews of books published in many languages, including French, German, Spanish, Italian, and English. The reviews, by scholars in the particular field, are brief but pithy. "An invaluable journal, both as a source of reviews and as an annotated guide to book purchase."

Choice. Chicago, Illinois: American Library Association, 1986–.

A leading book review media for public, college, university libraries. Each issue reviews 500 to 700 American-based books; annotations average 75 to 150 words in length. Full list of issue's contributors is given in back of each issue.

Classical Philology. Chicago, Illinois. 1923—.

A quarterly journal devoted to research in the languages, literatures, and life of classical antiquity. About half of the journal is given to signed book reviews, some rather lengthy. List of books received.

Classical Review. London, 1887—.

Published for the Classical Association, among the principal objects of which are to promulgate the role of classical studies in education and to encourage the exchange of ideas among classical students. Most of the journal is devoted to reviews. List of books received.

Classical Weekly. New York: Classical Association of the Atlantic States, 1907—.

Contains brief, scholarly articles on classics generally, survey articles of a bibliographical nature, and articles and notes on the teaching of the classics; book reviews and list of books received.

College and Research Libraries. Chicago: American Library Association, 1939—.
Includes general articles, official reports and addresses and, twice yearly, a listing and brief description of selected new periodicals; also an annual list of new reference works and publication of the statistics of a large number of college and university libraries. Signed critical book reviews; list of books received.

College English. Champaign, Illinois: National Council of Teachers of English, 1939—.

Articles on literature, on the teaching of English, and news, comments, and discussions of interest to members. Book reviews.

Comparative Literature. Eugene, Oregon, 1949—.

A quarterly journal devoted to the "manifold interrelations of literature . . . the theory of literature, movements, genres, periods and authors—from the earliest times to the present." Lengthy, critical signed book reviews; list of books received.

Contemporary Review Incorporating The Fortnightly. London, 1866—.

Brief articles on contemporary and historical subjects and, to a lesser degree, on literature, education, and science. Each issue contains a literary supplement with short signed reviews. Itself an old standard of acceptable literary merit and general interest, it incorporated in 1954 *The* FORTNIGHTLY, one of Britain's most esteemed literary and political journals.

Diogenes. Chicago, Illinois: Published under the auspices of the International Council for Philosophy and Humanistic Studies, 1953—.

A quarterly journal devoted to interdisciplinary articles, erudite, well-written, by outstanding scholars and literati from all nations. The review articles and the lengthy book reviews are both of exceptional quality.

Encounter. England, 1953—.

"Journal of theological scholarship discussing vital issues among Christians of various communions throughout the world. Each issue is designed to cover a specific area of religious thought." Includes superior creative writing and criticism and excellent book reviews. Many of the contributors are outstanding authors, commentators, and scholars.

English. London, 1936—.

Articles on writers and their works, the teaching of literature, the theory of literature, original poetry and short stories. Good signed book reviews. ENGLISH is published for the English Association, the equivalent in England of our National Council of Teachers of English.

English Language Notes. Boulder, Colorado: University of Colorado Press, 1963–. (For annotation see page 111.)

English Studies. A Publication of the English Association. London: John Murray, 1948—.

"A journal of English letters and philology." The scholarly articles are mainly by English and continental contributors. A regular emphasis is the analysis of modern English syntax. Excellent book reviews. (For fuller annotation, see entry in the "Serials" section.)

Essays in Criticism. Oxford: Blackwell Press, 1951—.

Articles, by scholars of all countries, stress English literature—criticism, literary theory and history, individual authors and works. The reviews, though few in number, are generally lengthy, detailed, and thoughtful. (For fuller annotation, see entry in the section "Serials.")

ETC: A Review of General Semantics. Chicago, Illinois, 1943—.

Official organ of the International Society for General Semantics. "Concerned with the role of language and other symbols in human behavior and human affairs." Includes poetry; discussions of previous articles; lengthy, signed critical book reviews.

Greece and Rome. Oxford, England, 1931—.

Published for the Classical Association. Articles, poetry, translation, reviews, competitions. Reviews indicate the suitableness of books for individuals and libraries.

Hudson Review. New York, 1948—.

Articles by outstanding writers and scholars in the fields of general literature, criticism and aesthetics. Excellent lengthy book reviews and review articles.

Journal of English and Germanic Philology. Urbana, Illinois: The University of Illinois Press, 1897—.

Almost half of the journal is devoted to book reviews, many of them exceptionally long and detailed. One of its features is the annual "Anglo-German literary bibliography." (For a fuller annotation, see the entry in section "Serials.")

Journal of Modern Literature. Philadelphia, Pa.: Temple University Press, 1970.-. (For annotation see page 115.)

Kenyon Review. Gambier, Ohio, 1939—.

A highly esteemed quarterly, emphasizing literary criticism. In addition to literature, it includes articles on music, painting, and general aesthetics. Extensive, critical reviews of fiction, poetry, criticism and essays, and scholarly works.

Library Journal. New York, 1876—.

A semi-monthly (monthly, July–August) covering the entire

field of library service. Among its special features are: the review section, "Professional reading," and "New books appraised;" also the three seasonal new book announcement issues, which include brief biographies of new novelists.

Library Quarterly. Chicago, Illinois, 1931—.

Emphasizes the historical, theoretical and biographical aspects of library sciences. Among the features are: signed, critical book reviews; list of books received; and the annual designation of "Graduate theses accepted by library schools in the United States."

Library Review. Glasgow, Scotland, 1927—.

A quarterly journal which stresses the practice and theory of librarianship, library and literary notes and news, and a classified booklist of selected new publications and important reprints. Excellent signed reviews of library materials and general works.

London Magazine. London, 1954—.

A "monthly review of literature;" includes articles, poetry, and fiction by well-known British writers. Many book reviews, some quite lengthy and thorough.

Modern Fiction Studies: A Critical Quarterly Devoted to Criticism, Scholarship and Bibliography of American, English, and European Fiction since about 1800. Lafayette, Indiana: Purdue versity Press, 1955-. (For annotation see page 116.)

Modern Language Forum. Los Angeles, California: Modern Language Association of Southern California, 1919—.

Scholarly articles on all areas of modern language and literature. An annual bibliography of "German Literature of the XIX century, 1830–1880," appeared through 1954. Classified listing of books received; signed, critical book reviews.

Modern Language Notes. Baltimore: The Johns Hopkins University Press, 1886—.

A monthly, scholarly publication (except July–October), emphasizing short articles on English literature. Signed book reviews; list of books received.

Modern Language Quarterly. Seattle, Washington: University of Washington Press, 1940—.

Includes American, Germanic, and Romance languages and literatures, but stresses English literature. Excellent, signed critical book reviews. (For fuller annotation see entry in the section "Serials.")

Modern Language Review. Cambridge, England: Modern Humanities Research Association, 1905—.

A large portion of the journal is devoted to signed, critical reviews, notices, and a broad listing of new publications, arranged by language. (For fuller annotation, see entry in the section "Serials.")

Modern Philology. A Journal Devoted to Research in Modern Languages and Literatures. Chicago: The University of Chicago Press, 1903—.

Contains articles, documents and other records, review articles, and lengthy, critical book reviews. (For fuller annotation, see entry in the section "Serials.")

New England Quarterly: A Historical Review of New England Life and Letters. Brunswick, Maine: The Colonial Society of Massachusetts, 1928—.

Scholarly articles and notes, essays, memoranda, and documents, all relating to the history or literature of New England. Includes an annual "Bibliography of New England," a classified arrangement of articles. Excellent signed book reviews.

New Republic. Washington, D.C., 1914—.

A weekly journal of commentary on politics, economics, and social thought, written by distinguished contributors. Impressive book reviews.

New Statesman. London, 1913—.

A weekly journal of political and social commentary; also includes literary articles, poetry, reviews of books. Before 1957, it was known as NEW STATESMAN AND NATION.

New Yorker. New York, 1925—.

Among the features of this sophisticated weekly are: biographical sketches, historical articles, political reports, art and book reviews. Highly regarded.

New York Herald Tribune Book Review. New York, 1924—.

Similar in general feature to the NEW YORK TIMES BOOK REVIEW, but lacking its embraciveness of coverage. Useful for the signed reviews of the very latest books.

New York Times Book Review. New York: New York Times, 1896—.

A section of the Sunday issue of the *New York Times*. Signed reviews of varying lengths; a selected listing of other books published during the week. Caters to popular taste, rather than to scholarship. (For a fuller annotation, see entry in the section "Serials.")

Nineteenth-Century Fiction. Berkeley, California: The University of California Press, 1945—.

Also known as THE TROLLOPIAN: A Journal of Victorian Fiction. Aims to provide a great variety in English literature for the years 1945–1957. Deals with major and minor authors of the period and with analyses of their works. Omits foreign language authors; includes Americans; stresses British authors. Reviews of the important works in the field are substantial; also contains notes and comments on other books.

Notes and Queries. London: Oxford University Press, 1849—.

The earlier subtitle was: A Medium of Inter-Communication for Literary Men, Artists, Antiquarians and Genealogists. A monthly from 1849 to 1935; a weekly from 1935 to 1943; a fortnightly since July, 1943.

Contains a large amount of interesting and useful information on miscellaneous small points—history, manners, customs, folklore, quotations, proverbs, bibliography, most of it in the form of signed answers to questions from readers, in which the sources of the information are given. Indexes are carefully compiled and quite useful.

Novel: A Forum on Fiction. Providence, Rhode Island: Brown University, 1967–. (For annotation see page 118.)

Philological Quarterly: A Journal Devoted to Scholarly Investigation in the Classical and Modern Languages and Literatures. Iowa City: State University of Iowa Press, 1922—.

Now publishes two annual bibliographies: "English Literature, 1660–1800," and, since 1956, the "Romantic Movement." Both include articles and books, domestic and foreign, with citations of reviews and frequent annotations. (For fuller annotation, see entry in the section "Serials".)

Poetry. Chicago, Illinois, 1912—.

Although it publishes the work of established poets, devoted to the introduction of experimental and important new poetry. Includes essays on poetry and critical reviews of published verse.

Renaissance News. New York, 1948—.

Renaissance Quarterly. New York, N.Y.: Renaissance Society of America, 1954–. (For annotation see page 119.)

Review of English Studies: A Quarterly Journal of English Literature and Language. Oxford: Clarendon Press, 1925—.

Scholarly articles and notes almost exclusively on literature. Some of the book reviews are exceptionally lengthy. List of books received. A regular feature is the "Summary of Periodical Literature," listing the contents of various journals in English literature and philology. (For a fuller annotation, see entry in the section "Serials".)

Saturday Review of Literature. New York, 1924—.

Still an important general book reviewing weekly, with the general semi-popular books being reviewed by professional reviewers, the scholarly works by specialists. Individual issues frequently give extended treatment to a single subject. (For a fuller annotation, see entry in the section "Serials.")

Sewanee Review. Sewanee, Tenn.: University of the South, 1892—.

The nation's oldest existing literary and critical quarterly. Contains verse, fiction, essays, arts, and criticism on modern literature and aesthetics. Both in creative and critical writing, it has "always been distinguished among American periodicals by a certain universality or catholicism." Excellent book review essays.

Shakespeare Quarterly. New York: Shakespeare Association of America, 1950—.

Critical and research articles by Shakespeare scholars from America and abroad on the poet's life, works, characters and on the interpretations and commentaries of his works. Lengthy, critical book reviews; notes and comments.

South Atlantic Quarterly. Durham, North Carolina, 1902—.

A literary, social-political journal contributed to mainly by members of college faculties. Signed book reviews.

Southern Review. Baton Rouge, Louisiana: Louisiana State University Press, 1965–. (For annotation see pages 119–120.)

Speculum: A Quarterly Journal of Mediaeval Studies. Cambridge, Massachusetts: The Mediaeval Academy of America, 1926—.

A major part of each issue is devoted to exceptional signed book reviews. Each issue also contains a bibliography of periodical literature in the field and a list of books received. (For fuller annotation, see entry in the "Serials" section.)

Studies in English Literature 1500–1900. Houston, Texas: Rice University Press, 1961–. (For annotation see page 121.)

Studies in Sho.. Fiction. Newberry, South Carolina: Newberry College, 1963–. (For annotation see page 122.)

Times Literary Supplement. London, 1902—.

Considered by many the world's leading book review source. Treats scholarly as well as popular works. Lists books received with critical annotation. (For a fuller comment, see entry in "Serials" section.)

Twentieth Century Literature: A Scholarly and Critical Journal. Los Angeles, California: IHC Press, 1955–. (For annotation see page 122.)

Virginia Quarterly Review: A National Journal of Literature and Discussion. Charlottesville, Virginia: University of Virginia, 1925–.

Covers much the same general area as the SEWANEE REVIEW and the SOUTHERN REVIEW—literature, social sciences, art, etc. Especially useful because of the short notes on books and the section "List of Reprints and New Editions." The reviews are as general in scope as the magazine.

Wilson Library Bulletin. New York, 1914—.

Among the monthly features are: review of recent reference books; selection of new books by competent authors, and biographical sketches of new writers.

Index to Authors

Index to Titles